PREACHING FOR TODAY

PREACHING FOR TODAY

CLYDE E. FANT

1817

Harper & Row, Publishers, San Francisco

Cambridge, Hagerstown, New York, Philadelphia, Washington
London, Mexico City, São Paulo, Singapore, Sydney

FIRST EDITION

Library of Congress Cataloging-in-Publication Data

Fant, Clyde E.
    Preaching for today.
    Bibliography: p.
    Includes index.
    1. Preaching. I. Title.
BV4211.2.F36 1987   251   86-43003
ISBN 0-06-062334-9

87 88 89 90 91 HC 10 9 8 7 6 5 4 3 2 1

To my mother and my father

Contents

IV. Saying the Sermon

Preface

Nothing is more sought today by laypeople and preachers alike than a meaningful sound from the pulpit. They both know, even if they cannot say it, that the Word is neither thunder nor angel speech. What it is, or what it should be, however, is another matter. This book is about that. *It is an attempt to unify the practice of preaching, from sermon construction to pulpit delivery, within a meaningful theology of proclamation.*

Most books about preaching are written by specialists in one preaching field or another—history of preaching, theology of proclamation, communication theory, innovative sermon form, sermon delivery, and so on—and those are the books that do me the most good. The thoroughness and depth with which they explore each of these areas enriches me and provokes me to further study.

Sometimes I do get the feeling, however, that preaching is a bit the victim of atomization or fragmentation. And I also get that impression from pastors and specialists in other theological areas whose picture of what preaching is about is at least partial, if not distorted.

That's certainly no one's fault in particular. But it has given preaching some problems, particularly in the division between the theoretical aspects of the theology of proclamation and the practical necessity of sermon construction and delivery. We clearly do not need more generalization, but it seems to me that a certain integration of these things on a common theological basis would help the wholeness of preaching.

The divorce between theology and practical homiletics is a primary reason for the parish minister's ongoing frustrations with preaching. Divorce may not be quite the proper term, however, since for many people theology and homiletics have never been wed. For some, they have never even been introduced. For all the prominence accorded the *theory* of preaching by theology, the *practice* of preaching has not enjoyed equal attention. The *what* of preaching is frequently regarded as concern enough; the *how* of preaching is merely a matter of rhetoric: "The renewal of our proclamation means that there remains only a question of what we proclaim, not the question of how we proclaim it."[1]

There are two reasons for this. First, homiletics is frequently regarded as a branch of rhetoric rather than of theology; and second, some theologians do not believe that preaching can be taught at all—which really means that the *what* of preaching can be taught, but the *how* of preaching cannot.

An example of this first point of view is to be found in Gustaf Wingren's book *The Living Word,* an excellent inquiry into "the essential theological nature of preaching."[2] Wingren asserts, however, that "such very practical questions as the construction of the sermon, its delivery and such like obviously do not fall within our field. Homiletics as a part of practical theology has its own specific problems *which are not theological in nature"* (italics mine).[3] In other words, homiletics is indeed a division of practical theology, but the practical questions of preaching, such as the construction of the sermon and its delivery, *are not theological in nature.*

Joseph Sittler presents the second point of view, that preaching cannot be taught, when he writes, "The expectation must not be cherished, that, save for modest and obvious instruction about voice, pace, organization, and such matters preaching as a lively art of the church can be taught at all. And therefore, seminary provisions for instruction in preaching, when these exist as separate curriculum items, should be examined."[4] On the other hand, he insists that "preaching is organic to the entire actuality of the preacher,"[5] and his provocative study of preaching gives strong support to the role of preaching in the church.

How shall we evaluate these arguments? Sittler is undoubtedly right when he says, "Disciplines correlative to preaching can be taught, but preaching as an act of witness cannot be taught."[6] It is also true that practical homiletics has been fragmented away from the whole of the theological enterprise as a separate discipline. But this is the very point I am making: the fragmentation of preaching is only made worse when the subject is either left in theological abstraction or relegated to "modest and obvious instruction about voice, pace, organization, and such matters."

Of course preaching cannot be taught—but then can theology? Technically, it cannot. Obviously systematic theology wishes to teach its students to "do theology," not merely to convey conclusions to them about theology, or to teach them the history of theology, or even to suggest to them helpful methodology for arriving at theological conclusions. At that point we are all equally helpless; we cannot teach a student to be a Barth or a Brunner in the theological study any more than we can teach him or her to be a Barth or a Brunner in the pulpit. All teachings shares this problem. Even if musicians could teach students *how* Bach did what he did, they still couldn't teach them to *do* what Bach did.

But is this not all beside the point? If theology does not unite the human dilemma with its ultimate concerns, is it truly theology? Likewise, if preaching has no theological basis for its considerations of form, method, and delivery, can it be justified as a practice at all?

We must remember that "preaching is preaching only when a sermon is being preached. No systematic consideration of preaching can afford to pass over this simple fact!" as Rudolf Bohren puts it. He adds, "Particular attention should be paid to the practical aspect of preaching. The act of preaching is a particularly important subject for systematic theology."[7] The practical aspects of speaking the sermon *must be united theologically* with the theoretical aspects of preaching.

If we do not do so, then preaching as a practical act within the church will be hopelessly schizoid. One half of its personality will be Hebrew-Christian, and the other half will be Greek-pagan. Perhaps the theoretical idea of preaching, or even the content of the sermon itself, may be solidly theological and Christian; but the *actual* sermon, the *preached* sermon, which cannot avoid its essential entanglement with questions of form, methodology, and delivery, will be weakly rhetorical and pagan. We will have "severed the head of preaching from theology and dropped it into the basket of rhetoric held by Aristotle."[8]

What is to be done in this case? Shall the Jew marry the Greek, and the Jew live tenuously, if not happily, ever after? Shall Judeo-Christian proclamation cohabit with Greco-pagan rhetoric? If so, it will never be more than a marriage of convenience, for the twain shall never become one flesh. There has never been, and there will never be, more than one possible result from this uneasy union. Preaching will go on being praised in theory and damned in practice.

But there is no need for this impossible situation. Theology itself provides us with the decisive clue. The divine-human nature of its concerns are precisely those of preaching: "The Word became flesh and dwelt among us (John 1:14, RSV)." *Form, methodology, and delivery are nothing more, and nothing less, than the word of God taking on flesh and dwelling among us.*

These practical questions are indeed the painful embarrassment of preaching, but no more so than the human form of Jesus of Nazareth was a stumbling block to the Jews and a joke to the Greeks. Any attempt on the part of theology, no matter how well intentioned, to sever these "human" questions from the "divine" nature of Christian proclamation can only be viewed as another error of abstract, speculative theology that would force preaching to live in a house it has just torn down for itself.

Freeing the pure soul of Christian proclamation—its content— from the wicked body of actual pulpit practice—its presentation —will not do. The salvation of preaching can only be the salvation of a living body, not an abstract soul. Then and only then can preaching at last be made whole.

I certainly do not believe that this book accomplishes such a large task. But I do think it is worth a try, and I hope that others will do more ably that which I believe I have realized to be worthwhile. As C. S. Lewis once put it, that part of the line where I thought I could serve best also seemed to be thinnest, and so to it I naturally went.

Perhaps one additional word of explanation is necessary. Throughout this work I use the term *incarnational preaching*. I believe the context will suggest, if not completely define, what I do and do not mean by it. But by no means do I intend to suggest a confusion between the unique event in Christ and what happens in preaching. I do believe, however, that the incarnation is the truest theological model for the mysterious divine-human preaching event, which is neither all of the human nor all of God, but which partakes of both with precisely the same degree of mystery and humility as that reality in Jesus of Nazareth.

It is always impossible to give adequate thanks to the many people who contribute to the writing of a work such as this. I dedicated the first edition of this book to the memory of my father, who died during the writing of it. He knew better than anyone I have ever known how to communicate with people—and I am not alone in this opinion. His twenty-five years of honorable public service proved that. And longer yet, he spoke in churches and taught the Bible to people in his own church. I am sure no one will object if I express my gratitude first for his lifelong contribution to this book—and me. Not only in speaking, but in understanding people, he was my first and greatest teacher.

This second edition of *Preaching for Today* I dedicate to my mother. In many ways that is meaningful. I have always said that my father was all Law, but my mother was all Grace. There has never been a kinder, more loving soul ever born on the face of this earth. Everyone who knows her shares that opinion. If my father spoke to my head, my mother spoke to my soul. Her love for all creatures of God's creation has no boundaries. She is the most truly liberal spirit I know.

I am grateful to those in my classes and graduate seminars for their contribution to this work. They suggested many ideas in the years that these concepts were being discussed with them, and they have offered good advice as they listened to the final copy read—even if I did get unmerciful kidding for reading a manuscript!

I would not have undertaken this revised edition without the encouragement of Harper & Row, particularly that of John Shopp. For several years I had wanted to make the language of the book more inclusive, but I would not have expanded this edition as I have without the publisher's support. (As to language in quotations, I have left it as it was. I did not feel responsible for revising others' speech—even though most of those authors from the past would likely have welcomed it.)

In many ways, the inclusive language in this new edition represents the entire movement of my thought in the past decade. As I have given lectures and conducted preaching workshops both in this country and abroad, my homiletical world has expanded greatly. I grew up in a world and in a tradition that did not recognize the sociological bias of its biblical interpretation or its role as the powerful among the powerless. We knew black preaching and loved it; but of course that was "their" preaching for "their" church. And of women's preaching? In my hometown we knew one woman preacher who both pastored and owned a church called The Plant of Renown, Inc. That just about says it all!

So I, like many other white male preachers of my generation, had a lot to learn, and I still do. But this book represents movement in my own understanding of the kerygma of God, largely due to the contributions of the varied people who have graced my world with theirs. They are too many to mention. Some of them live in tiny villages or great cities far away. Some of them exist for me only in their shared witness, their books. Some I know and count as friends. I hope I have listened well and spoken honestly.

Closer to home, I express thanks to Stetson University, in whose chapel I preach each week and where I enjoy, both in the classroom and on the campus, the stimulation of those who seek under the motto, "For God and for Truth." I am grateful for the encouragement of my colleagues in the Department of Religion, whose insights I value. Sims Kline, University Librarian, saved the day on more than one occasion with his sleuthing into obscure resources. Harry Grage, Stetson student and a person who actually understands computers, saved this revision from an "irretrievably damaged disk." Laura Rogers and Gabrielle King kept an office running while I was occupied with this writing. But my strongest thanks must go to my wife, Cheryl, herself an ordained minister in the Christian Church (Disciples of Christ), for her processing and managing of these materials, but most of all for the keen insights of her mind and spirit into the substance of this revision.

I. THE PROMISE OF PREACHING

1. What Can Preaching Do?

What can preaching do? For some who hear the Word of God in it, preaching can be a costly experience. I've never ministered in churches normally thought of as congregations of oppressed people; far from it. But I've found that for those who take the gospel seriously, even in those churches of professionals and managers, living out the faith is as costly as ever.

I received a letter recently from a research chemist with an oil company—at least he used to be a chemist with an oil company. A reorganization "eliminated" his position. I was his pastor once, and so he wrote to tell me about his life.

Much of the story, like all our stories, was familiar: he had a strict upbringing in a narrow religious world; he was mostly indifferent toward the church but had a good family life, quick success, and increasing responsibilities; then came growing uncertainty, and finally crisis. Some of the story, like all our stories, was unique: he felt a growing awareness of God in his world; he suddenly heard the Word of grace in two sermons a month apart, and rearranged all aspects of his life, including changing his management style to "building people" rather than the "manipulative, exploitative" style of the past; then he received an appointment to an important management position. Will we hear the usual ending to a testimony of success?

Not quite. Oil prices collapsed, fortunes reversed, everybody blamed everybody else, and vicious "lose-lose games" were played. "There arose over Egypt," as he wrote, "a new Pharaoh that knew not Joseph": the vice president who had approved his management style changes was deposed, and the "jungle fighters" came out to settle old debts. The new manager (with the old, "proven" methods) got rid of anybody who was guilty of the "softer" management style—which of course, as everyone knew, was responsible for their corporate problems in the first place.

And what of my friend now, and what of his faith? He writes, in part:

Did I lose? Yes, and my family has been disadvantaged. I lost in the sense that I was overpowered by authority. But, I won in that I did not revert to an exploitative management style and was true to what I believe spiritually, professionally, and personally. . . .

As I reflect on all this, it is hard to take in. It suggests that the Lord has been working with and on me, preparing and testing me. For what? Have I fought the good fight? I have tried hard to keep the faith. . . . I trust the Lord's grace and wisdom and I seek God's will. It may not have begun with two sermons six years ago, but they were certainly milestones beginning a new era. Opportunities have been presented and denied in what can only be described as a pattern leading away from the person I was before then. But toward what?

Who would like to answer his question? Few would be so bold, but there are some things we can say for sure. One man has moved from "the hidden agenda of power, force, and authority" to "the principle of commitment to a continuing struggle in this life by grace and love." Only God knows where that will lead.

There is also one other thing: one preacher will never doubt that God may choose to bring the Word of the costly gospel through even our poor words.

So what can preaching do? It can be itself. Or it can be something else. That is, all pulpit address is not preaching. Before we can know what preaching can do, we must first understand what preaching is and is not. Otherwise, we will never know the difference between what preaching can do and what nonpreaching always does.

WHAT PREACHING IS AND IS NOT

The content of preaching is bound to the wisdom of God. It rests upon the institution of God: preaching can only do what God has chosen for it and enabled it to do. God has chosen through "the foolishness of preaching" (1 Cor. 1:21) to establish the gospel of reconciliation and grace.

The "foolishness" of preaching is the foolishness of the thing preached. Preaching is to tell us a strange sort of "good news." It speaks of the humiliation, suffering, and death of Jesus as well as of his resurrection. "The word of the cross is foolishness to those who are lost" (1 Cor. 1:18), to Jews and Gentiles alike (1:23), and to the natural reasoning, the conventional wisdom of the average person (the "natural man," 2:14).

The "word of the cross" was also foolishness to both Jews and Greeks because it meant that the one who was on the cross was obviously a human being, and if he was a human being, where was God in that? The writer of the prologue to the Gospel of John tackled that question head on: "And the Word became flesh and dwelt among us, full of grace and truth; we have beheld his glory, glory as of the only Son from the Father" (John 1:14). So the writer asserts that God could no longer be regarded as impassive, invulnerable, aloof. Now the suffering of God would become visible in Jesus Christ, in his hunger, thirst, and pain, even in his death.

Obviously, such a message was ridiculous to Jews and Greeks alike. They were familiar with the concepts of both "Word" and "flesh." But never in the wildest imaginings of either were "Word" and "flesh" united. "Word" for the Greeks, particularly in the philosophy of the Stoics, meant the highest individual good, the attainment of the ultimate self-actualization, the discovery of "truth-for-me." For the Jews, particularly for the Pharisees of the first century, the "Word" meant the Law, the writings of Moses. By the time of Christ, the Pharisees regarded the Law as preexistent, virtually coexistent with God. Therefore, although in radically different ways, "Word" had a kind of immortality for both Jews and Greeks. It is not difficult, then, to imagine the scorn that fell upon the preaching of the cross. If Jesus was in the flesh—which he obviously was, particularly if he was crucified—then he could not be the "Word," not for Jew and not for Greek. The whole business was regarded as ridiculous, impertinent, and even blasphemous.

It didn't take long before this issue moved out of the realm of philosophic speculation and became acutely existential for everybody involved. Paul experienced it personally. He was mocked by the philosophers at Athens (Acts 17:18), where he was referred to as a gutter sparrow, a "seed-picker," a "babbler" of secondhand ideas (from *spermologos,* literally, "seed-talk," i.e., scatter-shooting nonsense). The proconsul Gallio, stepbrother of Seneca, regarded the argument of Paul with the Jews (Acts 18:15) as Jewish *morologia* ("moron-talk"). Festus regarded Paul as out of his mind, *maine,* a maniac (Acts 26:24).

Furthermore, Paul struggled against "super-apostles" in Corinth (2 Cor. 11:5, 12:11), who ridiculed his "weakness" and tried to make him look like nothing before the Corinthian church. Paul called them "peddlers" of the gospel (2 Cor. 2:17). For the Jews who required signs (spiritual proof) and the Greeks who sought wisdom (intellectual proof), they provided certainty. Their spellbinding oratory and slick performances provided both the emotional satisfaction and the rationalistic evidences the Corinthians craved. Paul, on the other hand, was left with only his human-sounding speech and his word of the cross.

We may be able to admire Paul's fidelity to the gospel in that setting, but in our contemporary situation we find it much more difficult to practice a similar fidelity. Corinthians sometimes seem to be everywhere, and super-apostles appear to be on every channel, if, indeed, on every corner. Much of the contemporary church seems to crave a return to nationalism, triumphalism, success-preaching, and promises of obtaining wealth and earthly riches—including promotions, higher commissions, bigger and better houses (or churches)—as well as absolute certainty as to life's direction and an answer to every question of the moment. These are examples of the use of preaching for its own gain through worldly wisdom.

By no means could such preaching be considered "foolishness." The crowds who flock to hear it in ever-growing churches and the preachers who preach it with ever-enlarging salaries attest to its practical "wisdom." Then, having defined what success is, strictly contrary to the life of Jesus and the words of Jesus, the modern super-apostles finally validate their message by pointing to the worldly symbols of success they or their churches have obtained, congratulating themselves and castigating others whose "faith" cannot be proved by their "success."

Great favor accrues to the preaching of such "successful" pastors, and their churches are frequently regarded as "exciting," in contrast to the churches without such preaching, which are labeled "boring." So prevelant is this thinking in some circles that "Be exciting" might well be considered the first and greatest commandment.

But obviously such excitement is truly worldly and makes null and void the preaching of the cross. That kind of excitement reminds me of the endless TV game shows and the ecstatic, hand-clapping, sobbing, leaping, and forever-grateful contestants for whom the curtain has just opened to reveal a new car. They are excited by this "good news," to be sure, but whose "gospel" is it?

Preaching can never be itself unless it understands clearly what its message is. The gospel is indeed "good news," but what does that mean? It is both "good" and "news." "Good" means something beneficial or advantageous; "news" means something not known. Everyone who preaches attempts to convey a message about *something* that is beneficial, *something* that is unexpected or not known. But *what* is beneficial? And *what* is not known?

The "news" of the gospel is that something surprising has happened, something contrary to normal expectations: we have been included, we have been reconciled by the love of God in Christ—quite apart from earning such favor or paying for it—and we may become what God has declared us to be. Whatever life brings, we will never have to go it alone. The gospel is therefore not a conditional sentence: "If you . . . then God"; it is a declarative sentence of great joy: "Because God . . . therefore you." We are enabled to become the New Persons in Christ; and our orientation to this world now shifts from the agendas of selfishness and power to the agendas of reconciliation and love.

Such preaching, however, is so contrary to our conventional wisdom that this message tends to get distorted, even in the pulpit. We want to give everyone *really* "good news." So we ask ourselves what they would like to hear. Our conventional wisdom soon produces the answer: they would like to hear that they can get what they want; that they are in total control of life; that they can always know without any doubt what choices they should make; that their happiness will be uninterrupted; that sickness and loss and death will pass them by (of course, they expect to die eventually, but not as long as their faith is strong; faith, apparently, also has a life expectancy). Now that would be "good news"!

But is it either? Since that message is what everyone wants, the only "news" is that they can get it. And is that "good"? The price tag is a little steep. God must simply cease to be God, and the world is populated by a million times a million gods, the ultimate individualism.

Preaching, we have said, is the proclamation of the Good News in Christ: that the One whom the world crucified has been raised up by God and highly exalted, "to give repentance to Israel and forgiveness of sins" (Acts 5:30–31). As a result, in him we also are released from the bondage of the past and given a new horizon for the future of life.

But this is a doctrine of *resurrection,* not of immortality, of the triumph of the righteousness of God, not of the invincibility of the person—not even of the person of faith. In fact, is not the preaching of the cross the very opposite—that the Righteous One, who was all of grace and love, was mocked and scorned and finally slain? And was it or was it not the demand of Jesus that we also must "take up the cross daily" (Luke 9:23) and follow him?

What do these words mean if not that we are to appear as foolish as he, the One for others, who was born in a stable, not a palace, whose story was not, as it has been said, "log cabin to White House," but quite the opposite? What meaning can his life's choices have for us, if not that we are to identify with the poor, the outcasts, the minorities, the marginalized? The trek of his life's journey makes the trajectory of preaching quite clear: what direction did *he* choose to go? To whom and to what purpose?

We must remember that it was unto Galilee that he journeyed for his ministry, not Jerusalem. That is, he centered his life and work among "the people who sat in darkness . . . Galilee of the

Gentiles" (Matt. 4:12–17), not in the courts of religion and cultural correctness, not among the people of power, not in the places of power, not using the principles of power. He "abandoned" Nazareth and moved steadily toward the peripheral people and away from nationalism and national expectations. Galilee was the place of freethinkers, rebels, nonconformists to religious tradition—and the place from which his disciples came. "The Galilean!" Are we even yet prepared for the radicalness of his message?

The wilderness temptations, likewise, show us that Jesus forever rejected the way of power, prosperity, and easy peace. "Bread!" cried Satan. "Provide manna as before and prove your power! . . . Leap!" cried Satan. "Become the lord of God and force God to act through the power of your faith! Behold, the powers of the world await your command. Strength comes only to the strong, power only to the powerful!"

But Jesus banished Satan with a word, not the literalistic words of the Bible taken out of context, as the Deceiver used them, but a word from the Spirit of God: "You shall not tempt the Lord your God!" That is, not even our faith entitles us to become the lord of God to succeed.

What does all of this do to our preaching? To our praying? We may pray, as he did in the garden, "Let this cup pass from me." But then we *must* pray, "Thy will be done" (Matt. 26:39–42). We may preach that the Lord wills the best for the children of God, but we may not preach the specious promise that those whose faith is great enough will always receive what they ask for. Nor, on the other hand, may we preach that those who don't receive what they ask for simply lack faith.

Such preaching implies that Paul did have his thorn in the flesh removed and that Jesus did not die at all (exactly what the Moslem faith declares). To the contrary of the preaching of the cross, it would have to assert that Jesus lived to a ripe old age, prosperous, untroubled, secure with his investments in Jewish nationalism, and always voting for the winner in every election.

We must be careful that our preaching does not wrap the gospel in the flag of nationalism and bury it in the sea of our own self-interests. We must be sure that the good news we preach is the gospel of Jesus Christ; that the power of God we proclaim is the preaching of the cross, the triumph from below, not above, the triumph of suffering love. Only in this way can we preach what Jesus preached, only in this way can we walk where Jesus walked, only in this way can we love as Jesus loved.

WHAT PREACHING CAN DO

At this point, no matter what anyone says, there are still plenty of people who will raise questions as to the efficacy of preaching, *any* preaching, regardless of its content. Isn't talking about God really useless, boring, and a waste of time? Isn't the world saturated with words? Hasn't preaching worn out its welcome, and isn't it time for preaching to stop dominating worship and quietly withdraw somewhere?

These questions are usually raised not so much out of basic antagonism to preaching as out of frustrated idealism about preaching. We have become cynical about words, not because of what they cannot do but because of what we know they can do. Language bears the deepest promise of any human practice. It reaches into the forgotten past, it touches the sensitive present, and it points toward the veiled future. Hands cannot bring the gifts that language offers. Words do not convey information; they convey existence.

Language is so fundamental to human existence that it may be said to constitute the most "human" aspects of it. Our deepest problems are revealed through language; our worst hurts and greatest hopes are transmitted through language. Language not only interprets reality, it creates reality. Mere words? Words are anything but "mere."

Elie Wiesel, survivor of the Holocaust, quotes one of his teachers on the power of language: "Be careful with words, they're dangerous. Be wary of them. They beget either demons or angels. It's up to you to give life to one or the other. Be careful, I tell you, nothing is as dangerous as giving free rein to words."[1]

Speaking is a unique *event.* Speaker and listener are united at an unrepeatable time and in an unrepeatable situation. The speaker chooses from virtually infinite fields of reference—subjects—and from an almost equally infinite array of signs—dictionary "words." Once placed in context, these signs will become words with meaning. So will the subject itself gain meaning in the context of the speaker, the situation, and the listeners.[2]

These virtually infinite permutations and combinations in speech make it ideally suited—indeed essential—for revealing God to us. For when we talk about God or the Church in Christ (beyond the empirical church), we stand at the borders of human experience. Unless we can point beyond ourselves and our doings, we cannot say God to people.

Preaching, then, appears weak because it disappears into the experience of others; it vanishes, seemingly without a trace: "Language seeks to disappear; it seeks to die as an object."[3] But this is precisely what makes preaching essential to the Christian faith. It shares a great mystery with the incarnation, "Word become flesh," and "eternal Word become subjective words." So preaching avoids the idolatry of fixation, the static representation of God by objects, however apt or beautiful. So preaching allows participation by the hearer, interpretation and appropriation. It is taken up in every generation by every individual who proclaims, not as object but as subject. It is therefore *open,* not closed; *I* may participate in this reality. "From its trajectory of death, resurrection and return, this story has a forward orientation; it is open to the future, and it is precisely its incompleteness which makes our participation possible."[4]

Language, however, must be careful of its own idolatry. Fixed formulations, slogans, and phrases must be avoided. Charles Haddon Spurgeon, that most noted of nineteenth century preachers, reported a favorite phrase of his day: "To go from heart to heart, as oil from vessel to vessel." After much research, Spurgeon said that he could not find any suggestion of the phrase in the Bible at all, and he suspected that it likely came from *Ali Baba and the Forty Thieves.*

Even biblical phrases must not become idolatrous. There must be no holy language, no language of Zion chosen by the very human high priests of our cult. Otherwise, the living Word is lost in dead cultural expression and we in our time are refused direct access to the Living One. We are rerouted through someone else's cultural terrain, made to travel in obsolete vehicles that usually break down short of their destination or, more often, that will not even start for us at all.

Preaching that addresses us in our own language on matters of ultimate importance to us and without the interference of meaningless clichés will be anything but boring or irrelevant. The doctor who calls the name of an anxious family in the waiting room and then gives them the condition of someone they love more than life itself will scarcely bore them.

No, if preaching is tedious and meaningless, it is not the fault of one individual speaking to others. It is the fault of the ultimate irrelevance of what is preached or of the impersonal way in which it is preached. Preaching that partakes of the living nature of the Living Word will be heard and heard gladly. What, then, can it do?

Preaching brings Good News. It is essential that those who preach understand the difference between conveying information and conveying news. The way people respond to each is of crucial importance to preaching. "The Message in a Bottle," an essay by Walker Percy, tells a story that makes the point clear.[5]

A man was shipwrecked upon a distant island, but without any memory of his past. He found a flourishing civilization there; he accustomed himself to it, married, and established a new life. But from time to time he would walk again upon the beach, and there he found many bottles washed ashore, each with a message inside. As he read the messages, he divided them into two groups. One he called "science"; it told him knowledge that anyone at any place and any time might derive from research or philosophy, such as "Lead melts at 330 degrees" or "Truth is beauty." The other he labeled "news"; it included messages that were significant for the castaway precisely in his present predicament, information that pertained to his particular situation, such as "There is fresh water in the next cove" or "A hostile war party is approaching."[6]

The difference between the two types of messages is the immediate relevance of news to the life situation of the hearer. For example, the message that the next cove contained water would be "science" to a geologist but "news" to a thirsty castaway. There is also a difference in the way in which each message is accepted. "Science" is verified by experimentation; "news" is accepted if it is relevant to one's own predicament and if the source of the message is regarded as credible. Finally, there is a difference in the response to each: the response to information is confirmation (or rejection, if it proves false); the response to news is action. The difference is critical for preaching.

If we preach a "science"—even the "science of God," an abstract theology—then our listeners may ponder this information, accept or reject it intellectually, file it or trash it. But if what we preach is "news" to them, relevant to precisely their life situation, their predicament now, they will act upon it. So the gospel is truly Good News, not merely Accurate Information. "What makes the word of God good news is not novelty" either, says Edward Schmidt, "but freshness for one's situation in life."[7]

Dietrich Bonhoeffer, in his lectures on preaching to the tiny Confessing Church's seminary at Finkenwalde, said that preaching should be like holding out a shiny red apple to a child and asking, "Wouldn't you like it?" or a cup of water to a thirsty man in a desert and asking, "Don't you want it?" Preaching should be just so concrete and relevant to the life situation of its hearers.

We dare not so abstract the news of the gospel that it becomes impersonal concepts or distant history. We bear a message of good news to those who most need it, those for whom it was intended. Percy reminds us that no castaway is ever quite at home on an island, no matter how comfortable life may be, and that "to be a castaway is to search for news from across the sea" and to live always in hope that such news will come. This is the task of preaching: to convey God's good news to those who wait.

But why do sermons have "texts?" Why is the Bible used in preaching? Is it simply an old custom, something expected, like black suits for funerals and white dresses for weddings?

Preaching allows us to hear from the historic community of faith. Preaching puts us in touch with the past tense of our faith. Through the preached word from the Bible we may share experience with others like us, with fellow pilgrims on this journey who have something to tell us about the road. They have asked the same questions, cried the same tears, celebrated the same joys, and anguished in the same darkness as we. They are witnesses to the way. "Wherefore," says the writer of Hebrews, "seeing that we are encircled by such a crowd of witnesses . . . let *us* run with patience the race that is set before *us."* (Heb. 12:1).

As the church in each generation has preached, it has preached from the Bible. The church's preaching both went into and came from the Bible. The Bible was very much the word *from* the church as well as the word *of* the church. Preaching, then, is a community affair: "No prophesy of the scripture is of any private interpretation" (2 Pet. 1:20). The source of a scripture is the word of the Holy Spirit in the community of faith. Preaching that ignores the Bible follows a radically individualistic course that contradicts the nature of the Christian faith.

It should be pointed out here that not all preaching that endlessly cites the Bible is biblical preaching. Some of the preachers who most argue for the inerrancy of the Bible and who most brag on their own use of the Bible seldom do biblical preaching. Jesus did not quote Bible verses simply to endorse the cultural traditions around him. He interpreted the scripture as a prophetic word for that day and for the very people who most thought themselves a part of that scriptural heritage.

For example, in his public sermon at Nazareth, Jesus did not shock the people by his reading of Isaiah 61:1–2, although it was far more expected to hear from the Law than the Prophets. Nor did they rise up when he said, "This day is this scripture fulfilled in your ears." In fact, all eyes were fixed on him, and they marveled at the "gracious words which came from his mouth." But when he *interpreted* those words as judgment on Israel, through his example of God's favor coming to the widow of Sidon and to Naaman the

Syrian when Israel was full of widows and lepers, they rioted (Luke 4:14–28). "God must favor our religion!" they cried. That is "biblical!"[8]

But preaching allows us to hear the truth of the Bible, both for us and against us. Any preaching that calls itself biblical and only endorses the political, economic, and social prejudices of its constituency had better listen again to the faith that gave it birth. It is essential that we not confuse cultural preaching with biblical preaching. The careful cultivation of regional and national prejudices may be observed every day on many religious television programs. "Whatever it takes to get them" seems to be the motto: promise them Jesus, but give them endorsement of their political, economic, and social views. In every case, you may be assured that these shortcuts to the Kingdom pass directly through the alleyways of our cultural prejudices and preferences.

Preaching introduces us to the Word become flesh. The story of Jesus is the story of someone who so partook of the divine as well as the human nature that the church has been trying to describe it ever since. The narratives of the Gospels, as well as the theology of Paul and others, struggled to express what they experienced. It is not likely that we will ever resolve the question to the satisfaction of the church.

On the other hand, the action of the church, and particularly the preaching of the church, has a better chance of expressing that elusive reality to us. For in itself, the church is the body of Christ, and through its commission, preaching is the work of God. The church is human, fallible, limited. It is a stumbling block to those who seek perfection. The preaching of the church likewise is human, fallible, limited. It too is a stumbling-block to those who expect the perfect.

Yet it is the very human nature of both the church and its preaching that permits their representation of the Living Word to us. Jesus Christ was the ultimate expression of God. Yet in the flesh, "he who was rich became poor for our sakes" (2 Cor. 8:9). The human nature of the preaching of the church is an offense to many, but such preaching can introduce us to the Christ in a way impossible for golden tablets, night visions, or even sacred books.

God has chosen through the foolishness of preaching to come to the people. The Word of God must be found in the Bible and interpreted afresh to a living community by a person who is one with them. Only living, human words can bear the historic Word, even as only a really human Jesus could bear the glory of God (John 1:14).

So preaching must, like Jesus, conduct itself in humility, not pride. Remember that Jesus always referred to his disciples as "little ones." Remember also that preaching speaks with authority, but not authoritarianism. Preaching reveals humanity; it does not pretend quasi-divinity.

Preaching tells us the way things are. Preaching points to the past, but also to the present. The "present" does not mean the trendy, superficial movements of the moment; rather, preaching proclaims the true structures of existence. The meaningfulness of preaching results not from its aptness in staying just abreast of the times, of being dressed in exactly the right fashions, but in its telling of the spiritual structure of the universe.

The nature of that reality is revealed to us through Jesus Christ. We do not intuit it; we do not extrapolate it from our own spiritual biographies. The truth of the moral universe can only be believed and acted upon. It is a matter of faith.

Preaching must tell us of the alienation of humankind from God and from one another. It must speak unflinchingly of the darkness of human nature and of the violence that has coursed in our veins from the dimmest beginning of time. It will see the beauties in sunrises and fields of flowers, yes; but it will also recognize the empty evil of war and greed that blasts those fields and obliterates those sunrises. It will speak of the catastrophic path of power as it changes compassionate human beings into cold merchants of misery.

But another truth must also be proclaimed, not as an equal part of a hopeless duality but as the larger truth of life, that is, that our alienation has been overcome in Christ and that grace will speak the final word. "God so loved the world . . . that whosoever believeth in God should not perish" (John 3:16). In Christ the war is over, both the war within and the war without. The alienation from God and from ourselves is ended and with it our alienation from others.

Once the true nature of life is made known to us in the preaching of the gospel, we are shown the possibility of a future. We who were dead in our sins are made alive in Christ (Rom. 6:11). Before, we were condemned to repeat a meaningless cycle of existence, not life; to fool ourselves into thinking we were gaining our lives while losing everything of worth in them; to suffer the emptiness of a society that accumulates things but never owns anything. But through the act of God in Christ humankind has been given a future, and all of the selfish power in the world cannot overcome that promise. That is the way things are. Preaching has both the solemn duty and the joyful privilege to tell it like it is.

Preaching offers a doxology unto God. Sometimes preaching is spoken of as if it only conveys information from one human brain to others, or else as if it merely provides stimulus from one set of emotions to those of others. True, preaching is integrative of all theological disciplines, and as such it performs an essential educative function. Also true, preaching cares about things that matter deeply, and as such it stimulates affective response. But both of these effects of preaching are too limited in their scope. Both make the listening congregation the sole end of preaching. If that is so, preaching fails in its place in worship.

For some churches and preachers, it is true that the sermon looks no further than teaching or motivating. No doubt it would come as a surprise to them how strongly humanistic and rationalistic such an approach really is. Even though they go on referring to the eleven o'clock hour on Sunday morning as the "worship service," there is virtually no worship of God in it. Some of these preachers are quite open about their feelings. One preacher even flatly declared that "churches that emphasize worship don't grow" (which, by the by, may be far more diagnostic of the true secrets of some "church growth" than many might care to admit).

Preaching, however, must ultimately offer itself unto God. God must be the subject of every subject. The sermon must be an offering of praise, thanksgiving, confession, and dedication unto the Most High: "The most, if not the only, appropriate posture for the speaker is that of worship. Regardless of the consituency of the . . . congregation, the real audience is God. What we say . . . we offer to God."[9] It must join with the other elements of Christian proclamation—music, singing, congregational participation in spoken liturgy, baptism, Communion, all forms of art and beauty utilized in the service of God—to form a unified offering of praise to the Creator, Redeemer, and Sustainer of life. "The proclamation of Christ occurs in a tense unity between doxological acclamation, grateful remembrance, and expectant prayer, on the one hand; and public confession, urgent appeal, and inviting offer, on the other. It is not only challenge and the promise and assurance of salvation. It is always also thanks and praise in response to Christ."[10]

Preaching must offer a doxology unto God, for if it does not, it will ultimately seek only to cultivate the favor of persons as an offering pleasing to them. Only when preaching directs itself initially as an offering pleasing to God can it find itself eventually prophetic to persons.

Preaching creates the church and sends it into the world. The church creates preaching, but preaching also creates the church. Out of the preaching of Jesus Christ the church is born. In the declaring of the reconciliation that has occurred through the grace of God, we who were once estranged and alienated are brought into the family of God.

Here we must be plain. It is God's family, the church, not ours. We may not say who may come in or who must stay out. Preaching is under the sternest mandate to keep the church as open as Christ established it. "And the Spirit and the bride say, Come. And let the one that heareth say, Come. And let the one that is athirst come. And whosoever will, let that one take of the water of life freely" (Rev. 22:17).

Those who thirst are invited to come and drink of the water of life freely. Preaching declares the goodness and the mercy of God, and need is the only qualification to partake. When preaching has spoken these words, the true church has been born. When it has not, some of the most monstrous societies on earth have been spawned. There is only one church, and it is God's. There are many religious societies, and they are ours. Nonpreaching gives birth to them; preaching gives birth to the church.

The mission of preaching does not end with the creation of the church, as if it were to exist for its own sake. Preaching sends the church into the world. Just as the church is not created as a club for selfish look-alikes, a Society of the Same, so it does not exist for itself and by itself. Only in the world can the church fulfill its mission. Jürgen Moltmann says, "Sermons mediate between the text of the biblical testimonies, and poor and helpless people today. It is out of this mediation that the community of Christ comes into being. People gather to listen to the words of the Bible . . . and they disperse again in order to bring the energies of the divine Spirit which they have experienced to the people with whom they share their day-to-day lives."[11]

What does this mean? It means that preaching must so inform the church that it dies to self. Even as "the Human Son came not to be ministered unto, but to minister and to give his life a ransom for many" (Matt. 20:28), so the church gives itself in the world. Preaching, therefore, does not encourage the church toward self-serving, isolated protectivism but toward existing in the world, for the world.

The old preaching of build-our-plant, feather-our-nest booster-ism must die. The foolish and even wicked expenditure of time and funds to get Christians to join our downtown branch and not the neighborhood branch of the same outfit, or vice versa, has got to go. The church is boring itself to death with this foolish number swapping while the work of God in the world goes largely unnoticed. The preaching of the Evangel is about more serious business than we have suspected. We are not and must not be talking about the single sharing of reassuring secrets, but the bold declaration that God is to be reckoned with in the widest corporate affairs of humankind and that we ignore that word only at our greatest peril.

"Going into all the world" is a Great Commission all right, but a dangerous one as well. Its implications are not only geographical, which are relatively unthreatening, but political and social— which are enormously threatening! Here preaching faces its strongest challenge; here preaching has most often failed. Our preaching must know no limits, accept no compromises with public or private interests.

What can preaching do? It can send the church into a real world, a world of starving children and murderous competition, of lonely rooms and smug clubs, of shattered dreams and burned out hopes. This is the final mark of true preaching, to send the church into the world. For that is where the Christ of the church is: "He goes before you into Galilee: there you shall see him" (Mark 16:7).

2. The Stubborn Pulpit

The last years of the twentieth century have seen a dramatic change in the fortunes of preaching. To the relief of everyone connected with it, preaching got up from its deathbed—as almost everyone regarded it—and, in the famous words of the black prayer, "thanked God its bed was not its cooling board" and that it "awoke clad in its right mind." (Whether it did so, or course, remains to be seen.)

At least preaching got a brief reprieve from its usual negative prognosis. Its illness proved once again not to be fatal, and its morbid self-doubts went into a brief remission. As the editor of a widely used series of homiletical volumes put it: "Preaching has captured the attention of increasingly large segments of the American public. Lay parish committees seeking pastoral leadership consistently rank preaching as the most desirable pastoral skill. Seminary courses and clergy conferences on preaching attract participants in larger numbers than ever. Millions of viewers watch television preachers every week."[1] He could have added that textbooks on preaching, a decade ago almost as extinct as the ivory-billed woodpecker, have proliferated, and that books of sermons have even sprouted alongside *The National Inquirer* in grocery check-out lines.

Before we hyperventilate over this heady turn of affairs, however, we'd best take a deep breath, sit back, and take a long look at the larger picture of preaching's path. Whatever virtues the pulpit may lack, stubbornness has not been one of them. The vine over Jonah's head would have withered in less than a day if it had suffered the heated blasts directed at the pulpit across the centuries. But for the most part, preachers have gone on sitting in the shade of sermonic vines, not sure if they were merely gnawed of worms or cursed of God—or both—even if they no longer flourished as they once did and even if the sultry east winds of criticism sometimes made them want to curse God and die.

No part of the worship of the church has been so generously and ecumenically roasted as preaching, but likewise no aspect of its worship has been so generally and ecumenically practiced. In fact, the act of preaching may be the most truly ecumenical observance of the church. It has a longer continuous history of virtually unanimous practice among all groups, both Protestant and Catholic, than any other element in its worship. Baptism and the Lord's Supper are as generally observed, but the meaning and method of observance of these rites vary widely from group to group. Enter any place of worship on any Sunday, however, and, like it or not, you probably can count on hearing a sermon not very different from the one you heard somewhere else the Sunday before.

Preaching, then, has a double stubbornness: it is stubbornly the same, and it is stubbornly there.

Whether this is good or bad depends on one's point of view. Legions of critics from the first century on have not liked it one bit. Despite the hoary history of pulpit bombardment, every generation of preachers seems to get caught by surprise in the attack. Previously this awareness crept up on most preachers about the age of pulpit puberty—which is an indeterminable age somewhere between pulpit innocence and pulpit senility—although some never seem to go through it at all.

If there was anything at all different, however, about the attacks on preaching in the middle years of the twentieth century, it was the around-the-clock nature of the bombing and the early seriousness with which young ministers regarded this criticism. It is hard to evaluate the self-doubt of previous generations; so we will never know how badly other generations of preachers were unnerved by the shelling of the pulpit. But obviously it didn't do much to encourage preaching in this century, as manifested by the widespread skepticism of the pulpit ministry among some and the decidedly apologetic tone of those writings that sought to defend preaching in the parish ministry.

If abundance of criticism is any criterion, however, no generation of preachers has ever had much ease in Zion. As a matter of fact, "to a large extent, the pulpit has from the first century received poor reviews (2 Cor. 10:9–10)."[2] Perhaps Selden overstated the case in his *Table Talk* when he asserted that "preaching in the first sense of the word ceased as soon as ever the gospel was written," but at least he proves that criticism wasn't long in beginning.[3] Brilioth quotes criticisms of various preachers and their preaching from the second century onward, including Tertullian's critique of Melito of Sardis and Porphyry's accusations against Origen.[4] In the fourth century preaching was said to have degenerated into a tool for ecclesiastical and political deceit.[5] The preachers of the seventh century were accused of "having too great a tendency to moralize, to allow every text in the Bible to become the starting point for an ethical admonition which was primarily intended to emphasize the church's precepts on penance, fasting, and good works."[6]

During the Middle Ages the sermon was attacked as mechanical, dull, and usually nothing more than a poor plagiarism of earlier works.[7] In the sixteenth century preaching was the butt of ridicule by the laity who found it to be incredibly boring and who passed the time away by sleeping, chattering, or playing simple games. Sometimes, if provoked, they even attacked the sermon during the service itself. One woman who had been rebuked in the midst of a sermon for gossiping with her neighbor promptly jumped up and said angrily, "Indeed sir, I know the one who has been doing the most babbling! For I do but whisper a word with my neighbor, and thou hast babbled there all this hour."[8] The sermons of this entire period were "no more than the dry bones of a decaying art."[9]

The preaching of the seventeenth century was criticized as one-sided and full of exaggeration.[10] In England, Robert South ridiculed the ignorance of the preachers of that age, saying that "to be blind was with them the proper qualification of a spiritual guide; and to be book-learned as they call it, and to be irreligious were almost synonymous terms."[11] For some years after 1660 the name of Charles I was more used in sermons than that of Christ. In 1670 John Eachard complained bitterly in his tract, "The

Grounds and Contempt of the Clergy Inquired Into," about the unintelligible, unnatural, and uncommunicative speech of the pulpit. In *The Reformed Pastor*, Richard Baxter devoted twenty-four closely printed pages to a survey of the sins of "ministers of the Gospel from the days of Christ until now."[12]

In 1761 John Harman wrote a scathing critique of preaching, *The Crooked Disciple's Remarks Upon the Blind Guides' Method of Preaching.* In 1799 Eli Forbes published *The Inoffensive Ministry Described*, which claimed that preaching had degenerated to a level far below that of previous years. One critic labeled the preaching of that age "dull, duller, dullest," and John Caird declared that "the pattern sermon of the Georgian era seems to have been constructed almost expressly to steer clear of all possible ways of getting human beings to listen to it."[13]

By now we might well wonder how long this cheery note continued. When *were* the "good old days" for preaching? Surely the nineteenth century was the Golden Age of Preaching! That era when sermons were the rage, and preaching was in its prime. Or was it?

A GOLDEN AGE OF PREACHING?

One reason for the perpetual trauma of pulpit puberty, or coming of age in the pulpit, is the incredibly persistent myth of the "Golden Age of Preaching," whenever that was. Ask any generation of preachers, and it was exactly three generations earlier. And that holds true all the way back, at least to within three generations of the apostolic age. (The apostles themselves were not troubled by such delusions—they just wanted to return to the Golden Age of Rabbinicism.)

The net result of this absolute figment of imagination is the feeling on the part of all preachers that they are among the first generation of preachers to be chained to the rock of the pulpit and have their livers torn out by the giant birds of criticism, only to have them grow back before the next Sunday. These preaching Prometheuses resent punishment for attempting to bring fire from the gods to earth, and they are sure that in the Golden Age of the ancients things were different.

This mythical era is usually located in the nineteenth century. Wasn't that the century of the "pulpit princes"? Weren't Spurgeon, Robertson, Beecher, Brooks, Maclaren, Liddon, Dale, Broadus, Parker, Talmage, Newman, Whyte, and Bushnell the glory of the pulpit? Wasn't "sermon tasting" the Sunday rage and the morning's sermon the subject of the afternoon's conversation? Didn't tours regularly stop at the churches of the famous pastors so that tourists could hear them? Was there ever such a time for preaching?

Nevertheless, the preachers who stood with both feet in the middle of that century did not see it as any "Golden Age," but just as another tough, demanding time to be a preacher. F. W. Robertson, probably the most widely used homiletical example from that century, saw his age as a time of declining influence for the pulpit: "By the change of the times the pulpit has lost its place. It only does part of that whole which used to be done by it alone. Once it was newspaper, schoolmaster, theological treatise, a stimulant to good works, historical lecture, metaphysics, etc., all in one. Now these are proportioned out to different officers, and the pulpit is no more the pulpit of three centuries back."[14] In a letter to a friend he wrote, "I wish I did not hate preaching so much, but the degradation of being a Brighton preacher is almost intolerable."[15]

Despondent, moody Robertson was not the only preacher of that time to mourn the passing of the pulpit. In 1882, when Mahaffy wrote "The Decay of Modern Preaching," Spurgeon, Liddon, Parker, Beecher, Maclaren, and Brooks were at the height of their careers. And in 1923 Joseph Fort Newton quoted the London *Times* as saying that, "For the present at least, the noble art of the pulpit must be considered as lost," and asking, "If the great sermons . . . of Bishop Butler were preached today, would they fill the smallest church in London?" Yet Newton reminds us that "in his own day the Bishop sat in his castle brooding over the decay of religion, while the miners, touched by the wondrous evangelism of Wesley, were singing hymns of praise almost under his window."[16]

If any further evidence is needed, a partial list of critical articles from the nineteenth century should be convincing:

1805, "Defects of Preaching" (London, *Christian Observer* 4:462–64)
1809, "On the Assumed Popularity of Evangelical Preaching" (London, *Christian Observer* 10:484–92, 627–28)
1811, "On the Little Success Which Attends the Preaching of the Gospel" (London, *Christian Observer* 10:746–49)
1868, "Bad Preaching" (London, *Broadway* 1:439ff.)
1868, John Caird, "The Declining Influence of the Pulpit in Modern Times" (London, *Good Works* 9:193–200)
1876, Charles H. Grundy, "Dull Sermons" (London, *Macmillan's Magazine* 34:264–67)
1877, James Baldwin Brown, "Is the Pulpit Losing Its Power?" (Boston, *Living Age* 133:304–13)
1878, "Is the Modern Pulpit a Failure?" (last chapter in *Lectures on Preaching* by Matthew Simpson: "It has become fashionable in certain circles to speak of the failure of the pulpit." He calls this an "old song.")
1896, *The Dead Pulpit*, Hugh Reginald Haweis, (London)
1899, Stephen J. Herben, "Is the Power of the Pulpit Waning?" (New York, *Methodist Review* 59:896–910)
And note this one:
1899, Walter Slater, "The Pulpit in the Good Old Days" (London, *Temple Bar* 85:557–59)

No age seems so golden as in the afterglow of its sunset. The nineteenth was indeed a strong century for preaching, but *no stronger than the twentieth.* Every teacher of preaching is pressed to answer the question, "Where are the great preachers today?" The answer is, "Right where they always have been—few and far between."

At the most, no one could produce more than fifteen to twenty truly memorable names from the nineteenth century of preaching. That is a fine number, actually, but nearly that many could be produced from the twentieth century. (Skeptical? How about Harry Emerson Fosdick, Dick Sheppard, William Temple, Studdert Kennedy, Karl Barth, Phoebe Palmer, Maude Royden, Georgia Harkness, Ronald Knox, Emil Brunner, George Buttrick, Paul Scherer, Reinhold Niebuhr, Samuel Shoemaker, Leslie Weatherhead, Fulton Sheen, James Stewart, William Sangster, D. T. Niles, Billy Graham, Helmut Thielicke, Martin Luther King, Martyn Lloyd-Jones. Don't agree with all of them? Did you with all of the nineteenth-century preachers?)

None of this should be understood as saying that all centuries are alike in the quality of their preaching or in the reception accorded to it. That is obviously untrue. Some ages have been bleak and others have been better. But it does say that every generation of preachers tends to romanticize the heroic past and to be overly pessimistic about the present.

This shortsightedness produces a kind of "cave mentality" for the ministry. The darkest view is always ahead, and the brightest light comes from behind us, from where we entered. We do not need to dispute the very real problems preaching has today, but we do need to lay to rest once and for all the unrealistic "Golden Age" myth and we do need to know that pulpit criticism was not born in our generation.

RECENT CRITICISM

This doesn't mean that we haven't had our share of it. Whatever preaching's problems in the twentieth century, at least it hasn't had any false delusions about itself as an age of preaching, golden or otherwise.

At the "turn of the century" (about as close to the popular idea of the Good Old Days as you can get), the Good Old Articles on preaching carried such encouraging titles as "The Decadence of Preaching" (1903);[17] "Is the Pulpit a Coward's Castle?" (1905);[18] "Why Sermons Make Us Go to Sleep" (1908);[19] "Is Preaching Obsolete?" (1911);[20] and the question most of the preachers must have been asking, "What Is to Become of the Preacher?" (1911).[21]

The two decades that followed sharpened the attack: "Is Preaching Futile?" (1920);[22] "Why the Pew Is Listless" (1924);[23] "The

Decline of Preaching" (1925)[24] (by now it should be apparent that preaching must be descending the world's longest hill—wherever and whenever its peak was); "The Futility of Sermons" (1925);[25] Fosdick's famous article, "What Is the Matter with Preaching?" (1928);[26] "Can the Protestant Sermon Survive?" (1932);[27] and the blunt question, "A Halt to Preaching?" (1936).[28]

More recent criticism of preaching has been characterized by increased perceptivity and articulateness. Some of it has continued to be marked by an unawareness of history and a desire to work out all of the problems of the church on preaching, but much of it has hit preaching where it hurts, or ought to hurt. What have been the sore spots for the critics?

Almost everything. Joseph Sittler has said, "Preaching is in trouble everywhere."[29] A partial list of the abundant complaints against it makes that perfectly clear. Clyde Reid listed seven categories of criticisms of preaching: (1) preachers tend to use complex, archaic language the average person does not understand; (2) most sermons today are dull, boring, and uninteresting; (3) most preaching today is irrelevant; (4) preaching today is not courageous preaching; (5) preaching does not communicate; (6) preaching does not lead to change in persons; (7) preaching has been overemphasized.[30]

Reuel Howe listed six complaints by laypersons concerning preaching: (1) sermons often contain too many complex ideas; (2) sermons have too much analysis and too little answer; (3) sermons are too formal and too impersonal; (4) sermons use too much theological jargon; (5) sermons are too propositional, not enough illustrations; (6) too many sermons simply reach a dead end and give no guidance to commitment and action.[31]

Others involved in counseling are quoted by Gene Bartlett as raising these criticisms from their experience: (1) preaching clearly seems directive; (2) all preaching generalizes (!); (3) much preaching is guilt producing; (4) listening to sermons may divert listeners away from their real problems; (5) the public preacher may violate his or her role as private listener.[32]

Besides these complaints, a summary list could be compiled

from the many other writers who have criticized preaching:

1. The *influence* of the sermon has been generally challenged. Does it *affect* anything? Does it change anything? Is it important enough to claim as much of the minister's time as it demands? Is it, in fact, a valid part of the Christian task? Berton,[33] Berger,[34] Glock and Stark,[35] Dittes,[36] and others have raised these questions.

2. The *form* of the sermon has been questioned. In its present form, can the sermon communicate? Earlier this question was raised by Reid and Howe who said that younger preachers were challenging the usefulness of traditional monological preaching.[37] New alternatives, notably utilization of small groups, were called for in various forms by Berton,[38] Symanowski,[39] Wenzel,[40] and Wedel.[41] More recently, idea-oriented sermons have been challenged by experience-oriented and narrative/story sermons; and deductive forms have been challenged by inductive forms, as in the writings of Craddock, Lowry, Wardlaw, Long, and many others (see chapter 12, "Once Upon A Time").

3. The *content* of the sermon has been sharply criticized. Harvey Cox says that preaching is weak because it does not "confront people with the new reality which has occurred and because the summons is issued in general rather than specific terms" and he adds, "We have departed today from the preaching of the Apostles."[42] Doberstein,[43] Jensen,[44] and Ebeling,[45] among others, emphasize that it is not preaching, but the weak content of our preaching that is at fault.

4. The *preacher* of the sermon has also come in for a considerable share of the criticism. In fact, increasingly the "declining" influence of preaching, the irrelevance of its content, and the problems with its form are being laid at the personal doorstep of the preacher. Helmut Thielicke has particularly located his criticism at that point.[46]

5. The *exclusiveness* of the sermon has been attacked. Feminist theologians—Ruether, Russell, Fiorenza, and others—have challenged sexist language and interpretation and male-dominated pulpits; liberation theologians—Gonzalez, Gutierrez, Cone,

Segundo, and others—contradict its political and class biases and urge it to translate works into action. Allan Boesak says of apartheid: "There are churches and individual Christians who defend this system as the will of God for South Africa, using arguments from the same gospel that for blacks has become God's incomparable word of liberation."[47]

In short, every aspect of preaching is under attack today just as it always has been from the beginning. Our review has made it abundantly plain that no age of pulpit proclamation has ever escaped heavy criticism.

This evidence should have two effects on today's preachers: first, *sobering,* when they realize how stubbornly unwilling or unable preaching has been to profit from its mistakes; and second, *reassuring,* when they realize that the first sound of criticism is not the last note of hope for the future of preaching. We need this balanced perspective to keep us from either unbounded optimism or unwarranted despair.

Nevertheless, although sharp criticism does not in itself signal the end of preaching, that is no excuse for continually ignoring it or not seeking to eliminate its causes. Preaching has stubbornly refused to acknowledge the validity of the charges against it and to repent, to change for the better, to be what it claims; and having failed to satisfy its critics with its life, it is now being invited to do so with its death.

Outside of obligingly stretching out prone, what else can preaching do to remedy its problems? It seems to me that we need an adequate perspective on the development of these problems if we are to deal with them seriously.

THE PREACHING CYCLE

The first step in this direction has already been taken; that is, we are aware of the long history of pulpit criticism and realize that we have not desecrated Eden, that we have not been driven out of the Golden Age of preaching by our sins, and that no angel with a flaming sword bars our return to a preaching paradise. When

Joseph Sittler says, "Preaching is in trouble everywhere," he goes on to add, "Of course preaching is in trouble. Whence did we ever manufacture the assumption that it was ever to be in anything but trouble?"[48] It is only our duty, as we shall see, to make sure it is in trouble for the right reasons.

The second step is to understand that preaching, like the church whose servant it is, participates in a definite cycle. At times, preaching has enjoyed great prominence in the church; at other times, it has been less than nothing. But when preaching becomes *everything* in the church, it quickly becomes *nothing* for the next generation. There is but one God, who will tolerate no other. The foolish idolizing of the pulpit and the fatuous worshiping of the cult of personality inevitably lead to the decline of preaching.

Nothing is surer than this. Only when the pulpit is servant is it given a place at the table; when it ceases to be the servant of the Word and fights for the chief seats, it is told to "go down there and sit." But when it becomes the servant of all, as in the parable, preaching finds its true greatness.

With respect to the proclamation of the gospel, a definite cycle can be observed for two thousand years: *search, discovery, excitement, routinization, boredom, disillusionment, search.* Naturally this order is not mechanically reproduced in every generation, but the broad outlines are plainly discernible in Christian history. Furthermore, there are smaller waves of this effect going on within the larger cycle. The church as a whole might be at one point, while individual locales might be at an altogether different stage of development.

Since this is a cycle, we might begin at any point in examining it, but *search* will do as a starting point. Preaching always begins in a search for an adequate means of conveying the Word. Since the gospel is good news, the Word is always in search of words to publish glad tidings; the church struggles to find expression for the faith once delivered in the midst of a living contemporary community.

This search, born of faith in the Word, leads to *discovery,* discovery of words for the realities it has grasped, however imperfectly, and of means for expressing these words to its age. New forms and methods of preaching are born.

Great *excitement* attends this discovery—which usually is made initially by a few—as others seize upon the words and means that have been found faithful servants of the Word.

A process of *routinization* follows, wherein that which was spontaneously done in its beginnings is made the common practice and eventually the official program for proclaiming the faith. Deviations in content, language, and even style are frowned upon as unorthodox, if not rejected outright or surpressed.

Boredom quickly sets in as the church suffers from the deadening routine of "the right way to do it." During this period the church frequently searches its memory to recall "how it was done" when its preaching was successful; and anyone who asks painful questions of the cultically correct method is quickly reminded that these approved practices are identically the same as those that produced the Golden Days, now receding rapidly into myth.

Disillusionment follows, as more and more of the faithful discover that the standard routine does not work any longer, that the words and means that were once strong and honest servants have now become tottering and powerless tyrants. These old systems are quickly deposed, but only cynicism inherits their empty thrones. For a while cynicism and nihilism reign, and only celebrating the emptiness brings any satisfaction. Sooner or later, however, the painful reality of this hollow meaninglessness seizes the church, and it is led again into the agonizing *search* for authentic words.

This search is always agonizing because the pioneers of this movement cannot resist substituting newer meaningless cultural clichés for the older cultic language they so emphatically reject. But when someone, somewhere, in this process realizes that these efforts are no more than updated versions of the same mistake that has held the Word captive all along and waits in humility to listen until it speaks fresh words to him or her, then the Word becomes flesh again and discovery begins.

It would take a prophet to say where we are now in this cycle. The answer would vary anyway from group to group, and even from person to person. Ten years ago, in the first edition of this book, it was my guess that preaching was "not at the crest of the wave and quite likely has emerged from its trough . . . somewhere in the process of search—either quite early in that stage, or perhaps, for a few, on the edge of discovery." That "edge of discovery" now has been crossed, in my opinion, by the rediscovery of narrative for the sermon, the value of inductive movement, and the importance of the oral nature of the sermon and its delivery. All of these contributions will be explored later. In fact, discovery has definitely led to excitement, at least for some; and there have been indications of even an approaching new synthesis for the future of preaching. But as we shall see, that synthesis remains yet to be achieved.

All of this, however, leads me to raise some early warning flags of danger. Everything that tells us that preaching is on its way up, that the popular interest in it has increased, also tells us that the downside of the cycle is imminent. We may ride the crest of this tide a good while longer—and I hope we do—but the pride of the pulpit has historically risen up at such times to undo it. We always seem to forget that it is God alone who can effect the proclamation of the gospel and that generally it is culture that affects its popularity.

For instance, has no one noticed that all religious movements are on the upswing now, even worldwide? That television evangelists are exercising unheard of clout in politics—even running for president!—and that conservative causes in general are in ascendance? Let the pulpit take fair warning from its own history: such periods of power do not bode well for preaching, and those who seek self-aggrandizement from the lofty perch of the pulpit will be brought low—and sadly, for a time, the pulpit with them.

In the face of its many failures, what can be the true confidence of preaching? What hope sustains it? What keeps the pulpit stubbornly there?

3. The Stubborn Hope

Can the stubbornness of the pulpit—not its stubbornness in resistance to change, but the stubbornness of its existence—simply be attributed to inertia, to habit, to some mysterious hold the pulpit continues to exercise through the centuries? Or is there something more basically stubborn about the pulpit? Does preaching sustain some kind of internal relationship with the Christian faith rather than merely being a cultic, temporal expression? Could it be that preaching itself is essentially and authentically Christian?

PREACHING AS AUTHENTICALLY CHRISTIAN

If we want to answer this question, we have to look at the origins of the Christian sermon. Did it arise from Hebrew soil, or is preaching nothing more than a Greek intrusion, a pagan rhetorical overlay on the Christian faith?

Amos Wilder insists that "the spoken and written word have a basic role in the Christian faith," and he sees the background for this role in the Old Testament:

The religion of Israel is very much a matter of hearing rather than of seeing. Even God's actions are spoken of by the prophets as his word. No man can see God and live, but he is known in his speaking. By contrast it is the gods of the nations that are mute, and their visible images are dumb. As we read in Psalm 115:7, "They do not make a sound in their throat." Throughout scripture, revelation is identified above all with speaking and hearing . . . rather than with the imagery of the visual arts. . . . Of course, like all religions Christianity has its sacred actions and spectacles, sacred places and times, sacred arts and objects, but it is in connection with God's speaking that they are sacred. . . . Language, then, is more fundamental than graphic representation, except where the latter is itself a transcript in some sense of the word of God.[1]

This emphasis on the priority of *word* in the Old Testament is apparent even in the creation narratives. In the book of Genesis, humankind is created by the word of God. All of God's creatures are called into being, and humans themselves are created in the image of God in that they also speak, name, and communicate.[2] Likewise, in Exodus 33:11 we are told that "the Lord used to speak to Moses face to face, as a person speaks with a friend." And Wilder says, "The rhetorics of the Old Testament represent the response of man to the address of God, and their form and style are elicited by the self-communication of God."[3]

Hebrew precedence for Christian preaching is also evident in the proclamations of the rulers of Israel as well as in the preaching of the prophets. In Isaiah, *proclamation* is used to describe the activity of the Servant of the Lord (Isa. 61:1). Jesus later declared that his ministry was the fulfillment of these prophetic words and thereby traced his ministry of proclaiming to Old Testament sources (Luke 4:21).[4] Brilioth agrees that "A clear line extends from Old Testament prophecy to the sermon in the Church."[5]

More directly, Christian preaching bears striking resemblance to the expositions of Scripture in the synagogue, perhaps even more so than the sometimes spontaneous oracles of the Old Testament prophets: "The origin of the Christian sermon, like nearly everything in the church services, is to be found in the Synagogue. We know from the Bible that it was customary to expound the lesson read in the services. In the Jewish church this developed into a hortatory address, very near to a modern sermon."[6]

The participation of Jesus in the worship of the synagogue at Nazareth is not only interesting as an example of the earliest Christian proclamation, but also because it is one of the very few contemporary records of a Jewish synagogue service. Three elements in that narrative are particularly instructive in showing us the relationship between Jewish synagogue worship and the contemporary sermon. The sermon of Jesus in the synagogue of Nazareth was *liturgical, exegetical,* and *prophetic;* that is, it formed a part of a worship experience and was itself a mode of worship; it started from and expounded a text of Scripture; and it was a message for the present time that made the scriptural text a living word in the contemporary situation.[7] Jesus regarded his proclamation as so closely related to the framework of the Judaism of his day that he could claim its message to be one of fulfillment (Matt. 5:17). Not only in its form, then, but also in its content, the basic message of the Christian faith had Hebrew origins.[8]

The conclusion of these studies, and others, is that preaching cannot be accused of being a "Greek intrusion." It is an authentic development from Hebrew tradition: "The Christian preacher is not the successor of the Greek orator, but of the Hebrew prophet."[9] Obviously the prevailing environment for the Christian church soon became Gentile rather than Jewish, but the primary kinship of New Testament proclamation is not with this new environment but rather with its Jewish heritage.[10]

There was, in fact, a fundamental difference between the Hebrew and Greek perceptions of reality: "For the Hebrew, the decisive reality of the world of experience was the *word;* for the Greek it was the *thing.* . . . We can conclude for the Hebrew the most important of his senses for the experience of truth was his hearing (as well as various kinds of feeling), but for the Greek it has to be his sight; or perhaps inversely, because the Greeks were organized in a predominantly visual way and the Hebrews in a predominantly auditory way, each peoples' conception of truth was formed in increasingly different ways."[11]

One distinctive difference between Old Testament and New Testament concepts, however, should be noted. The Old Testament rarely uses the expression "to preach." P. H. Menoud says that the term was not used more because the Old Testament prophets were not heralds of *good news* as were the New Testament preachers: "Their commission was to exhort the elect people to remain faithful to their God. . . . These prophets were not bringing news; they asked for a better and stricter obedience to the given law."[12]

This fact bears an interesting relationship to another curiosity in the New Testament. Since the most common expression translated "to preach" in the New Testament is *kerussin,* it could be expected that the most common New Testament word for preacher would be *keryx* ("herald"). But this term only occurs three times in the New Testament (1 Tim. 2:7; 2 Tim. 1:11; 2 Pet. 2:5). All of these occurrences are obviously extremely late. Why is this so?

Apparently the term was avoided because it was widely used by the pagan Stoic preachers of that day and also because the New Testament writers wished to distinguish Christian preaching from the rather mechanical heralding of the Greeks, which was principally repetition by rote and as such thereby violated the personal dynamic inherent in Christian proclamation.[13]

Because of its Hebrew heritage, early Christian preaching was also afraid of any particular vocabulary that was thought of as sacred or pious; that is, there is no precedent in early Christian speech for what is now termed "the language of Zion." To create such a language would be to engage in idolatry.

If the Hebrew tradition feared images because they promoted idolatry, the Hebrews were no less strict with their own concepts regarding words. Once any term took on a fixed or magical character for Israel, its value was forfeited: "The repertory of images used in the prophets and the old tradition of Israel—such images for Israel as the vine or vineyard, the foundling or orphan, the wife —these were not allowed to become a 'holy language' or stereotypes in the postexilic writers. They were continually reshaped and combined with new and fresh figures and expressions. The new utterance which Jesus and his followers brought into the world similarly re-created the religious vocabulary of the Old Testament."[14]

When Jesus came forth speaking, therefore, he placed himself fully in the primal oral tradition that preceded him. This in itself bears a profound theological significance: "For one thing speaking is more direct than writing, and we would expect this in him through whom God openly staged his greatest controversy with his people. . . . Jesus was a voice not a penman, a herald not a scribe, a watchman with his call in the marketplace and the Temple, and not a cry of alarm in the wilderness like John the Baptist."[15]

There was an urgency about the word of Jesus, an immediacy, a personal note that nothing but the living voice could achieve. His ministry was consistently characterized by "teaching . . . preaching . . . healing" (Matt. 4:23). In fact, Mark omits "teaching" and alters "healing" to "casting out demons" (1:39), and Luke retains only "preaching" (4:44). Mounce says, "This suggests that preaching is the most important of the three activities."[16] Jesus himself declared that it was for this reason that he had come (Mark 1:38). He committed himself freely to speech, and in this sense the early Christians also lived on the "free bounty of God."[17]

Fuchs has observed that Jesus wrote nothing and that even Paul wrote reluctantly; Paul was distressed by any circumstances that prevented face-to-face address (Gal. 4:20), and his writing itself has direct oral style, typified by imagined dialogue, direct discourse, rhetorical questions, and exclamations.[18] In this emphasis on oral style, Paul and the other disciples followed in the footsteps of Jesus: "The apostles came preaching."[19]

Although the preaching tradition of the church is clearly Hebraic in origin, this *does not mean* that there was no Greek influence upon it at all or that any such influence would render preaching invalid. Why should it? Did Egyptian influence render invalid the sacrificial system of Israel? Of course Greek rhetoric could be abused and was; but its strong emphasis on the hearers and the plainest means of conveying a message to them was adopted by the Christian church only because this emphasis was fully in keeping with the purposes of preaching.

But it should not be overlooked that it was Greek *rhetoric* upon which the church fastened and in so doing again asserted for itself the primacy of speech: "It is true that when the church took over the heritage of classical culture—ancient rhetoric, architecture, painting, and sculpture—it related itself to all the arts and has exploited them all ever since in changing situations. But the thesis still holds that the faith identifies fundamentally with the arts of hearing and against those of sight and touch. Even when the Christian paints, or carves, or dances, or sings he does so to a text, and identifies himself with an archetypal dialogue between God and man."[20]

From its Hebrew origins to its Greek influences in the later New Testament era, then, preaching is an insistence on the priority of word over image. Recent psychological studies corroborate the validity of this ancient viewpoint: "Reality becomes a meaningful part of consciousness only through the interpretation of real contacts by language. . . . A world without sound is a dead world: when sound is eliminated from our experience, it becomes clear how inadequate and ambiguous is the visual experience if not accompanied by auditory interpretation. . . . Vision alone without acoustic perceptions does not provide understanding."[21]

What significance does this study have for the contemporary preacher? Two implications are of particular importance. First, preaching is authentically Christian because it represents face-to-face encounter and thereby participates in the historic medium through which God disclosed God's self to us: "The word of the Lord came unto me, saying . . ." Human speech permits a degree of encounter that is profound without being idolatrous.

This leads to a second implication for preaching. The spontaneity of speech and freshness of form that Jesus employed must never be violated by crystallizing terms and forms into a "language of Zion." The tradition that commits Christian preachers to speaking also commits us to listening. "He who aspires to the enunciation of the word must first learn to hear it; he who hears it will have found the means to articulate it."[22] When we have heard the words of others around us as well as the Word of God, then we are ready to speak with the same freshness and freedom demanded by the preaching of the gospel in every age.

The authentically Christian nature of proclamation is a basic reason for the stubborn existence of preaching, but there is also another cause for its persistence: the importance accorded to it by theology.

PREACHING AS THEOLOGICALLY SIGNIFICANT

It is probably safe to say that theologians have been more enthusiastic about preaching than have preachers. Preachers would
likely counter by replying that if they are frustrated with preaching, it is because they have to *do* it rather than write about it. To
a certain extent, of course, they are right, and only the most
obscure theologian could fail to have sympathy with them.

But one reason for the stubborn problems of the pulpit, and a
major one, is the low self-esteem of preachers, both of themselves
in general and of the preaching task in particular. And conversely,
one reason that the pulpit is still stubbornly *there* after nearly two
thousand years of Christian history is the seriousness with which
theologians have regarded the place of preaching in the church. In
fact, at this point there is an amazing agreement among theologians, of whatever persuasion—right, left, and all points in between. Only the pervasiveness of the practice of preaching can
rival the uniformly high place accorded to preaching in Christian
theology. But I do not believe that preachers are generally aware
of the striking ecumenicity among theologians at this point. How
many preachers are as aware of the prominence of preaching in the
theology of Bonhoeffer or Bultmann as in the theology of Barth?

If you want to present a real theological riddle, ask someone
sometime what Barth, Bultmann, Ferré, Ott, Ebeling, Bonhoeffer,
Niebuhr, Farmer, Tillich, Wingren, Brunner, and Gilkey have in
common. If you get any answer at all (you probably won't, and
you probably won't be invited back for coffee, either), it might be
that they are all Christian—although a good many people
wouldn't even agree on that. And if you reply to your own riddle,
"They all have a high view of preaching," get ready for a dubious
look followed by a vigorous argument.

But it is true, and that doesn't strike me at all as incidental. We
could not think so little of what we do in the pulpit, nor could we
take it so lightly, if we understood the convictions on preaching
of this incredibly broad array of theologians. No one would claim

that these theologians understand the task of preaching in the same way. They most certainly do not. But they all share a view of preaching that can only be described as high, and that in itself bears its own message.

Since theological studies do not usually pull together the ideas of these people on preaching, I think it is necessary to briefly document this claim before going on to draw conclusions from it. But anyone who really wishes to know whether it is so will have to examine the writings themselves—which is precisely my reason for mentioning the subject in the first place.

It comes as no surprise to anyone that Karl Barth had a high view of preaching. In fact, he insists that if we would understand his theology we must hear all through it the question, "What is preaching?" Dip into his theology almost anywhere and you will find evidence of his regard for preaching.

For example, "Preaching is the Word of God which he himself has spoken."[23] Again, "When the gospel is preached, God speaks: there is no question of the preacher revealing anything or of a revelation being conveyed through him. . . . Our preaching does not differ in essence from that of the prophets and apostles who 'saw and touched'; the difference is due to the different historical setting in which it takes place."[24] Furthermore, "Preaching is 'God's own word.' That is to say through the activity of preaching, God himself speaks."[25] With reference to the effect of preaching Barth says, "It was pointed out above that the Church needs to be constantly renewed; it is always being created by the preaching and hearing of the Word." In this regard, for Barth "the only thing that counts is to make the Word of God heard."[26]

Barth's position is so well known that it may not come as a surprise, but it may be more difficult to believe Carl Braaten when he says, "Bultmann has always agreed with Barth at the decisive point. Both are ultimately concerned about the living Word of God as it encounters real men."[27] Or to agree that Barth and Bultmann share a "common subscription to the Later Helvetic Confession: 'Preaching the Word of God is the Word of God.' "[28]

But Bultmann is indeed unequivocal at this point: "The redemptive event is only present in the word of preaching, the word of address and claim and promise."[29] He insists that the word of preaching confronts us as the word of God. We are not to question its credentials; it is we who are questioned. We are asked whether we will believe the word or reject it. He writes, "Is not the encounter with God possible only in the fellowship where faith in God is living and preached? . . . Faith is faith in the Word of God which encounters me through the preaching of it, and preaching occurs only in the Church. . . . I should like to add: the preaching of the community enables me to participate in the eschatalogical event that has its origin in Jesus."[30] And he adds, "That means the eschatalogical occurrence continues to take place in preaching, in the address which proclaims. Preaching, therefore . . . is always the word of man and at the same time it is to be understood as God's address."[31] (At this point we should probably remind ourselves that we are quoting from Bultmann, not Barth.)

For Bultmann, preaching is also a unique kind of communication: "Christian preaching is the communication of a historical fact, so that its communication is something more than mere communication."[32] Finally, and most emphatically, "The crucified and resurrected Christ encounters us in the word of preaching, and never in any other way."[33] When theologians as diverse as Barth and Bultmann agree so emphatically on anything, we should all take notice.

Bonhoeffer has scarcely been more often identified with preaching than Bultmann. And yet for all of his critical questions to the church and its preaching, Bonhoeffer maintained a view of Christian proclamation as high as anyone since Luther.[34] Eberhard Bethge writes: "Bonhoeffer loved to preach. When he found out that a relative of his might have a few months to live, he wrote, 'What would I do if I learned that in four to six months my life would reach the end? I believe I would still try to teach theology as I once did and to preach often.' "[35] Bethge insists that for Bonhoeffer, "discipleship, suffering, silence, worldliness—all that does not take the place of the sermon, but serves for its enthronement." His concern for the sermon "was not a matter of fearfulness," but of confidence in the ultimate value of the sermon.[36] As for his "secular interpretation of biblical concepts," Bethge says, "The secular interpretation of biblical concepts does not mean the discontinuation of preaching, but the first step toward its renewal for the world."[37]

Bonhoeffer himself wrote, "The proclaimed Word is the Incarnate Christ himself. . . . the preached Christ is the historical Christ and the present Christ. . . . He is the entrance to the historical Jesus. Therefore the proclaimed Word is not a medium of expression for something else, something which lies behind it, but it is the Christ himself walking through his congregation as the Word."[38]

Typical of the "new hermeneutics" and its emphasis upon preaching, Gerhard Ebeling also stresses the priority of preaching: "Proclamation is the Alpha and Omega of the church's *praxis.*"[39] Like Bonhoeffer, Ebeling identifies the purpose of theology with the function of preaching: "Theology is necessary only to the extent that it makes itself superfluous and makes proclamation necessary."[40] For Ebeling, the oral character of the Word is decisive since the Word is an "acoustical event."

Similarly, Heinrich Ott says, "In so far as preaching of the gospel is a constitutive function of the Church (and there is no church without gospel proclamation; the church is essentially the sphere where the gospel is proclaimed; to declare the gospel is the church's business) gospel proclamation and theology are most closely interrelated. The coordination of theology in the church is effected through gospel proclamation."[41]

Paul Tillich exercised considerable criticism upon the day-to-day preaching of the church. A recurring theme in his writings is the insistence that the church has not proclaimed the healing, reconciling work of the gospel with sufficient courage, selflessness, and truthfulness. Nevertheless, Tillich had a high view of the place of Christian proclamation; he saw the value for every theology as "determined for what it can do for preaching."[42] The measure of the success or failure of preaching is always the accuracy of the preacher's grasp; first, of the content of the message he or she has to deliver and, second, of the human situation to which he or she speaks.

Many other theologians are equally emphatic in stressing the place of preaching in the church. For example, Gustaf Wingren writes, "The task the preacher faces is that of bringing about a meeting between the Word and men. . . . The Word exists to be made known; only when it is preached is its objective content fully disclosed."[43] P. T. Forsyth calls preaching "the most distinctive institution in Christianity," and says "that with its preaching Christianity stands or falls."[44] Emil Brunner claims that wherever there is true preaching and the word of God is genuinely proclaimed, "in spite of all appearances to the contrary, the most important thing that ever happens upon this earth takes place."[45] H. H. Farmer says that for the church, "the prime task is to preach the gospel."[46]

Contemporary American theologians have agreed. Martin E. Marty writes: "The Christian cannot usually get away from verbal witness. . . . The Christian is commanded to preach. Preaching is a virtually universal activity for the churches."[47] Similarly, Harvey Cox reminds us that "the biblical faith, unlike Buddhism, must *speak* of God. It cannot withdraw into silence or cryptic aphorisms. A God to whom human words cannot point is not the God of the Bible."[48]

John Bright says that "the strength of the church lies in the gospel it proclaims—thus in its preaching—today, as it always has. . . . The church lives, let it be repeated, in her preaching—always has, and always will."[49] Nels Ferré says, "Preaching cannot take the place of the acted Word in sacrament nor the lived Word in Christian fellowship, but preaching is indispensable as the communication of the Word—the meaning and purpose of God."[50]

Likewise, Langdon Gilkey views the preacher as a mediator of the Word, since he believes that Christ is related to the church through the word of God as it is preached. This viewpoint has led Clyde Reid to conclude that Gilkey holds "a very high view of preaching. . . . His emphasis on the preacher as the mediator of the word would seem to place him with those who regard preaching not only as essential but as an integral part of the Christian message."[51] And Joseph Sittler sees preaching as integrative to the ministry of the preacher: "Preaching is not merely something a preacher does; it is a function of a preacher's whole existence concentrated at the point of declaration and interpretation."[52]

Peter Berger's shift of emphasis on preaching represents one of the most striking and potentially significant statements of recent times. In a speech to the Consultation on Church Union (COCU) meeting in Denver in 1971, Berger said, "Ages of faith are not marked by dialogue, but by proclamation"; and further, "I believe a new stance is called for in our situation . . . a stance of authority." While he did not deny "the ever-new ways in which . . . (the Christian message] may be told," he asserted that "when all is said and done, the Christian community consists of those people who keep on telling this story to each other and some of whom climb up on various boxes to tell the story to others." He insisted that "if there is to be a renaissance of religion, its bearers will not be the people who have been falling all over each other to be 'relevant to modern man.' "[53]

Berger would be grossly misunderstood if his emphasis was interpreted as a call for "authoritarianism" or conservatism in theology. But just because it is not, it is all the more remarkable when he calls for authority and proclamation to cure the "demoralization and loss of nerve" of the church.

Now this in itself is noteworthy, but all the more so in light of the sweeping change of emphasis in the ten years since the publication of *The Precarious Vision,* Berger's work of 1961, in which he states:

But it is possible to ask even while accepting the traditional Protestant posture of the kerygma, whether an acceptance of the "world come of age" may not also involve what can be called a nonkerygmatic posture— that is, a stance on the part of the Christian which deliberately and meticulously *surrenders any claim to authority* [italics my own].

It would seem that only in such a posture is genuine dialogue possible. . . . A claim to religious authority, carried into a dialogue however polite, is a club held under the table. A claim to authority always projects the point at which coercion will replace communication.[54]

It would be extremely unfair to imply that this earlier statement is at absolute variance with the opinions expressed in 1971 or to fail to note that an emphasis needed by the church at one time might not have changed in ten years. But the direction of the change is significant. Likewise, it illustrates the cycles of opinion to which proclamation is subjected, largely due to its own cycling between "authoritarianism" and "loss of nerve."

Anyone, with a little effort, can discover many other extensive references similar to these. What conclusion can we draw from this impressive testimony? What is it about preaching that causes it to be regarded with such seriousness? (For an examination of the specific hopes and concerns of women theologians for preaching, see "Women and Preaching" in the following chapter.)

Obviously each of these theologians would want to answer that question for himself. And their answers would be radically different, poles apart. But however the replies might be worded, two elements would appear to me to be indispensable to the answer: *preaching bears the eternal Word,* and *preaching touches the living situation.* That is, the historic given of the Christian faith encounters the experiential given of the contemporary situation through preaching. "Faith comes by hearing" (Rom. 10:17), and "The one that hears you hears me" (Luke 10:16).

Preaching is not essential to the church or to theology because the church has always done it, or because the early apostles did it, or even because Jesus did it. Preaching continues to have an irreplaceable position in Christian theology and Christian worship because it does what God did in self-disclosure to Israel and in the fullness of that revelation in Jesus. It provides a medium for revelation that enables the eternal Word to maintain its living, dynamic character and encounter our concrete situation.

When the Word would make its fullness known, it took on flesh and dwelt among us; and to make itself known *now,* the Word must *keep on* becoming flesh among us. As we shall see, only when preaching is incarnational is it truly preaching.

It is not merely a parable to say that preaching "becomes flesh and dwells among us." The two determinative elements of revelation are present in that statement: the Word and the human situation. "The Word" speaks of God's gracious self-disclosure; "dwells among us" is the human dimension essential to our understanding. True preaching participates in both.

Preaching is often criticized for its inability to get people to *do* something—"people do not do something just because they are told." But this critique betrays a shallow concept of preaching and ultimately turns back on itself. That is, preaching is *not* "telling people what to do"[55]—although at its worst it degenerates into that. In preaching, Person comes to persons through person. Preaching is personal encounter, word-event, ongoing revelation.

The ultimate promise of language is not that it conveys *something* to us, but *someone:* "The Word as an event is always something said from one to another. . . . The Word which is concerned with God would then in this sense *say God to us,* so that *God comes to the one addressed and is with him,* and the one addressed is with God."[56] But if we promise ourselves to another, we lie. Even at our best we cannot fulfill that promise: "Only the Word by which God comes to man, and promises himself, is able to do this. That this Word has happened, and can therefore be spoken again and again, that a man can therefore promise God to another as the One who promises himself—this is the certainty of the Christian faith."[57]

God's Good News is no less that the promise of the Person who can, and will, come to the people. No one can do more for another than that.

Theology, then, takes preaching seriously because through it Christ comes to the people. The preacher who has the faith to believe that this is so can share the theologian's enthusiasm for preaching.

But hope is difficult to maintain in the face of frustrated experience, and preachers may be forgiven if sometimes their own experience of preaching causes their faith to shrink smaller than the proverbial mustard seed. What is harder to believe than that my words can bear the divine Word? Little wonder that we stumble: "Lord, I believe; help thou mine unbelief!" Preaching is the ultimate act of faith.

The past two chapters have revealed at least two of the primary reasons for the double stubbornness of the pulpit. Its authentic Christian nature and the lofty promise accorded it by theology have kept it stubbornly *there,* but its stubborn unwillingness or inability to fulfill the promise of its heritage has subjected it to an increasing barrage of criticism. At its best, the stubbornness of the pulpit is the result of its hope. At its worst, the stubbornness of the pulpit is the result of its pride. Its pride, unless overcome, will kill it; its hope, unless misplaced, will save it. It is apparent that the recovery of its true voice is mandatory for the survival of the contemporary pulpit. But how?

4. Proclamation, Manifestation, and Action

As we have seen, the stubborn hope of the pulpit has been strongly undergirded by various theologies of proclamation. But there are other voices from theology, some raising pointed questions for preaching, and it is to these theologies we must now turn.

Theologies of proclamation and manifestation, as Paul Ricoeur has designated them, look at revealed truth in quite different ways.[1] The classical theologies of Barth and Bonhoeffer and, in a different but no less emphatic way, of Bultmann and Tillich are *theologies of proclamation,* theologies of the Word. (For that matter, so are the theologies of virtually everyone cited in the last chapter.) These theologies are directed by the experience of God's decisive word of address in Jesus Christ; only through the Word, we are told, do we find true reconciliation and true liberation. The only appropriate response to this word of address, with its gift and demand, is faith. In spite of the invectives applied to them by fundamentalism, these radical theologies of proclamation destroyed the "easy peace with culture" of classic liberalism, so aptly described by H. Richard Niebuhr: "A God without wrath brought men without sin into a kingdom without judgment through the ministrations of a Christ without a cross."[2] As a result, preaching took on new vigor and earnestness. At the same time, a much needed reemphasis was placed on the centrality of theology for an understanding of preaching.

As we have seen, these theologians were followed in their proclamation emphasis by Ebeling, Fuchs, and others of the "new hermeneutic" school, as well as a majority of Protestant theologians up to Jürgen Moltmann. Preaching has been enriched by their contributions and generally has tended to look no further for its theological guidance.

THEOLOGIES OF MANIFESTATION

Nevertheless, this stance is not the only possibility open to theology. Significant *theologies of manifestation* have also been developed. Ricoeur says that these theologies are concerned with "the logic of meaning in the sacred universe."[3] The writings of Mircea Eliade have been foundational to an understanding of this tradition, particularly *The Quest, The Sacred and the Profane, A History of Religious Ideas,* and *Patterns in Comparative Religion.* Most recently, David Tracy has pursued these lines in *The Analogical Imagination.*[4] In certain Old Testament studies as well there has been a discernible shift from the verbal—with "an accent upon speech and writing, and generally upon the Word of God," as in Gerhard von Rad and Bruce Vawter—to manifestation or presence emphases, as in Claus Westermann and Robert Cohn.[5]

Manifestation emphasizes image rather than word, vision rather than hearing, sacrament rather than preaching. The prophetic-ethical-historical emphasis of proclamation theologies is matched by the mystical-priestly-aesthetic-metaphysical emphasis of manifestation theologies.[6] These differences obviously correspond, but not exclusively, with Protestant and Catholic theologies. Tracy says he could describe the Catholic Reformation as "image-event" just as Gerhard Ebeling can describe the Protestant Reformation as "word-event."[7] (Neither theology is the exclusive property of any Christian group, as is evident by the extensive emphasis on aesthetics/liturgy in some Protestant circles and the prophetic/proclamational emphasis in current Catholicism.)

From the philosophical reflection of Charles Hartshorne and Alfred North Whitehead and the journey toward transcendent mystery in Karl Rahner, to poets with the sense of the extraordinary in the ordinary like T. S. Elliot and Gerald Manley Hopkins, to the studies of Marcel Proust and Mircea Eliade on privileged moments and rituals, to sections of the works of Hans Küng,

Edward Schillebeeckx, Schubert Ogden, Langdon Gilkey, and John Cobb, manifestation theology reflects upon the wonder of all creation as gifted and all reality as graced. It therefore "transforms the stuttering self into a creature alive to and with a fundamental trust in the ultimate reality manifesting itself/himself/herself as none other than an incomprehensible, a pure, unbounded, powerful love decisively re-presented as my God in the event of Jesus Christ."[8]

As might be expected, theologies of manifestation do not immediately apply themselves as directly to preaching as theologies of proclamation. This shift of attention may explain some of the comparative lack recently of significant input from theology to preaching theory. (On the other hand, much more input has come from language theories of various kinds, especially in the works of Paul Ricoeur, Jacques Ellul, and Walter Ong, among others.) Nonetheless, in the larger task of proclamation these approaches have much to suggest, and even the most practical tasks of preaching can be enriched by the insights of manifestation theologies. Certainly Barth's view of the Word is mystical and performatory, and Bonhoeffer's theory of that moment one begins "to see" the message of a text of Scripture is highly mystical. At the same time, Tracy affirms the need for the authentic proclaiming word: "The emphasis upon the proclaimed word in Judaism and Christianity will occasion expressions in words via different genres—narrative, prophecy, hymn, prescriptions, proverb, parable. . . . And these normative words, these scriptures, will themselves be continually reinterpreted, applied and preached by the individuals and communities empowered by a word of proclamation."[9] Likewise he affirms that theologies of both proclamation and manifestation "must prevail in Christian consciousness."[10]

These directions seem highly suggestive for contemporary preaching, and current image-oriented approaches to preaching might profit greatly from a further integration of theologies of manifestation and proclamation.

THEOLOGIES OF ACTION: LIBERATION THEOLOGY

A third category of contemporary theology that speaks to our understanding of preaching is that of *action*—personal, social, and political. The theologies of action are generally referred to as liberation theology. Gustavo Gutierrez defines it: "The theology of liberation is an attempt to understand the faith from within the concrete historical, liberating, and subversive praxis of the poor of this world—the exploited classes, despised ethnic groups, and marginalized cultures. It is born of a disquieting, unsettling hope of liberation. It is born of the struggles, the failures, and the successes of the oppressed themselves."[11]

The theologians of this movement travel a somewhat different route from those theologians of proclamation or manifestation. These liberation theologians, whether their efforts stem from Third World, black, or feminist concerns, emphasize Christian *action* and the primacy of the praxis of the faith, by which they mean action in behalf of the faith. For them, neither the visions of manifestations nor the words of proclamation are sufficient. We must be doers of the word, they say, but not in the limited individualistic, mystical, interiorized ways of the past. Gutierrez says, "Only from a point of departure at the level of practice, only from deed, can the proclamation by word be understood. In the deed our faith becomes truth, not only for others, but for ourselves as well. We become Christians by acting as Christians. Proclamation in word only means taking account of this fact and proclaiming it. Without the deed, proclamation of the word is something empty, something without substance."[12]

Redemption cannot, must not be purely or even primarily personal. True redemption includes liberation from all bondages of sin and suffering and especially from all inhuman structures and systems of society. Third World theologians such as Gutierrez place particular emphasis at this point: "The proclamation of the gospel from the standpoint of identification with the poor summons the church to solidarity with the lower classes of the continent, solidarity with their aspirations and struggles to be present in Latin American history. The church is called to contribute from its own task, the proclamation of the gospel, to the abolition of a society built by and for benefit of a few, and to the construction of a different social order, juster and more human for all."[13]

Liberation theology is frequently noted for its sharp critiques of traditional Christian praxis, but the theologians of that movement believe the Christian faith itself demands such critiques. Therefore all expressions by Christians that are recorded by liberation theologians as racist, sexist, anti-Semitic, pro-power, or triumphal have come in for strong criticism, as have certain patriarchal, anti-Jewish, and pro-Roman interpretations of the biblical witness.

Naturally, along with these biblical and systematic critiques, liberation theology also raises strenuous objection to any Christian preaching that reflects these tendencies. This is not because liberation theologians are hostile to preaching, however. These theologians may begin, indeed, from theologies of proclamation or manifestation, but because they have heard the Word of proclamation or seen the vision of manifestation or both, they move on to social and political practice. (For example, liberation theologians such as Johann Christian Metz and Gustavo Gutierrez clearly seem to have begun from manifestation theology; Jürgen Moltmann, Dorothee Soelle, Rosemary Radford Ruether, and James Cone from proclamation theologies.) As Tracy points out: "Above all, for all political and liberation theologians, the word event of proclamation commands, the gift event of manifestation demands a singular recognition; the recognition of the primacy of praxis, action in and for a church and a global society groaning to be set free from the alienating events and oppressive structures in the contemporary situation."[14]

Moltmann, for example, insists that the word of the gospel is a word of promise that commands action in history and a word that contradicts our contradictions of it. Ruether and Cone insist that our Western, male, white theologies and interpretations of the Bible do not correspond to the reality of oppression experienced by blacks, women, and other marginalized groups around the world.[15] Liberation theologians argue that new interpretations and new actions are required by Christians to correct these injustices.

As an example of the movement made by many of these theologians, Moltmann serves an interesting role as a kind of "John the Baptist" transitional figure between classic proclamation theologies and liberation theologies. From his statement on the radical hope proclaimed in the resurrection in *Theology of Hope,* to its corrective counterpart in the dialectic of the cross presented in *The Crucified God,* and more recently to his liberation understanding of the relationship of church and world in *The Church and the Power of the Spirit,* Moltmann has demonstrated the conviction of many contemporary theologians that the proclaimed Word is a suffering Word as well as an ultimately victorious one and that any proclaimed words must eventually also be liberating words if they are the Word of Jesus Christ. He writes: "The aim of the sermon is not merely to make a statement. Sermons are also meant to communicate something that has been experienced. What they seek to state is found in the biblical testimonies which relate the history of powerless men and women with a God who makes them live. What they intend to convey is experienced in the presence of the divine Spirit, who calls the unworthy, opens people who are closed in on themselves, disarms the aggressive and encourages the powerless to hope."[16]

For liberation theologians, these concerns imply a shift of attention for proclamation. For example, Bonhoeffer's theology of proclamation focused on the problem of communicating the gospel to the person who is nonreligious in "a world come of age." But for liberation theology, the question is how to communicate the gospel to a person who is not a person, or at least not recognized as such by the existing social order. The challenge in Latin America, according to Gutierrez, does not come primarily from the person who does not believe (religiously), but from the person who does not believe that he or she is a person, from those in the ranks of the poor and the exploited. Their challenge "is not aimed first at our religious world, but at our *economic, social, political and cultural* world; therefore it is an appeal for the revolutionary transformation of the very bases of a dehumanizing society."[17] From South

Africa, Allan Boesak asks, "What are Christians to do when they have to live under oppression—*and* when oppression claims to be 'Christian'?"[18]

Liberation theologians insist that our concerns must therefore shift from religious/nonreligious to human/inhuman issues. And this takes a rereading of the gospel. Christian redemption must mean the redemption of all structures and systems of society and the liberation of every oppressed person in that society. Major focus is placed by liberation preaching on the marginalized in society: women, blacks, and members of the Third World.

With their emphasis on action and their scorn of idle words, liberation theologies might seem to have little place for preaching. But that has not been true. Gutierrez says, "But this understanding of the faith from within concrete historical praxis leads to a proclamation of the gospel at the very heart of this praxis. It is a proclamation that is at once both voice and vigilance, active deed, in concrete solidarity with the interests and struggles of the populous classes. It is *word* concretized in *gesture:* it determines attitudes and is celebrated in thanksgiving."[19]

That he is correct is clearly evident: some of the most notable examples of preaching have issued from the very groups most involved in liberation theology. Perhaps the most striking feature on the preaching scene today is the remarkable dynamism of preaching among women, black, and Third World preachers. Any such list of preachers is dangerous because it is invariably limited and arbitrary. But those risks are worthwhile, I believe, to call our attention to the importance of liberation preaching. (At this point I cite only preachers principally concerned with Third World issues, since I will treat black preaching and women's preaching later.) Notable preachers, among many others, must include Orlando Costas, Jose Miguez-Bonino, Elsa Tamez, Pablo Deiros, Bishop Desmond Tutu, Allan Boesak, Samuel Escobar, Louise Ahrens, Mortimer Arias, and Kosuke Koyama. Of course, many of the authors previously cited are themselves preachers of note. This list, although admittedly selective, does illustrate the place of preaching in Third World liberation theology.

In fact, by their insistent emphasis upon the preaching of Jesus to the poor and the outcasts, upon the prophetic tradition of declaring God's favor and mercy upon the needy and oppressed, and upon the Old Testament tradition of retelling the story of the liberating God of Exodus, liberation theologians have reemphasized the true importance of preaching. Justo and Catherine Gonzalez insist that "liberation theology can lead to biblical renewal in the task and art of preaching."[20] How is that so?

The Gonzalezes suggest, "The white male preacher has general credibility until he shows himself incompetent. Therefore, he may be tempted to rely upon public presence, jokes, irrelevant illustrations, voice characteristics, and so forth, and not on the biblical text itself."[21] These words are truer than most of us would care to admit. But is it not true that if we "white male preachers" would lay aside the cultural power given to us we could not preach so many nonbiblical sermons—sermons on "what to do" and "how to succeed," which have scant or no biblical basis, but which in fact "preach," *if they do,* because we are regarded as authorities— a luxury most women and minority persons do not have? Would there not be more biblical preaching also if we relied less on our public presence and rhetorical effects and more on the witness of the biblical text?

In any case, liberation theology engages preaching at virtually every point, and its significant questions cannot be overlooked. It is my opinion that these issues cannot continue to be regarded as peripheral interests for preaching, an elective course on the boundaries of homiletics. This shift, I suspect, will be even more difficult and demanding for us than we now imagine. But the truths of the gospel and its liberation are as inevitable as those that destroyed the slavery of the Civil War era. The church ignores them at its own peril. Unless preaching speaks in the cause of the oppressed, the poor, and the marginalized of every society, it will become a seldom visited cultural ghetto in less than a century.

We must turn next to a more specific focus on the distinct emphases of black and feminist liberation theology with reference to preaching. While "liberation" concerns were identified initially with Third World theologians and issues, similar concerns have been strongly advanced by preachers and theologians among blacks and women.[22]

WOMEN AND PREACHING

Regarding the importance of women in the interpretation and proclamation of the gospel, Letty M. Russell writes:

The universal message of God's love for all humankind will continue to be heard through the power of the Holy Spirit, but the fashion in which it is heard depends on our willingness to speak and act the Word in ways concretely addressed to the struggles and longings of men and women today. Today, that speaking and acting can no longer ignore the existence of women as part of the people of God. *Women are no longer willing to be invisible either in the work and life of church in society or in the interpretation and proclamation of the gospel* [emphasis mine]. The Word must be concretely addressed to their journey toward freedom as well as to that of others.[23]

As one who served for ten years as pastor of the Presbyterian Church of the Ascension of the East Harlem Protestant parish, Letty Russell summarizes the convictions of countless women in ministry. The question of the role of women in the Christian faith has already proved to be one of the most crucial issues for the church. My brief remarks do not pretend to be an adequate statement of the many concerns of women for the life of the church or, for that matter, of the concerns of women for preaching. That is obviously beyond the scope of this work. However, it is my intention to illustrate those concerns—especially the difficult struggle of women to achieve the right to preach—and the seriousness with which the church must take those concerns.

Rosemary Radford Ruether defines the church as liberation community:

Feminist liberation theology starts with the understanding of Church as liberation community as the context for understanding questions of ministry, creed, worship, or mission. Without a community committed to liberation from sexism, all questions such as the forms of ministry or mission are meaningless. Conversion from sexism means both freeing oneself from the ideologies and roles of patriarchy and also struggling to liberate social structures from these patterns. A feminist liberation Church must see itself as engaged in both of these struggles as the center of its identity as Church. Joining the Church means entrance into a community of people who share this commitment and support one another in it.[24]

The very statement of these concerns introduces new issues for historical Christianity. What is a "feminist"? Letty Russell says, "The word 'feminist' signifies anyone advocating changes that will establish political, economic, social, and ecclesiastical equality of the sexes." What is "sexism"? It is "any attitude, action, or institutional structure that systematically subordinates a person or group on grounds of sex." Feminists seek to end sexism in the Christian faith through a "nonsexist" interpretation of the Bible: *"Nonsexist interpretation is prohuman interpretation* that views male and female as equally made in God's image." For many Christians, this sort of definition of the nature of the Christian community calls for a radical restructuring of thought and action.[25]

The evidence that this is so is easy to find. One only needs to examine the long struggle of women to find places in Christian ministry. As Ruether says, "The patriarchal history that has prevailed throughout most of Christian history in most Christian traditions has rigidly barred women from ministry. The arguments for this exclusion are identical with the arguments with patriarchal anthropology."[26] These arguments generally stem from a theology of male headship and female subordination: "This subordination, while attributed to women's physiological role in procreation, extends to an inferiority of mind and soul as well. Women are categorized as less capable than men of moral self-control and reason. They can play only a passive role in the giving and receiving of ministry. They should keep silent."[27]

An alternate tradition within early Christianity has been pointed out by recent feminist scholarship:

This alternative Christianity could have suggested a very different construction of Christian theology: women as equal with men in the divine mandate of creation, restored to this equality in Christ; the gifts of the spirit poured out on men and women alike; the church as the messianic society, not over against creation but over against the systems of domination. We see hints of this vision in the New Testament. But the Deutero-Pauline recasting of Christianity in patriarchal terms made this inclusive theology nonnormative.[28]

Other traditions dominated in the Christian movement, and although women were never denied participation in the outpouring of the gifts of the Spirit, the rising tide of episcopal power and succession marginalized any expression of women's public ministry.

There were exceptions, however. Considering the generally conservative nature of many Baptist and other evangelical free-church traditions today, it seems strange to remember that they represented the left wing of the Reformation, the radical Reformation. It is also instructive to note that when the Anabaptists were persecuted during the Reformation, women rose to take the places of men who were killed or imprisoned. But they were also deemed worthy of execution because of their ability to teach subversive doctrines," and one out of three Anabaptist martyrs was a woman.

Since free-church groups believed that God directly called ministers without mediation of the church, women were occasionally found as preachers among Baptists and Quakers, as during the seventeenth-century English Civil War—nearly 150 years before Methodist or Holiness women preachers. Female Baptist preachers were denounced in the treatise *A Discovery of Six Women Preachers in Middlesex, Kent, Cambridgeshire and Salisbury* (London: n.p., 1641).[29]

But as these groups themselves became more mainstream in their concepts of Christian ordination, the phenomenon of women as preachers in early America was largely limited to the Pentecostal and Holiness movements. Where Spirit was regarded as the empowering force in preaching, women might preach; where institution was regarded as the authorizing power for public ministry, women might not preach.[30] And although Wesley himself encouraged women as preachers (and got himself barred from several of his own Methodists churches for it too), his vision did not last through the next generation.

Nevertheless, women such as Phoebe Palmer, "the mother of the Holiness movement," did preach (even if without a preaching license), declaring that Wesley himself licensed Sarah Mallet to preach at the Manchester Conference in 1787 and citing Wesley's letter to one of his women preachers: "But it [conscience] will not permit you to be silent when God commands you to speak."[31]

Phoebe Palmer's model for women in ministry was the prophet. She found the scriptural idea of the terms *to preach* and *to prophesy* inseparably connected as one and the same thing. She argued that at Pentecost "they were *all* filled with the Holy Ghost" when the cloven tongues *"sat upon each of them,"* and men and women alike "went everywhere preaching the word" (Acts 8:4). As a result of this line of argument, sometimes women even outnumbered men as preachers in such Pentecostal churches as the Assemblies of God and in such Holiness movement groups as the Salvation Army and the Church of the Nazarene.

Other images of women in preaching were projected by women such as Frances Willard, who was born a full generation after Phoebe Palmer and who became president of the Women's Christian Temperance Union in 1879. Her influential book *Woman in the Pulpit* urged the pastoral ministry upon women even though she herself felt "too timid" to act on those longings within herself "without a call [to a church]."

Willard cleverly reversed the rhetoric of "the cult of domesticity," which said that the nature of women best fitted them for the gentle duties of the home, and argued persuasively that it was radically inconsistent of the church to allow women to serve as frontier missionary-evangelists, a ministry that sent them through snowdrifts and into dangerous territory, while insisting at the same time that "women are timid and shrinking, delicate, modest, sensitive, home-loving, nestling, timid little things." She questioned the church's consistency in sending them out to "wild and naked barbarians" while denying them the right "to engage in the motherly work of the pastorate." Willard argued, in fact, that the pastorate *was* "motherly work," for which women were uniquely and ideally suited.[32]

In spite of these arguments and the eloquent pleas of such women as Anna Oliver for ordination, these women were generally frustrated in their requests. Phoebe Palmer once cried out in her frustration, "The church in many ways is a sort of potter's field where the gifts of woman, as so many strangers, are buried. How long, O Lord, how long before man shall roll away the stone that we may see a resurrection?"[33]

However, due to the incredible evangelistic skills of women such as Maggie Newton Van Cott, some women began to be licensed and even ordained. During one twelve-month period from 1871 to 1872, the journal of Maggie Van Cott records that she had "seen 3,085 seeking at the altar the Saviour's love, who have professed to being blessed. Of this number I have been privileged to extend the right hand of love and welcome on probation into the Methodist Episcopal church to 1,113 souls."[34] When Van Cott was eventually handed her preacher's license, she asked: "Will this [preacher's license] make me more efficient in winning souls for Christ?" "I cannot say that it will," replied Presiding Elder A. H. Ferguson. "Well, then, sir, I value it but very little."[35] Although she was not the first woman to be licensed to preach, her extraordinary prominence, as well as that of other charismatic women preachers such as Sojourner Truth, forced the church to consider the place of women with such evident gifts of ministry.

The history of American women in religion is obviously a complicated one, but five major stages have been identified and are useful in understanding the development of women's role in the church:[35]

Stage One: This is an incredibly lengthy period of little change, from the beginning of the Republic through the 1950s, characterized as "prehistory." During this period social reform, women's rights, and evangelical religion were mutually supportive of each other among the concerns and activities of women.

Barbara Welter concludes that American religion became "feminized" in the nineteenth century, "not only because the majority of revival converts and church members were women, but also in the sense that more genteel theology now replaced the harsher religious styles of colonial puritanism."[37] Donald Matthews likewise concludes in *Religion in the Old South* that churches were the principle means of establishing a public life for women: evangelicalism provided a framework for social organizations and experiences that were exclusively for women as they were brought together in churches, women's seminaries, and societies.

Stage Two: Beginning in the 1960s, women's rights were viewed through feminist eyes. "The Cult of True Womanhood," a well-known article by Barbara Welter, surveyed women's magazines and showed how they shaped contemporary social and religious ideas about women. In this stage women were made aware of the limitations of this "cult," but they were also challenged to become more active in social institutions.

Stage Three: In the 1970s, evangelical religion emerged as an important agency through which women entered the public domain of American society and politics. Questions were raised about the ways in which religion had oppressed women, but also about the ways in which women had benefited personally and socially from their religious beliefs.

Stage Four: In the 1980s women have looked at questions of the effects of race, class, and community upon women's experiences in religion and society. How has the female religious experience varied by race, class, and denomination? What actions should be taken by women to ensure their full equality in society?

Stage Five: Most recently, women have begun looking toward a synthesis of the liberation concerns of black women and Third World women with those of the previous feminist leadership, which was largely Anglo and white.[39] Progress has been made, but some inevitable tensions have become evident.

Although this historical sketch traces only the largest outlines of the issues regarding women and the church, it does show us the background for the ongoing issues for women in preaching. How can the stereotypical images of male and female service to the church be modified? How can "ideological suspicion" be used to deconstruct sexist biblical interpretations and then be saved to serve as positive critique for its reconstruction? How can sexist language be overcome in popular use, in the liturgies of the church, and in the reading of the Bible? How can women's specific contributions to an understanding of war and peace, a theology of nature, the questions of grace and justice in society, and many other issues be communicated to a church that needs to hear "the whole counsel of God"—as revealed to the women upon whom God's Spirit is poured out, even as it is upon men?

The Church has already heard from voices as diverse as those of the charismatic Phoebe Palmer, the gentle Frances Willard, the mystical Sojourner Truth, the fiery Maggie Van Cott. There were many others, too, like the famous missionary Ann Hasseltine Judson, "the premiere model of the American female missionary and an early articulator of religious feminism,"[40] the noted educator Mary McLeod Bethune,[41] and the gifted and articulate theologian Georgia Harkness.[42] Now we are again hearing from women's voices in proclamation, no less gifted and no less diverse, such as Virginia Mollenkott, Elsa Tamez, Elizabeth Achtemeier, Dorothee Soelle, Letha Scanzoni, Letty Russell, Louise Ahrens . . . the list goes on. And it will not stop. Because the same God who ordained the women at the tomb as the first preachers of the resurrection —and to male apostles at that—and who alone ordains who is to preach will keep on sending women with their Good News to our world in these "last days" when God's Spirit has been "poured out upon all flesh, and your sons and your daughters shall prophesy" (Acts 2:17).

BLACK PREACHING

If there is one place in Christianity where the enthusiasm for preaching has never waned, it is in the black church. According to Henry Mitchell, it was preaching that first attracted Negro slaves in significant number to Christianity—not just any preaching, but preaching influenced by that of George Whitefield: "All African speech was characterized by a tonality, and to follow Whitefield's preaching example was literally to 'go home to African facsimiles,' in contrast to the cold and unmodulated utterances of the Anglicans, whose churches had dominated slave territory prior to the harvest of the Great Awakening. The nourishment of identity and the nostalgic appeal of Whitefieldian preaching was like a drink of water from home."[43]

For the first time blacks saw preaching with which they could identify: "The spontaneous (no manuscript), inventive utterance and vivid description were, with their results, a way in which blacks could finally feel at home in Christianity. . . . It was only important that he [Whitefield] had taken the faith from the chilly modes of the prior experiences and given it a 'soul' model on which they were able thereafter to build a faith truly Christian and truly African."[44] It was no coincidence that the greatest preacher in the early history of the black church in America, serving the largest black congregation of that time, was Andrew Marshall of Savannah, Georgia, the city that was Whitefield's headquarters.[45]

That may have been the beginning, but it was certainly not the end of a long and distinguished pulpit tradition in American. Other early pioneers in black preaching included the distinguished Bishop Richard Allen, AME, Henry Highland Garnet, Samuel Ringold Ward, C. T. Walker, and other striking characters such as Black Harry, who was said to have memorized all of the sermons of Bishop Asbury,[46] and the dramatic John Jasper, whose sermons brought both black and white listeners from all over the nation.

This tradition continues today, just as exciting and varied as then. Martin Luther King, Jr., is unquestionably the best known preacher of this century, worldwide, either black or white, but his efforts have been accompanied by those of many others: Sandy F. Ray, William Holmes Borders. Howard Thurman, Henry Mitchell, Peter Gomes, James Cone, James Forbes, Gardner Taylor; and from South Africa, Allan Boesak and Bishop Desmond Tutu. These only suggest but by no means exhaust the lengthy list of distinguished contributors to black preaching.

How might the contributions of black preaching be summarized? The following suggests some central principles:[47]

1. *Black preaching proclaims a God who is actively involved in the continuing process of the liberation of humankind.* Because of the black people's long experience of oppression, black preaching reached out early in its

history to the Old Testament texts about the liberating God of Israel. The *power* of God, especially as liberator, has been particularly emphasized. Nevertheless, in spite of the inequities of life, black Christianity proclaims life as good because the Creator of life is good (a tradition that originated in Africa and was enriched by its contact with Christian tradition). Therefore the *providence* of God as all-sufficient is strongly emphasized in black preaching. But this God is not a God of an abstraction but of reality, a God who seeks nothing less than the *wholeness* of the person and of life. This God cares for body as well as soul and for soul as well as body.

I still vividly recall an experience twenty-five years ago of preaching to an enormous congregation of blacks of all ages in a rural school auditorium in Louisiana. The material they had ordered for their Vacation Bible School Congress, to which "folks from the granddaddies to the babies" had been invited, had not arrived, and I was a desperate last-minute substitute. I had only briefly met the pastor at my office, but he gave me, a fledgling preacher in my twenties, the full-fledged "works" for an introduction: "You have all heard of President Kennedy" (sounds of murmured "uh-huhs" and shouts of "Yes!"). "Well," said the patriarch, "the man we have here today is greater than President Kennedy!" I was stunned. "Because President Kennedy is concerned about your body, but this man is concerned about your soul!" Somehow I managed to preach, but afterward I had the distinct impression that the group would much rather have heard President Kennedy.

2. *Black preaching seeks to create a living experience with the Word, first in the preacher, and then in the lives of those to whom the message is directed.* These sermons are intended to be happenings, events. Black listeners are not expected to be passive listeners but active participants. "Black people, owing to African continuity, are not spectators by nature; they are participators. The images created in an event gain in spiritual and physical potency through active participation in the mode."[48] The relationship of preacher and congregation is at all times dialogical. Using a call and response pattern, the

preacher's sense of timing allows room in the sermon for punctuation by "Amens" and other expressions of agreement. Sonja Stone says, "Improvisation is a major component in the vehicle which enables the collective to expand its creative powers, ultimately, in order to tap the reservoir of divine creativity."[49] Historically then, black preachers locate the sermon in the midst of a communal atmosphere.

James Cone says that the black church emphasizes the role of the Spirit in this living experience of preaching: "It is the people's response to the presence of the Spirit that creates the unique style of black worship. . . . There is no authentic black worship service apart from the presence of the Spirit, God's power to be with and for the people."[50] Through the Spirit, preacher and people unite in an *experience* of the word.

3. *Black preaching emphasizes the importance of identification with the text as the word of God.* The black preacher speaks from *within* the Tradition, not from without. The preacher is to be one who has not only heard but seen the events of the text. Then and only then can the truth of the text be seen in its contemporary context. Henry Mitchell refers to this as an "eyewitness account." James Sanders refers to it as using the biblical text as "mirrors for identity" rather than as models for morality. Through empathetic application of the word and a knowledge of the audience, black preachers use one of two basic hermeneutic models: the constitutive, or supportive, interpretation and the prophetic, or challenging, interpretation. For example, in the story of the Israelites crossing of the Red Sea, the black preacher might preach the text to comfort the oppressed or to warn the oppressors.[51] But in either case the identification of the preacher with the living situation of the text is the key for preaching.

4. *Black preaching proclaims the word in the common language of those who hear the message.* Preaching becomes a translation of the intended of the text. The language of the text must be interpreted and in such a way that the hearers will identify with and participate in the happening. Henry Mitchell has leveled scathing criticism at white preaching for consciously seeking to use a vocabulary and an

intellectualized content above the "less intellectual" worldview of the average member: "Seminaries often hold before their students models of graduate study as opposed to ministry—men who are obligated to speak a language foreign to the pew. The most scholarly effective black preacher knows and affirms the folk religion and language of his people." But he also insists that cultural and social identification with the people does not relieve the black preacher of the obligation "to advance the flock spiritually, morally, and even intellectually. He simply does not call to them across a deep chasm in words and tones that are strange to their ears"; the black preacher uses "inside rather than alien communication."[52]

5. *Black preaching regards the sermon as dialogue with the congregation, and both voice and body are used to interpret the meaning of the message.* Oral tradition is much stronger in the black church than in white churches. This is partly because of the African tradition, but once severed from its African origins, continued reliance on the oral tradition was necessitated by the illiteracy in which the slaves were kept in America. Since they could not read, generations of blacks taught one another by calling line and response. Even today observers of the black church continue to marvel at the extent to which Bible texts have been memorized by black preachers and their congregations.

Recent emphases on narrative preaching, then, come as no innovation to the black church. As Cone puts it, "Telling the story" is the essence of black preaching. It means proclaiming with appropriate rhythm and passion the connection between the Bible and the history of black people."[53] For that reason black congregations always ask of every preacher: "Can the Reverend tell the story?" These stories of the Bible were learned as they would be told—orally. In *Jesus and the Disinherited,* Howard Thurman tells how he came to know the *real* Bible as that portion his ex-slave grandmother loved and quoted.[54]

Black preaching understands that the sermonic process is not completed by the writing of a sermonic essay in the privacy of the preacher's study, nor even when it is read aloud—still a written product—to a congregation. It is understood as a *process,* one that begins with the preacher's own hearing and "seeing" of the story, continues as that story is recast into contemporary oral images, and then is transmitted through a dynamic oral process of speaking to a congregation who will first experience it themselves and then tell it to others. This alone is the true end of the hermeneutical process.

This brief survey highlights only a few of the distinctive contributions of black preaching in America. These insights, and many others, are a part of the legacy of the black church. It shows us that black preaching can no longer be understood as a marginal, other-cultural phenomenon in Christian preaching. It is time for white preaching to appropriate more of those insights, not as "truth for black preaching," but as truth for Christian preaching. This does not mean, of course, that there are no differences in the ways that black and white preachers should address their congregations or that white preachers should conform to every distinctive of black preaching anymore than black preaching should conform to every detail of white preaching. But there are truths beyond the details, principles beyond the practice.

First, white preaching offered black preachers the tradition of its rhetoric; now black preaching is offering white preachers their gift of its soul. It is a gift that should not be refused.

Having now listened to the varied theologies of proclamation, manifestation, and action, it is time to seek a unifying concept for a theology of preaching. I believe that such a model is to be found in God's ultimate communication with humankind: the incarnation event of Jesus Christ.

5. Toward Incarnational Preaching

The struggles of the early church against heresy principally involved the question of the nature of Christ. For centuries the ancient theological councils wrestled with the dialectic in the name *Jesus Christ: Jesus*—is he not the carpenter's son? And *Christ*—is he not the Promised One? Was he God, human, or the God-human? How could the divine Word take on human flesh?

The early heresies made short work of that paradox. For some groups, like the Ebionites, Jesus, was human, nothing more. He may have appeared to be divine, but he was not; his divinity was only imagined from his impressive humanity. For others, like the Docetics, he was divine, nothing less. He might have appeared to be human, but he was not; his humanity was only an accommodating illusion. In both heresies, the reality of the incarnation was denied.

These same dangers threaten proclamation. Preaching must recognize that it stands between the attraction of two powerful poles: to its right, "the faith once delivered," the historical given of the eternal Word; to its left, the present situation, the existential given of our own contemporary culture. Christian proclamation is intimately connected with both.

But preaching fails the dual promise accorded it by theology—that it bears the eternal Word and that it touches the contemporary situation—when it betrays the wholeness of its calling by affirming part of its nature and denying the other. To the left, preaching becomes all human; to the right, all divine. To the left, there is nothing of God; to the right, there is nothing for humankind.

Even God had to become incarnate to communicate with us at

the most profound level. The incarnation was the supreme revelation of God because it was God's ultimate means of communication. Nothing else could rival this ultimate revelation, that "God was in Christ," that "the Word was made flesh and dwelt among us" (John 1:14), not even the history of God's self-disclosure to Israel. Neither the historic pronouncements of the lawgivers nor the contemporary utterances of inspired prophets could approach the fullness of revelation of the incarnate Christ.

The incarnation, therefore, is the truest theological model for preaching because it was God's ultimate act of communication. Jesus, who was the Christ, most perfectly said God to us because the eternal Word took on human flesh in a contemporary situation. Preaching cannot do otherwise.

But each of us as proclaimers is pulled between the poles, tempted to one heresy or the other due to personality, temperament, or confessional tradition. We are torn between the historical and the contemporary, the Word and culture, the human and the divine, objectivity and subjectivity, authoritarianism and autonomy. Preachers should understand themselves well enough to recognize the particular direction of this fierce pull upon their own preaching.

Are we fascinated with the smallest historic details in the Bible but uninterested in the largest current issues of our own time? Is Jerusalem more familiar territory to us than the avenues of our own hometown? Are we able to shed honest tears of compassionate understanding over the prodigals of the New Testament at the same time we are unable to do more than shake our fists at the prodigals on the highways of our own world?

Or on the other hand, are we intrigued by the contemporary scene but impatient with the ancient Word? Are we eager to find God in every contemporary movement but reluctant to identify God in the historic revelation? Has the Bible become a virtual embarrassment to our preaching, while every contemporary source is regarded as authoritative for it?

Like the early church, preaching is constantly tempted toward incarnational heresy. But the Word must go on becoming flesh, and the preacher who succumbs to homiletical heresy destroys any possibility of that happening.

HOMILETICAL HERESY

On either side of the pulpit we are threatened by homiletical heresies that stand left and right of incarnational preaching: to the right, the preoccupation with the historic and the divine; to the left, the preoccupation with the contemporary and the human. This is the true split chancel of the church. To the right, "Beware of the leaven of the Pharisees"; but likewise to the left, "Beware of the leaven of the Sadducees" (Matt. 16:6). Let us examine the dangers each of these tendencies poses for preaching.

THE LEAVEN OF THE PHARISEES

When Jesus warned his disciples to "Beware of the leaven of the Pharisees," they were being warned against losing themselves in legalistic preoccupation with the letter of the Law. For the Pharisees, nothing could rival the ancient Law in importance. The books of the Prophets were rarely used in the synagogues; the Writings, virtually never. Even the Messiah, when he came, would do nothing more than interpret the law of Moses. He could add nothing new; he could only interpret what was already written. It is little wonder that the freshness of revelation that Jesus brought to the contemporary scene met with fierce opposition from the Pharisees. The contemporary meant nothing; the historical meant everything.

This slavish devotion to the historical letter of the law actually resulted from the Pharisee's fear of human fallibility. Their memories of the Babylonian captivity were so bitter that they were fanatically determined to build a hedge about the Law to prevent the possibility of any future human intrusion. This same fear of the human factor soon manifested itself in Christian circles in the Docetism of the second century, which was another attempt to preserve the divine by eliminating the human.

The perpetuation of this error is a major source of the problems of preaching. Whenever the pulpit is not aware of the leaven of the Pharisees, it falls victim to a deadening legalism, homiletical Docetism, and cultural ghettoism. When preaching turns its back on the contemporary given, its own human involvement with the living situation, and exclusively embraces the pole of its historical given, then proclamation becomes partial, inadequate, and distorted.

Both the theological right and the theological left can be guilty of this error. It is not the exclusive property of any one theological position, although this misunderstanding may manifest itself in different ways. But the basic problem is the same, and it exhibits two common traits.

First, *it fears the human factor.* This homiletical Docetism is afraid that the power of preaching will be lost or its message corrupted if it admits its humanity. Such fear results in a cult of objectivity. For the theological right, this fear usually manifests itself in a literalistic fundamentalism. The Bible "says what it means and means what it says." The necessity for interpretation may be denied altogether; all that is necessary is to "say what the Bible says." After all, if preachers themselves got involved in the process, how could they be certain that they were preaching God's absolute, objective truth?

But this same fault is exhibited in the preaching of some who are by no means fundamentalists. Neoorthodoxy has a particular problem at this point. About the only thing that can be said about the preacher's role in proclamation is that he or she needs to get out of the way. The writings of many theologians of this school, Barth's in particular, are filled with such expressions as "the Word arises out of the Bible," and "the preacher simply must not hinder its way into the congregation." These expressions reveal a false objectivity with reference to the preaching of the word. (Strictly speaking, Barth is a homiletical fundamentalist, as strange as that may seem. There is no position farther to the homiletical right than his. In fact, if the preacher were any less involved, he or she would simply have to stand mute at the pulpit while the Bible spoke for itself.)

Bonhoeffer also shows these tendencies. He speaks of the relief that came to him following the sermon when he was able to serve the Lord's Supper and know that something was occurring that did not depend upon his subjective involvement. It is apparent that he regarded the human factor as a minus in the preaching equation, a necessary evil at best.

It is extremely curious that those who would be the first to insist upon the reality of the humanity of Jesus should have such evident difficulty with the human element in the contemporary revelation of the Word. And theologians who would be the last to deny the human instrumentality of the writers of the biblical revelation should not be the first to fear the human instrumentality of the preacher of that revelation.

Second, *this homiletical heresy ignores its own cultural emphasis.* When Jesus preached, it was said that he "taught them as one having authority, and not as the scribes" (Matt. 7:29). What does that mean? Principally it implies that he did not speak in footnotes as the scribes did, endlessly drawing authority from previously recognized rabbis and thereby building his message from culturally accepted truisms. But this scripture also reveals that the Pharisees, who purportedly scorned cultural influences and dealt only with the pure Law, were actually enslaved to their own cultural, inherited tradition. They overlooked their dependence on the oral law which had become more important than the word of God itself.

The same was true of the Puritans. They purported to say nothing that the Bible did not say, but they actually created a body of human tradition that ranged far afield of the Bible. Likewise, fundamentalists who "only say what the Bible says" obviously do not merely stand in the pulpit reading the Bible aloud. They are actually transmitting a body of culturally inherited dogma—usually from oral tradition—without realizing it, and all of their statements from the pulpit that are not direct quotations of Scripture are human interpretations, theological statements from their own tradition. Not only do most of these statements have difficulty finding their way back to biblical origins, many of them actually do not date beyond the preacher's own grandfather.

The more critically enlightened positions on the homiletical right, such as neoorthodoxy, also cannot escape their cultural environment. Every act of interpretation carries with it an entire body of inherited presuppositions and subjective statements. No informed theology would deny that, but it is inconsistent to admit it readily with reference to theological affirmations made in the study and attempt to minimize it when those same affirmations are made from the pulpit.

Let us be quite honest about this. There is a touch of magic here, as if God mysteriously grants someone the ability to be less subjective in preaching than in writing. The passionate desire to ensure that the pure word of God is proclaimed to the congregation has resulted in an almost superstitious depersonalization of the act of preaching. As a matter of practical fact, the Word does not "arise out of the Bible and proceed into the congregation." It proceeds into the congregation on the words of a very subjective human being who has struggled to interpret those words he or she has found in the Bible and God graces with God's presence as the Word.

This one-sided emphasis on the historical given of Christian proclamation, particularly in its less-informed expressions, has produced several interesting and quite specific results:

1. *Extreme emphasis on the original language of the text.* For some preachers this has meant nothing more than a careful attention to exegesis, with perhaps some overemphasis on historical footnoting in the sermon, but in other cases it has resulted in the various dictation theories of inspiration. Because the human element is so feared, these mechanical theories had to be concocted to protect the transmission of the word from human instrumentality. This is the reason that the expression "inspired in the autographs" is so popular among some groups, and also why the most extremely conservative theological seminaries devote such a preponderance of the curriculum to original language studies. There is safety in the original, literal words; there is danger in the interpretation of them. In this case, "the spirit killeth, but the letter bringeth life."

Elaborate, rigid grammatical systems also have been devised as a mechanical means for arriving at correct interpretation. This slide-rule method of solving all questions of interpretation attempts to achieve an impersonal, objective—and therefore infallible—statement of the meaning of the Bible.

2. *A reliance upon cultic language.* Since the preachers who are involved in this heresy eventually realize that no one can simply "preach the Bible" (unless they do nothing more than read the Bible aloud from the pulpit), but that they must use their own fallible human words, they take another step to remove the human element from preaching. They employ cultic language, language formulas handed down by their tradition. Then they cannot be held accountable for their words since even when they are not quoting Scripture they are also not using their own words but the words given to them by their tradition.

This cultic language may express itself in the conventional clichés of a language of Zion or the more sophisticated formulations of a neolanguage of Zion, the most updated terminology for expressing one's faith "with integrity." But in both cases an oral tradition is being followed. And some groups who pride themselves upon having "no human creeds" influencing their preaching have instead an oral tradition of dogma and language far more rigid and intimidating than any written creed.

3. *The use of a "holy tone" in delivery.* In addition to trying to excuse themselves from the preaching formula through a reliance upon mechanical inspiration and cultic language, some preachers makes one final attempt to completely objectify the preaching experience. They rely upon a voice whose tone and cadence mark it as something definitely more than human.

The famous "ministerial tune" is another attempt at false objectification, the last weapon in the minister's arsenal of defenses against human involvement in preaching. The singsong cadence of the ministerial tune and the orotund tone of the ministerial voice betray the insecurity of preachers who wants to hide from their personal responsibility in proclaiming the word.

As Bonhoeffer has pointed out, this false objectivity in preaching may even yearn for its liturgical ancestor, the Latin language of the Catholic Mass (which *really* obscured the human component); or it may move steadily toward music as a more objective and therefore less vulnerable medium for the word. The contemporary spoken word is not good enough for the holy act of worship; a chanted tone must be employed. Bonhoeffer cites the liturgical chants of the Middle Ages as an example. *The ministerial tune is the medieval chant of Protestant worship.* By falling into the singing cadence, preachers are subconsciously striving to further objectify their words so that they will not seem so subjective.

The errors of this extreme objectivism are pathetic efforts to ensure that nothing but the divine occurs in preaching, no matter how human the body of proclamation might appear. But at the opposite pole, the contemporary or existential given of the preaching task, a second homiletical heresy tempts the preacher: an emphasis upon the contemporary and the human to the exclusion of the historical and the divine.

The Leaven of the Sadducees

The Pharisees were ill at ease with their contemporary, pluralistic culture, but the Sadducees certainly were not. They were eager to embrace the Hellenistic culture of their modern era, to wear the Greek hat and hurl the javelin. The Sadducees were as willing to conform to culture as the Pharisees were determined to ignore it.

Likewise, in Christian circles the desire to relate to the contemporary, no matter what the cost, was not long in surfacing. This tendency found its most extreme expression in the Montanism of the second century. Montanus and his followers believed that they had received direct revelation from God apart from any historical connection whatsoever. Their delusion became so extreme, in fact, that Montanus finally believed himself to be none other than the Holy Spirit.

These tendencies are very much a part of the contemporary scene for preaching. Because of our "recent bad history" of authoritarianism and absolutism in the pulpit we fear the leaven of the Pharisees extraordinarily. The past few decades have witnessed an era of overreaction to literalism, legalism, and extreme Puritanism. As a result, preaching has been lured into cultural accommodation and a "too-easy peace with culture," to use Niebuhr's term; or what Peter Berger has referred to as "culture Protestantism." Berger has been sharply critical of the tendency to make "modern man" and "modern consciousness" into "golden calves around which a depressing number of Christian thinkers have staged an ongoing dance celebration"; and he has described "the more bizarre exaggerations of religious accommodation to the modern spirit" as having reached the point of absurdity.[1]

The influence of contemporary culture is an inescapable reality for the preacher. We cannot deny the human factor in our preaching. Every ministry has a specific cultural setting; we ourselves are very much the product of it and so is the congregation to whom we speak. But if we becomes preoccupied with an immediate revelation, with contemporary visions that divorce our bit of history from the historic revelation of God, then our preaching falls prey to homiletical Montanism.

What are the characteristics of this error? Precisely the opposite of the one-sided emphasis on the historical dimension of preaching.

1. *Emphasis on the immediacy of revelation.* The biblical revelation is virtually ignored in homiletical Montanism; the key question becomes, "How do *I* understand God?" All self-appointed, popular prophetic figures are equally dangerous to the church, regardless of which side of the theological stage they stand upon. This is true of the wildly apocalyptic preachers who ignore the historic meanings of the biblical images they torture into contorted shapes; but it is equally true of sophisticated preachers who believe that the Bible is hopelessly irrelevant and that revelation is the product of their own enlightened self-understanding.

We must test the spirits; and if they do not speak of Jesus Christ, they are not of the Spirit of God. *Without the humility that places it beneath the Word, only the demonic can and will occur in preaching.*

2. *Exaggeration of the human factor.* If homiletical Docetism fears the human factor, homiletical Montanism is intoxicated with it. It

believes that if anything is going to happen in preaching, the preacher must *make* it happen. Therefore this preaching is success-oriented. It strives for effect. It constantly holds a mirror before its face to see how attractive it is.

In its cruder forms, this preaching is deliberately and consciously manipulative; in its more sophisticated forms, it is subtly intimidating in its cultural correctness. Its insecurity may drive it into a restless search for innovative forms—not to better communicate the gospel, but to please its crowd—just as the rhyming sermons of Wycliff's day were intended to entertain and gain popular approval.

3. *Ignoring of its own dependence on authority.* Because this preaching is so "humanistic," it prefers to believe that it is not authoritarian. In an age of rapid change, certainty is an embarrassment and ambiguity a pride. Sophistication and ambiguity are twins. But sophistication is knowing, and so is ambiguity. Ambiguity is knowing what not to know. This is merely another subtle and powerful kind of authoritarianism.

It is amazing how oblivious this preaching is to its own desperate search for authority. For sophisticated, "progressive" preachers, this need is usually satisfied by fact stacking and contemporary authority citing. On the other hand, "conservative" preachers who have in fact actually abandoned the authority of the Word attempt to fill this void by endlessly citing personal experiences, either their own or those of others. The word of God is largely ignored in this kind of preaching; our experiences become the authority for the sermon. It is fearful preaching, too; fearful that without this constant experience-mongering, God disappears. Primitive religion always lacks faith and therefore demands miraculous experiences. Miracle-mongering, likewise, whether of the Shantung revival or of medieval Catholicism, reveals the same anxiety—that without such human proofs, the Word is impotent.

Even the noble insistence upon the "priesthood of the believer," the belief in the competency of individuals to interpret the Bible for themselves, can lead to self-pride and a distorted sense of authority. This invariably occurs when we arrogantly insist on our subjective rights and refuse to listen to the testimony of the historic word but instead bring our previously held notions to it, and then come forth proclaiming the accuracy of our cultural totems. In this case, the "priest" ceases to be priest and becomes God.

More could be said about each of these extremes, but perhaps this description will help us to identify the dangers of homiletical extremism.

I would hope that one thing is now clear. Neither the historical nor the contemporary, neither the Bible nor humankind is served by these distortions. The Pharisees believed themselves to be faithful to the Law and above the dangers of cultural corruption, but in fact they made both themselves and the Law captive to the oral traditions of their own culture. And the Sadducee merely added a thin cultural veneer over their own rigidly legalistic interpretation of life.

The same is true today. Those preachers who seek to save the word of God from the human and the contemporary merely lock it up in some human tradition from the past, which is no more sacred or less human because it is hallowed by time. But likewise some preachers who wish to escape the archaic stance of biblical authoritarianism really betray the contemporary by their legalistic insistence upon the *new* "right" way of saying things. The tragedy of these one-sided efforts is that in both cases the communication of the living Word to the living situation never happens.

To be sure, neither of these, the Pharisee or the Sadducee, actually exists in such broad portraits. But each of us participates enough in one or the other of them—or both—to know that these figures are real, and let those who think they stand at balanced midpoint take heed lest they fall.

THE TWO POLES

I have tried to demonstrate that preaching, like all of theology, is pulled between two powerful poles of attraction: the divine and the human, the Creator and the creation. All of our other terms of classification—liberal and conservative, left and right, the histori-

cal and the contemporary—are usually only means of describing
a dominant emphasis on one or the other of these poles.

So whether we refer to the homiletical right, or the historical
pole for preaching, we are referring to the attempt of proclamation
to be faithful to the divine dimension of its character. Conversely,
to speak of the homiletical left, or the contemporary pole of
preaching, is to refer to proclamation's efforts to be faithful to its
humanity.

There is a positive value for us in the negative study of the
heresies that result when preaching becomes a divided self. We
realize that both of these extremes have seized upon something
essential to the nature of proclamation.

The homiletical right has grasped the importance of the historic
revelation, of the priority of the actions of God, and of the confrontation of contemporary culture with the word of God. The
homiletical left has realized that preaching is a ministry God has
graciously given to human servants, that it must speak to the
actual needs of the real people of its own time, and therefore that
it must have a sensitivity to people and a willingness to experiment with contemporary means of communicating with them. The
right sees the importance of the historical and the divine; the left
sees the value of the contemporary and the human.

But no preaching can be truly whole, and therefore truly itself,
until it has thoroughly committed itself to *both* of these realities.
This means that an incarnational approach to preaching must be
based upon two primary affirmations: *first, that Christian proclamation
recognizes the priority of the actions of God; and second, that Christian proclamation recognizes the possibility of the irrelevance of our human preaching.* Let us
examine each of these affirmations.

1. *Christian proclamation recognizes the priority of the actions of God.* God
has acted. God has acted in Israel; God has acted in Christ. Christian speaking begins with the speaking of God; we speak because
we have been addressed. Our preaching does not merely speak of
our own subjective inquiry, *but it is based upon the reality that was
brought to light in the actions of God.*

In referring to the preaching of the apostles concerning the resurrection, Jürgen Moltmann writes: "They did not merely wish to tell of their own new self-understanding in the Easter faith, but in that faith and as a result of it they reported something also about the way of Jesus and about the event of the raising of Jesus. Their statements contain not only existential certainty in the sense of saying, 'I am certain,' but also and together with this objective certainty in the sense of saying, 'It is certain.' "[2]

This does not mean that we are committed to a mere historical recital in preaching (nor that historical "proof" is either possible or essential), but that preaching will seek to express that reality that was brought to light in the prior revealing actions of God.

2. *Christian proclamation recognizes the possibility of the irrelevance of our human preaching.* Contemporary preaching has already wasted far too much time in the pointless debate on whether or not the word of God "has to be made relevant." How could a word from God be irrelevant?

But we will avoid a great deal of lost motion if we direct ourselves to another question. Is all preaching invariably the word of God? And therefore, is all preaching invariably relevant? Does the word of God invariably encounter me every time the preacher mounts the pulpit steps and opens his or her mouth, no matter what he or she says to me or how I am addressed?

Obviously not. This means that there is a real human dimension to proclamation and that the question of relevance is inescapably bound up with it. *The preaching of the word of God is the interpretation of a historical event to a contemporary situation by a person who must be intimately familiar with both.* Any separation on the part of the preacher from either of these situations results in irrelevant preaching.

If my preaching does not understand the reality revealed in the historic word of God, it cannot speak to the ultimate needs of my contemporary congregation. But if I am alienated from my own times so that I cannot understand the unique language with which the contemporary expresses its alienation from God, then I cannot find understandable words to speak the historic revelation: "As God in Christ entered into a specific culture at a given time and place, so the message of the revelatory-redemptive act must become incarnate in and for each generation by entering the culture of that generation and redeeming it."[3]

The word of God is never irrelevant, but my preaching may well be. And it will be, if it does not bear the eternal Word, and if it does not touch the living situation. Only the word that dwells among us is the word of Christian preaching.

MIDPOINT: COMMUNICATION

But it is not enough simply to set the two poles of the historical given and the contemporary given of Christian proclamation and to assert that they are both important. We must also ask how they are related. This is the essential problem for Christian preaching: "Christianity, whether defined as church, creed, ethics or movement of thought, itself moves between the poles of Christ and culture. The *relation* of these two constitutes the problem."[4]

What is the relationship between these two poles? In other words, what assurance can the preacher have that the "square peg" of the ancient word will fit the round hole of contemporary needs?

The preacher must understand that the historic word and the contemporary situation are not mutually exclusive and that preaching unites the two in the act of communication. These are the two primary guideposts toward incarnational preaching: the first points to *what* is preached, to the message itself; the second, to the *act* of preaching. Each requires some attention.

1. *The historic word and the contemporary situation are not mutually exclusive.* Preaching must not allow itself to be forced into a false antithesis between the objective and the subjective, between the word and persons.[5] Subjective preaching invariably results in the cultivation of persons; objective preaching invariably results in the coercion of persons. But *subjective* and *objective* are really useless terms for the preacher because of the unity between the "objective" word and the "subjective" congregation.

The contemporary preacher must realize that the congregation he or she addresses is already present in the word of God in the

Bible: "When the Bible lies open on the preacher's desk and the preparation of the sermon is about to begin, the worshipers have already come in; the passage contains these people since it is God's word to his people."[6] The subjective congregation is already present in the objective word because it is the word of God to humankind.

Not only is the congregation present in the word, however, but what the word offers is precisely what the congregation needs. Humanity was created in the image of God. Our emptiness is our alienation from God, and all of our incompleteness, whether we realizes it or not, is the result of the absence of the word.

If the word and humankind were related as objective and subjective, as philosophical absolutes, then there would be no hope for preaching at all. After all, why should the contemporary preacher go to the Bible in the first place? What hope do we have that the ancient record contains a message for our contemporary congregations? And what hope do we have that the message preached is the message needed? But we are able to believe that the word addresses all people in all cultural situations and at all times—even our own contemporary congregations—when we understand the essential human dimensions in the provision of the word, and the essential eternal dimension in the needs of humankind.

There are three implications from this understanding of the essential unity of the word and humankind for the Christian message:

(a) *Preachers must correctly position themselves relative to the world.* We have already affirmed the priority of the actions of God. "It is God that hath made us, and not we ourselves" (Ps. 100:3). The same must be true of the Christian message.

The preacher must stand beneath the word he or she preaches, not above it. To stand above the word means to reject it, to ignore its message for ourselves, or to use it to manipulate people for our own ends. Then the essential order in proclamation is reversed, and we become the lord rather than the servant of the word. We violate both the essential nature of our humanity and God's sovereignty when we do not stand beneath the word.

To stand beneath the word means that we must acknowledge our own humanity. To acknowledge our humanity is to confess our sinfulness. To confess our sinfulness is to make plain to the congregation that we stand beneath the very judgment of the word we proclaim.

(b) *The preaching of the word demands a partial participation in culture.* Just as preachers may take a false stance relative to the word, so they may also position themselves incorrectly in relation to culture.

It is possible to be both overimpressed and underimpressed with culture. Being overimpressed with culture causes the preacher to be dominated by it; being underimpressed with culture causes the preacher to ignore it. Where culture has dominated, the ultimate significance of proclamation has been lost; where culture has been ignored, true communication of the message has been lost.

Preaching that is overly impressed with culture becomes weak and despairing and therefore incurs the scorn of the world. Preaching that is underimpressed with culture becomes arrogant and pharisaical, remote and cultic, and therefore incurs the hatred of the world.

The sermon is to have a note of certainty and joy. It is also to be prophetic. Neither of these notes can be sounded when preaching is overimpressed with culture. That is the reason for the failure of the world-weary and uncertain preacher. And conversely, it is the reason for the success of some fraudulent and simplistic preachers. Their prophetic certainty and joy may be feigned, but they are perceived as people who will confront the world with the declaration of the gospel.

Nevertheless, no truly prophetic preaching can ever occur, or has ever occurred, unless a preacher sufficiently participates in the culture to understand its unique language and respond understandably. The solution to this dilemma is a *partial participation* in culture on the part of the preacher. If we did not participate at all in our culture, it would be impossible to communicate with it: "Communication is a matter of participation. Where there is no participation there is no communication."[7] But if there is an absolute identification of the preacher and his or her message with the contemporary culture, then the Christian gospel is lost in a capitulation to culture: "We can speak to people only if we participate in their concern. . . . We can point to the Christian answer only if, on the other hand, we are not identical with them."[8]

This partial participation in culture on our part permits the communication of the Christian message and a confrontation of culture: "We must participate but we must not be identical, and we must use this double attitude to undercut the complacency of those who assume that they know all the answers and are not aware of their existential conflicts."[9] Or, as Wingren puts it, "The priest may venture to belong to his own age and mix in the ordinary life of society without thereby losing the divine life. . . . When preaching willingly concerns itself with the needs and problems of its time, there takes place once more what ought to take place: Christ sits at the table with publicans and sinners, that is, with us. In the human, the divine is present."[10]

(c) *The subjectivity of our existence is a blessing rather than a curse, and so is the objectivity of the word.* For some preachers, the subjectivity of their existence is viewed as a liability, a handicap in the task of preaching. For others, the objectivity of the historical revelation, the particularity of the Word becoming flesh in the history of Israel and in the person of Jesus, is regarded as an ongoing hindrance to contemporary communication. Both of these stances are false.

In the first place, without my personal, subjective involvement with my congregation, with my culture, with these people here and now, I could not communicate at all. Preaching would be more futile than a Bedouin trying to describe a camel to an Eskimo, or an Eskimo attempting to describe a walrus to a Bedouin, when neither spoke the language of the other.

I do not enjoy many advantages over the apostle Paul, but there is one: I am here and now, and he is not. And if the reality he expressed in his life and in his theology is to come forth for my congregation, it will only be because his language and symbols have been translated and interpreted meaningfully for our time.

Just as transliteration of language is not adequate translation of the Bible, mere historical recital is not adequate proclamation of the gospel. Of course my subjective participation in culture and my interpretation of the Bible presents risks and dangers; but nevertheless, the subjectivity of my contemporary existence is a permit for preaching, not a prohibition of it.

Likewise, preachers who feel themselves limited by the historical given of revelation do not understand the facts of the case. It is *because* God was particularized in Israel and in Jesus of Nazareth that we may have confidence in addressing the particular situation of the here and now. The God we proclaim is not abstract; this God is not embarrassed to be involved in history; this God is not too impersonal to enter into the sufferings of every human life.

And if I did not know that God exists as Word quite apart from my own human understanding and fallibilities, as a preacher I should be of all people most miserable. Then the communication of the gospel would be entirely a matter of my own persuasive abilities, of my own sweaty exertions in the pulpit. But when I know that the presence of the Word in my preaching is entirely a matter of the sovereign grace of God, then I may have a confidence that transcends self-confidence. Then I may commit my preaching to God's promise and rest my trust in God.

2. *The historic word and the contemporary situation become united in the act of communication.* This is the second of our guideposts toward incarnational preaching. Again, the incarnational model demonstrates the truthfulness of this claim.

(a) *Speech was an essential part of the communication of the human and the divine in the incarnation of Jesus.* The words of Jesus apart from his life would have been empty; but the life of Jesus apart from his words would have been unintelligible. We cannot imagine a mute, silent Jesus. The Good News apart from words is inconceivable. Perpetual silence from Jesus could only have led to ambiguity; speech led to the cross. None of his deeds, neither the miraculous nor the compassionate, could have unmistakably said God to us apart from the interpretation his words provide. "No one ever spoke like this man" (John 7:46); and with all of our difficulties in interpreting those words, imagine the confusion we would suffer apart from them.

Speech connected him to the inner being of humans. Beyond everything people could observe in his actions, the words of Jesus identified with hurts in the human spirit and ministered to them at those subtle depths of the human predicament where hands can no longer reach. And at this depth, we find him most identified with our humanity; but paradoxically, it is also in this dimension that we realize most fully that he is God.

True, there were times when Jesus was silent—as before Pilate, when every word might appear to be a plea for deliverance. Then he would not allow words to be misunderstood as a capitulation of the Word to culture; then he was silent. But silence was never normative for his ministry.

That is not surprising to us because silence is never normative for a human being. Nor is it for the church as the body of Christ. Speech is indeed the greatest danger of the church because it is the most human. "Language is the basic cultural creation" of humanity; and whether the symbols used are silent or spoken, "every act of man's spiritual life is carried by language."[11] Words are wily, potential, but human. This leads us to a second implication:

(b) *Speech is an essential part of the communication of the Word by the church.* As the body of Christ, the human church has form, it acts and it speaks. Its form is uncomely because it is human—it is not God, nor angel, nor even intermediate being. It acts and fails because it is human. It confesses its sinfulness and acts again. So when it speaks and fails, it must also speak again. God does not refuse God's self to the church even in its weakness and its humanity, and the Word does not deny itself to the fallibility of human speech. "A bruised reed shall God not break, and the smoking flax shall God not quench . . ." (Isa. 42:3; Matt. 12:20).

The nervousness of the church over its proclamation is partly proper and partly false, partly proper because it correctly recognizes its frequent failures and often abuse of the office of preaching, partly false because it realizes that the explicitness and concreteness of speech will make clear the distinctiveness of the gospel. It is good that the church fears its former exaggerations (it has said too much, and it has caused many to stumble over itself).

But the church cannot simply act and leave its actions in ambiguity. A speechless, formless, disembodied church is a heresy. True, it is not as risky—but it is also not as human. The risk of humanness was essential to the incarnation, and there is no true humanness without speech.

Furthermore, without speech the church cannot reveal the divine source of its life. Just because we are not God, none of us can perfectly incarnate the Word in our deeds. We must always point beyond ourselves with words to the fullness of the revelation of God. And with all of the serious difficulties the church faces in finding suitable language to speak of God, it really has no other choice: "The Biblical faith . . . must speak of God. . . . A God to whom human words cannot point is not the God of the Bible."[12]

Since the word of God is intended, in Brunner's words, to "make himself accessible to me," and "the sole analogy is the encounter between human beings, the meeting of person with persons," then the spoken word is especially suited for the communication of that word.[13] It is "right within the core of the I-thou relationship, and the written or printed word is always a poor substitute for it."[14] In fact, Kyle Haselden makes the bold assertion that in the presentation of the gospel, "the spoken word is the best weapon, the superlative tool; in this area it has superiority over all other forms of communication."[15]

This suggests our final conclusion concerning the speech of the church:

(c) *Proper speech is essential to overcome the wrong stumbling block to the gospel, our inability to communicate.* But it is at this point that theology begins to raise its red flags of warning. Eberhard Bethge says that Dietrich Bonhoeffer never asked, "How can we better communicate to modern man the message we possess? That question would turn the interpreter into a salesman to the have-nots."[16] This suspicion of any studied approach to the oral communication of the gospel is widespread in theology.

In an article entitled, "Theology vs. Communication Theories,"

Ronald E. Sleeth lists six current criticisms of theology at this point: (1) Theology has expressed its disapproval of the application of communication theories to preaching by ignoring them; (2) this indifference is actually based upon the fear that the study of oral communication elevates the human and minimizes the divine; (3) theology regards the task of communication as a theological one, and it sees communication theory as affirming that right techniques rightly learned are sufficient for communicating the message of the gospel; (4) theology is suspicious of communication because of its apparent instrumental or pragmatic use of the religious message; (5) theologians are afraid of the study of communication because of their fear of manipulation; (6) theology is concerned about the humanistic implications of some speech theories because of their preoccupation with the behavioral and social sciences.[17]

These are warnings not to be ignored. We can readily agree with Tillich when he says, "The question cannot be: How do we communicate the Gospel so that others will accept it? For this there is no method. To communicate the Gospel means putting it before the people so that they are able to decide for or against it. . . . All that we who communicate this Gospel can do is to make possible the genuine decision."[18]

But must we not also agree with Tillich when he says that there are two kinds of "stumbling blocks" in Christianity: "One is genuine. . . . There is always a genuine decision against the gospel for those for whom it is a stumbling block. But this decision should not be dependent upon the wrong stumbling block, namely, the wrong way of our communication of the gospel—our inability to communicate." He insists that this wrong stumbling block must be overcome to bring people face to face with the right stumbling block, the gospel itself, and he asks, "Will the Christian churches be able to remove the wrong stumbling blocks in their attempt to communicate the gospel?"[19]

In other words, Tillich is saying that communication does not mean persuasion; that is, even if a person says no to the gospel, it has still been communicated—*if* it is the gospel he or she is rejecting and not merely our presentation of it. But it has not been communicated if he or she never gets to the gospel at all because of stumbling over my presentation of it.

If Tillich is right at this point, and I believe that he is, then this has important implications for the responsible involvement of theology in the practical dimensions of preaching. If our methods of communicating the gospel can set a false stumbling block in the paths of people so that they are never able to hear the gospel at all, *then our presentation of the message is an essential part of the contemporary hearing of the living Word.*

No theologian would argue that an unstudied exposition of a biblical text is superior to one that gives careful attention to the text in light of the most recent contributions of critical research and modern hermeneutical theories. But is it not utterly contradictory of theology to insist that it is our right—indeed, our absolute responsibility—to use the best of recent research in arriving at the proper *interpretation* of the Christian message, and yet to object to the use of the best of recent research in arriving at a proper *presentation* of the Christian message?

Theology must realize that an understanding of communication is to the presentation of the sermon what critical research is to the content of the sermon, and with the same attendant benefits and dangers. Critical research helps the preacher in the interpretation of the Christian message; communication theory helps the preacher in the presentation of the Christian message.

Of course there are dangers in the use of communication theory, just as in the use of critical research. But how are these dangers to be avoided? Do we avoid false interpretation by refusing to study the principles of interpretation? Is a spontaneous interpretation free of error? Likewise, can we prevent manipulation in the act of preaching by an unstudied, spontaneous presentation? Or is my involvement simply not needed in the pulpit? When I stand to speak, does the divine immediately take over? If not, then theology must give more attention to the practical act of preaching if Christian proclamation is to be made whole.

How then can theology inform practical homiletics? The reality of the historic word and the contemporary situation must become incarnate in the person who preaches, in the shape of the sermon he or she preaches, and in the language with which he or she preaches.

But we must begin with the person. If these realities are not incarnate in the person, they can never become incarnated in his or her preaching.

II. THE PERSON WHO PREACHES

6. "We Are Human Beings Like Yourselves"

The greatest confession of the early church was the Caesarean confession of Simon, "Thou art the Christ, the Son of the living God" (Matt. 16:16). But if that is its greatest confession, the Lyconian confession of the apostle Paul ranks second only to it: "We are human beings like yourselves . . ." (Acts 14:15). In fact, no one can make that exalted confession of Simon without first having made this contrite confession of Paul, "We are human beings . . ."

For the preacher, this Lyconian confession takes on added significance. Without it, we can never point beyond ourselves or escape the despair that playing God brings. Sooner or later in life, we will all make this confession. It may come as a shattering realization or as a buried neuroticism, but it will come. It may come early in life, with life's first frustrations and failures; or it may come with the assumption of family responsibilities, or the disappointments of ambition or career, or the crises of the thirties or the fears of the forties; or with gathering years and declining health —or with death near—but it will come. Unfortunately most of life is spent either in the postponement of this confession or in the self-deception that it is not true. Nothing could be more destructive to Christian ministry.

To understand how this is so, look at the experiences of Paul and Barnabas in Lyconia that produced this confession. They had healed a crippled man by the gate. The priests of Jupiter had tried to crown them with garlands, thinking that the gods had finally fulfilled all the old legends and come down to earth in human form. Then Paul rent his clothes and ran into the midst of the excited crowd, shouting, "Stop! Why are you doing these things?

We are human beings like yourselves, and we are here to tell you of the true and living God whom we serve." But the Scripture says, "Even with these words they scarcely restrained the crowd from worshiping them" (Acts 14:8–22).

Imagine, however, what would have happened if Paul and Barnabas had not confessed their humanity. At first their authority would have been infinitely greater. Huge crowds would have gathered to see them. Of course there would have been demands —for healing, miraculous displays, prophetic visions. They could have concealed their humanity and stalled, reminding the throngs of the last wonder and promising more. And that would have satisfied the mob—for a while. But sooner or later there would have come that knock on the door that said, "Produce—or else."

Then what? Theudas, who disappointed his hoard of avid followers by failing to collapse the walls of Jerusalem as promised and was stoned to death for his failure, was not the last religious figure to learn the penalty for playing god.

HUMANITY: PREVENTING DESPAIR

Confessing our humanity is the only way we preachers can prevent complete despair in ministry. Only when we can say, "I am human. I can make mistakes. I can fail," are we able to eliminate the burden of divinity. That burden is simply to heavy to bear. No minister really thinks of himself or herself as God. A few, perhaps, may regard themselves as a little more than human. According to reliable reports, at least one or two have been seen traveling with their feet a few inches above the ground.

Particularly adroit preachers may get away with this masquerade for a brief time—particularly if they move frequently—but eventually their clay toes will peep out from their dusty sandals. Then their authority disappears along with their divinity, and both they and their followers are destroyed by the unmasking.

This error is particularly pernicious in those immature younger godlings with gigantic egos who have been bragged on too much because they are ninety-day statistical wonders or because they are wizards at lay manipulation through psychological tricks. But "maturity" also tends to promote pride. The longer preachers live and work in churches, the more decisions they must make. So they make them, and some of them even turn out right. They gain the approval of their religious culture; they are "successful." And after a while, unless they are careful, they make a very slight error: they confuse their words with the divine word, their will with God's will.

When the prophetic mantle falls on some preachers, it drops right over their heads. They can see neither the people nor the word of God.

I will not debate whether pride *(hubris)* or sloth *(acedia)* is the chief sin of the ministry. (As a matter of fact where there is one there is frequently the other.) But in its extreme forms, there is nothing worse than pride. It often shows itself in the arrogance of those word manipulators whose speech and dress exploit the insecurities of middle-class or working congregations until they becomes demigodlings whose piousness and pompousness even God would not use (and *did* not, in Christ). Or it may show itself in the arrogance of those subtle cynics whose speech and dress exploit the insecurities of upper-class or intellectual congregations until they are the ultimate Person whose hypersophistication and blasé ways are the envy of their self-established in-cults with their obscure symbolism and new holy-language, which even God would not use ("and the common people heard him gladly" [Mark 12:37])

But in spite of their apparent differences both of these preachers are first cousins, sick unto death, leaving sickness in their wake and making their converts (not God's) tenfold more children of hell than before. If the light that shines from these windows, either stained-glass traditional or contemporary abstract, be darkness, how great is that darkness!

Both god-players find immense personal gratification in their cults; both scorn the opposite social pole; both attract fanatical personal allegiance from their followers whose insecurities are at last gratified by a superego that interprets all of life for them. And hell hath no fury like the cult follower whose living space is intruded upon.

Needless to say, both would-be deities also build "great" churches or audiences, at least for a time. But people's taste in gods —when there is more than one—is notoriously fickle, and at the first sign of failure or fatigue in the leader they are off, racing after the latest phenomenon to alleviate their lifeless boredom and give them the "spiritual" thrill they once felt. Meanwhile the dropped divinities may struggle all the more frantically to regain their niche by using ever cheaper and shabbier tricks. At this point, despair knows no lower depths, not even in Dante's lowest levels of hell.

The mob that worships most often stones when its gods fail them. That crowd that shouted "Hosanna!" to Jesus was yelling "Crucify him, crucify him!" next. He had frustrated their misguided expectations. Or the prodigal son with his carousing friends—where were they when he wandered about begging and finally crawled into a pigsty? Let the godlings who play roles and who pretend to be God fail and see what will happen.

Many Christian workers are obsessed with the terror of inconsistency: "What if I can't produce?" "What if giving or attendance fall below last year's?" "What if the next church goes down instead of up?" Such is the fear of the person who wears the mask of God, and behind it is a very human, frightened, insecure individual. It will destroy anyone who has the least shred of integrity, and it will destroy any church or denomination that becomes deluded by this pretension.

But when we confesses our humanity, we alleviate the fear of inconsistency. No matter how alluring the role of local divinity, deep inside each of us knows ourself to be both human and fallible, empowered only by the Spirit of God. When we are able to confess that to ourselves and others, we can end the anxiety of the divine masquerade.

But confessing our humanity is not only essential to prevent despair, it is also crucial for another reason. It is the only stance that permits our complete testimony to God.

HUMANITY: PERMITTING TESTIMONY

Paul and Barnabas never could have witnessed to the true and living God if they had masqueraded as gods. But when they admitted their humanity, they were simultaneously set free to point beyond themselves to God. Paul said, "We are not here to be worshiped but that you should turn from these meaningless things to serve the true and living God" (Acts 14:15). Curiously enough, when we most accept our humanity, we are most enabled to participate in the divine task.

This issue is so profound for the ministry that we must not be the least uncertain about it. As preachers of the incarnate Word, we must involve ourselves in incarnational preaching. We must be committed to the historical word and the contemporary world. Without the word, we have no message. Without the world, we have no ministry.

The insecurity of some preachers will not allow them to confess their humanity. The insecurity of other preachers will not allow them to admit their involvement with the divine. Both are afraid of their ministry groups, and both fall into a heresy of ministry.

That is, without a recognition of our humanity we are condemned to deception, frustration, and depression. Feelings of guilt always result in depression. When we try to carry the burden of divinity and inevitably fail, we feel guilty and are dropped into depression, sometimes minor and transitory but sometimes extremely serious and disabling.

On the other hand, without a recognition that we are children of God, disciples, joint heirs with Christ and part of his body, we are likewise frustrated and depressed. We may be human enough —but what is the basis for our ministry? Without a steady confidence in our calling, in the guidance of God's hand in our lives, and the assurance of a strength beyond our own, our sense of purpose gradually erodes until we are baffled, depressed, and bored.

The boredom of the ministry—and it is at epidemic proportions

—can be traced directly to spiritual sickness. No one who has a sense of vital, useful purpose can be bored except for normal periods of mental or physical fatigue. Any preacher who says he or she has never experienced such periods of boredom or depression is either manic or dishonest, or both. Even the most purposeful routine is still routine, and eventually it gets repetitious and tedious.

But this occasional boredom is different from the settled, aching misery that some ministers struggle to live with. This emptiness of life, however, is precisely that which the coming of Christ was intended to fill: "I am come that they may have life, and that more abundantly" (John 10:10). Does not this promise apply also to Christ's ministers? Accepting one's humanity does not mean accepting a life of boredom in ministry. On the contrary, true humanity, humanity as it ought to be, is always in Christ, and the life in Christ is not one of boredom.

Nor, it should be added, is it one of perpetual excitement. The highly artificial happiness cult in the church is spurious Christianity, and those preachers who perpetually try to see how many upper teeth they can show in one smooth movement of the mouth do neither themselves nor their congregations a favor. The kingdom does not come with much grinning. Rather than conquering depression and boredom, this pose only deepens despair.

Unfortunately for the truly bored preacher, that feeling is transmitted all efforts to conceal it. The result is a skepticism on the part of the laity that the minister really lives in the world he or she recommends to others. Helmut Thielicke says: "This is the point, it seems to me, where the secret distrust of Christian preaching is smoldering. Behind all the obvious and superficial criticism—such as that the sermon is boring, remote from life, irrelevant—there is, I am convinced, this ultimate reservation, namely, that the man who bores others must be boring himself. And the man who bore himself is not really living in what he—so boringly—hand out. 'Where your treasure is, there will your heart be also'—in this case the treasure of the heart seems not to be identical with what it is commending to others."[1]

This points us toward the true stance for the preaching minister. We must really live, as Christ did, in the real world. We must be fully involved, fully knowledgeable, fully sympathetic inhabitants of our own time. If we cannot affirm our humanity in the time and place given to us, we will never minister to the human beings who do live there. No matter how much our love for Zion, we must also love our home town. But if we are not also citizens of the kingdom of God, if we cannot feel ourselves a part of the ongoing purposeful movement of that kingdom in our own time, we will likewise never preach the redeeming word to a divided humanity.

This is a most solemn and profound realization. It challenges us to assert for ourselves a full participation in the divine Body as well as to confess of ourselves a completely human existence. We do not speak lightly when we speak of incarnational preaching, and that should be obvious at this point as at no other. We do not equate ourselves with Christ nor challenge the unique authority of God when we assert our participation in the divine Body. God has given this to us. We become the temple of the Spirit; Christ lives in us: "Nevertheless I live; yet not I, but Christ liveth in me" (Gal. 2:20).

Nevertheless, it is foolish, misguided theology to assert that Paul meant that my personality is unimportant, that God wants the death of my individuality, that in fact "I" am dead. The new life that is promised is for *me. I* am the person who is "born again." My own, my unique, my God-given self is made alive. I am no piece of dead equipment with the Holy Spirit sitting inside at the controls, pulling levers and moving my frame through its paces. What is dead is my alienation from God, from others, even from myself.

Preachers can attempt to use the Holy Spirit, however, for their own purposes. There is nothing more demonic than preachers who chant the magic words of Scripture to cause the Spirit to do their bidding, all the while asserting, "The Spirit has never failed me. We must all *pay the price* to be empowered by the Spirit."

But the sin of Simon Magus was nothing more or less than

attempting to purchase the Spirit *for his own use* (Acts 8:18 ff.). The key to authentic ministry is not how much is wrought, but *what* is wrought, and *for whom,* and *to what end.* The price of commitment paid by preachers must always be for one purpose and one purpose only—that they might be servants of God's will, and not of their own ambition. Samson "wist not that the Lord was departed from him" (Judg. 16:20) in his selfishness; but he was not the first, nor the last, servant of God to have that experience. George Buttrick writes, "The purity of a man's motives outweighs all other elements in his influence and almost completely cancels out other factors of difference."[2] The preacher's motivation can only be to point beyond himself or herself to the Lord whom he or she serves. And only the preacher who has confessed his or her humanity is able to confess Christ.

After all, we must remember that Simon Peter himself, who made life's greatest confession—"Thou are the Christ"—had first already fallen upon his face and cried out, "Depart from me; for I am a sinful man, O Lord" (Luke 5:8). Only the preacher who has confessed that can confess him. But what does it mean to be human?

HUMANITY AND PERSONALITY

Listing character traits needed by the preacher is exactly as futile as listing the attributes of God, no matter how time-honored the practice. And for exactly the same reason. God cannot be described by any list of attributes, no matter how exhaustive the list. Neither can human personality. The traditional listings of personal characteristics needed by the minister generally become superficial and usually wind up sounding like the Boy Scout oath, "Brave, clean, and reverent."

At this point, an incarnational approach is again essential in understanding the preaching task. The humanity of the preacher is critical because we participate in the person of Christ. We do not understand the humanity of Christ because we understand ourselves; we understand what humanity means by looking at Jesus. Servants cannot be greater than their master. Preachers cannot be less human than their Lord. This is the great law for the personality of the preacher.

What does it mean for a preacher to be truly human?

1. First of all, no one needs to *become* human. We are already human. We simply need to be *honest*, to avoid playing dishonest games with ourselves and others that deceive us into believing otherwise and that retard or block entirely the process of becoming a maturing human. Spurgeon says:

There is such a thing as trying to be too much a minister, and becoming too little a man; though the more of a true man you are, the more truly will you be what a servant of the Lord should be. Schoolmasters and ministers have generally an appearance peculiarly their own; in the wrong sense, they are "not as other men are." They are too often speckled birds, looking as if they were not at home among the other inhabitants of the country, but awkward and peculiar. When I have seen a flamingo gravely stalking along, an owl blinking in the shade, or a stork demurely lost in thought, I have been irresistibly led to remember some of my dignified brethren of the teaching and preaching fraternity, who are so marvelously proper at all times that they are just a shade amusing. Their very respectable, stilted, dignified, important, self-restrained manner is easily acquired, but is it worth acquiring?[3]

Trying to be impressive is a great sin, and one that is easily self-excused. Do we not need to be "powerful" in our preaching? Do we not need to "impress" others with the gospel? Does not God use personality, our personality in that?

Yes, to all three questions. But that is the danger. The human element in proclamation is real, inescapable, important—and dangerous. P. T. Forsyth warns of the dangers of personality when he writes: "No man has any right in the pulpit in virtue of his personality or manhood itself. . . . To be ready to accept any kind of message from a magnetic man is to lose the Gospel in mere impressionism. . . . And it is fatal to the authority either of the pulpit or of the Gospel. The church does not live by its preachers, but by its Word."[4]

Likewise, Bonhoeffer warns in strongest terms against developing a "cult of personality": "Every cult of personality that emphasizes the distinguished qualities, virtues, and talents of another person, even though these be of an altogether spiritual nature, is worldly and has no place in the Christian community; indeed, it poisons the Christian community."[5]

The grave danger is that we will not be servants of the Word, but of ourselves; that we will not invest our talents in God's interests, but in ours; that we will not allow God to use us to preach the Word, but that we use God to project our words. Then if challenged, dishonest preachers can always plead divine right and interpose God between themselves and their people. Very convenient—and very dishonest.

2. After honesty, *naturalness* is the second requirement for true humanity. Preachers are indeed to "be themselves." But what self? We are all so divided that it is usually a hollow claim to plead that "I was just being myself." What does it mean to "be yourself," to be "natural"?

Naturalness means not adding to or subtracting from your personality. It means being neither more nor less than you are. Some try to be more than they are; they want to appear holier, or more profound, or more dynamic. Others are scared to death to seem to be as much as they are; they do not want to be regarded as zealous or devout. Both project a false, unnatural personality.

But how do I know what my natural personality is? We are all plagued by the ambiguity of selfhood.

Perhaps Bonhoeffer provides the best clue when he says, "In the service of Jesus I become natural."[6] Only the New Person in Christ is truly natural. The only self that is appropriate is that new self. This means that I do not need to imitate anyone else; neither do I need to imitate the ideal minister.

Imitation is not only the sincerest form of flattery, it is also the sincerest form of insecurity. Yet no one is completely free of imitation, especially in his or her early development, and modeling is a healthy and essential step in the maturing process of any minister. A preacher is lucky if the model chosen is a good one. Paul urged his followers to be imitators of him even as he was an imitator of Christ (1 Cor. 11:1).

But there is still a real danger in imitation. When preachers continually ape the preaching manner of another, they are betraying a lack of personal security and identity. The natural desire for acceptance can lead to the unnatural imitation of others. Beyond the beginning stages of ministry, this practice indicates a warped concept of ministry and an unhealthy striving for prestige.

Many ministers preach with anything but the natural personality that is theirs. Either they speak with the personality of some preacher they admire (which is bad, but least worst), or more horribly, they adopt the collective personality they imagine a preacher should have. Mary Shelley wrote about a similar attempt. Dr. Frankenstein pieced together the parts from a number of cadavers to make a man, but instead he created a monster, but no more so than preachers whose personalities are a composite of the bits and pieces of others, some long dead and nearly decomposed. And then when that monster roars and stalks about, they should not be surprised when children will not play about their feet.

3. The preacher will struggle all of his or her life with the inevitable tension between ego and humility, but true *humility* is another essential to true humanity. The answer certainly does not lie in unbridled self-assertion, but it is also most definitely not to be found in a Publicanish pride, a kind of "of course I am less than nothing," inverted pride, either. That is only a subtle way to force humility to serve pride.

Nor can humility be taken care of by semantic dodges. For example, saying "we" when a preacher means "I" cannot cloak a preacher's outsized ego. The preacher who is always saying such things as "We are humbled by this opportunity to stand before you this morning . . ." or "We are grateful that you have listened to our words . . ." sounds like a speech choir. There is nothing humble about becoming a committee instead of an individual. Mark Twain once said that only three people were entitled to use the editorial "we": an editor, God, and a person with a tapeworm. Perhaps the "we" preachers do not consider themselves either editorial or divine—they may be merely revealing a parasitic problem.

C. S. Lewis said that truly humble individuals will not be the greasy, "smarmy" kinds of people who are always telling you that of course they are nobody; but if anything, they will strike you as cheerful, intelligent persons who enjoy life and who take a real interest in what *you* say to them. Being humble has nothing to do with believing yourself to be worthless. Only an incredibly obtuse preacher could fail to know his or her own obvious talents. Ministerial humility simply means recognizing the source of these gifts and firmly committing them to the service of Christ.

The theme of humility is a frequent one in Christian theology and has an ancient tradition. Chrysostom said in his homilies on Acts that some preachers lived for applause: "If they get applause from the multitude, it is to them as if they gained the very kingdom of heaven, but if silence follows the close of their speech, it is worse than hell itself, the dejection that falls upon their spirits from the silence." He himself had to forbid all applause from his audience—and this announcement itself brought the house down with applause![7]

When Henry Parry Liddon was about to deliver his first sermon at St. Paul's Cathedral, he wrote in his diary on the evening before, April 18, 1863; "Feel very unequal to preaching at St. Paul's tomorrow, both spiritually and physically. O Lord Jesus, help me— a poor sinner."[8] Similarly, D. T. Niles said of himself: "That is what I am. I am a sinner for whom Jesus died. I am just one of those who has been loved of God in Jesus at the cross. That is the central truth about me. All the rest is peripheral."[9] And Karl Barth has written, "We are *worthy* of being believed only as we are aware of our unworthiness. There is no such thing as *convincing* utterance about God except as Christian preaching feels its *need* . . ."[10]

4. When Christian preachers are able to admit their own needs, they can stop feeling guilty about needing rest. This is another essential in true humanity—being human means *being able to rest.* Gods do not need rest; humans do. And no one needs to be rested more, in spirit and mind and body, than God's preachers. When we understand our part in ministry—which is not attempting to manage the whole world, but letting God be God—we can rest, physically and psychologically.

Compulsive recreation is not rest. Play is involved in rest, but without an understanding of our humanity, rest is impossible. We are never at ease, never at rest. But when God is God and I am God's servant—I hope a hardworking and faithful one, but still only a servant— I can be at ease. "The earth is the Lord's, and the fullness thereof; the world, and they that dwell therein" (Ps. 24:1). When we really know that, we can be at rest with the peace that is not understood. At work we can be at ease, and at rest we can be set free to play.

5. Being human also means *allowing others to be persons.* Some who would stoutly insist on their own humanity are chronically unwilling to let anyone else be persons. "Don't preach at me" is a common, unfunny idiom. What it means is, "Don't overturn my personality! Who are you to be playing God? I am a person, and so are you."

Many preachers who would never recognize themselves as god-players nevertheless want to call all the shots and make all the decisions for every living creature. They are master of the house, the dog, and the church, and there is not much difference in the way they speak to each. Allowing others to be persons means respecting the uniqueness of their selfhood. It means never using approaches in preaching that are inappropriate for communication with other persons, approaches that are dictatorial or imperious, artificially sincere or seductive.

Letting God be God also means letting persons be persons. And the most miserable human being alive is the preacher who cannot be God and will not be a person.

6. As a matter of fact, preaching that really matters to people does not result from high-handed techniques, but from caring. *True humanity means caring.* A great deal has been written about caring, so much that unfortunately "caring" has virtually become another fad word. Preachers who try to mentally psych themselves into deeply "caring" about a sermon subject to be more persuasive are in trouble. Nothing is worse than the pose of phony concern. No one can care equally about all subjects, or doctrines, or even texts. Our caring about subjects varies with our interests. Anyone who attempts to appear equally passionate about every sermon subject destroys both perspective and credibility at the same time.

But if we have been honestly apprehended by the word of God so that we ultimately care about it, and if, at the most foundational levels of our being, that apprehension has led to its corollary, that we has been enabled to care about people, our concern cannot be concealed.

In short, you cannot develop concern from external enthusiasm for your subject. Caring about people and the word that God has spoken and will speak for them results in honest caring. Where a person's treasure is, his or her caring will be observed close by.

7. This kind of concern can only come from genuine involvement in the lives of the people to whom we minister. Paul Sherer says, "You may begin your career with a doctrinaire interest in theology or in preaching as one of the fine arts. But pray God you may find yourself, little by little, drawn to human lives and human hopes and human fears."[11] If people suspect that we do not care, they will not listen—and properly so. Brand Blanshard writes, "But how often writers on religion, morals, or art leave one with the bleak impression that they have never come within miles of what these experiences are like to the people who have them!"[12] *Involvement with reality* is the final mark of true humanity.

Of course no one could experience all of life—just as no one could grasp all of the Scripture—but that is not the point. If we seem not to understand either the real life of real people or the word of God for that existence, we are disqualified from proclamation of the gospel. But if we have known suffering, happiness,

frustration, satisfaction—of whatever sort—and if we can bring
the word of God to bear on these and other real conditions of
human existence, we will be heard, and heard gladly. "The secret
of reality in preaching is intelligibility, and the secret of intelligibility is interest. 'Interest,' 'interesting,' are to be understood in
their etymological sense—*inter est*—that which is common to the
speaker and hearer, that which they have between them."[13] When
we speak of those things that we and our people have in common,
interest always results.

To develop this mutuality of interest, the preacher needs sympathy—he or she must "feel with" others. The classic remark on
this subject is that of John Broadus: "If I were asked what is the
first thing in effective preaching, I should say sympathy; and what
is the second thing, I should say sympathy; and what is the third
thing, I should say sympathy."[14] Jesus could not have preached
with the aliveness he did unless he also had his sympathetic interest in the human situation. Children and the common people
heard him gladly because he welcomed little children and dined
with publicans and sinners.

The first step—and a big one—toward increasing interest in
preaching, and curing obscurity in language as well, is a reinvolve-
ment in the common experiences of people as well as a renewed
study of the living word. No one ever has a language problem
alone. A context problem is invariably present. What a person is
becomes language. If we are out of phase with our context, ourselves, and the word of God, our language will reflect our confusion. Insecurity, anxiety, striving for prestige, anger, fear, inability
to relate to others, and unwillingness to obey God all result in
language failure. Brand Blanshard strikes it correctly: "Persistently
obscure writers will usually be found to be defective human beings."[15] Tampering with vocabulary won't help that. The cure is
far more radical. God must make us right within our own skins.
Then our language will make sense.

In summary, then, only a thoroughgoing commitment to the
Bible as the word of God makes the present truly real, and only
a thoroughgoing commitment to the present makes the message of

the Bible fully intelligible. When we as preachers position ourselves at midpoint between our contemporary given and the historical given of the Gospel, we will find—perhaps to our surprise
—that we are completely immersed in both. Perhaps even more
surprisingly, we will find, as the early disciples did, that our
human involvement enables our testimony to the divine Word.

7. Credibility and Charisma

As we have seen, it was characteristic of the early disciples to refuse to play God. Paul's concern for the present and his commitment to the revealed Word refused to allow him to shift the focus from God to himself. As a result he gained a hearing for the gospel and established his own credibility at the same time.

In his day, just the reverse seemed to be the custom. Halford Luccock points out that Paul and Nero pursued opposite courses, and at that time Nero seemed to be right and Paul wrong. The contrast between the two is a fascinating study in credibility. Nero claimed divinity for himself, and Paul refused to do so when he had the chance. In that age Nero certainly appeared to have the last word. Yet no one would argue that Paul's credibility since that time hasn't been considerably better than Nero's, and Luccock reminds us that today people name their sons Paul and their dogs Nero.

There is a profound lesson here for the preacher who will listen. "The one who will be greatest, let that one be servant of all" (Mark 10:44). This truth applies also to preaching. The great sermon is the servant sermon. If the preacher would preach a great sermon, let him or her preach one that serves. Christ understood human ego drive and did not deny it, but he showed it the proper channel. When we lose our lives for his sake, and the sake of the gospel, we find it. But preachers who seek to elevate themselves for the sake of their own lives lose everything.

Nor do we speak parabolically in saying this, but factually and practically. As we will see, credibility and charisma are both involved in this principle, which Christ established for his servants. What is this element of credibility that Paul had and Nero lacked? Can it be analyzed?[1]

To understand this important concept, several terms need definition. *Credibility* may be defined as the weight given to the assertions of a speaker and the acceptance accorded them by hearers. It is composed of two factors, trustworthiness and expertness. The greater the trustworthiness and expertness of the speaker, the greater his or her credibility. *Expertness* is the extent to which a communicator is perceived to be capable of being a source of valid assertions; *trustworthiness* is the degree of confidence the listeners have in the intent of the speaker to communicate valid assertions.

Credibility is highly important in communication: the listener's acceptance of the message of a high-credibility communicator can be as much as four times greater than that of a low-credibility communicator, one who is perceived as seriously lacking in trustworthiness and expertness. The credibility of any communicator is not static, however, but varies from situation to situation.

In the first place, no one is perceived as equally expert in all situations. A Supreme Court justice would usually be regarded as more expert than a plumber, but again, that all depends on whether a legal case is involved or a sink. Trustworthiness is generally a more stable factor in credibility than expertness, but not invariably so; it may also vary with the situation or the group.

The importance of these credibility factors for the minister is obvious. Unless we are perceived as both trustworthy and expert by the people to whom we minister, our influence will be seriously impaired. We cannot hope to communicate the gospel with any degree of credibility if we are neither trustworthy nor expert. Obviously no one is completely expert on all questions—even within his or her own field of competence—and no one is perceived as equally trustworthy by all individuals. But the degree to which our listeners regard us as persons whose assertions are accurate and dependable will largely influence the degree of acceptance our message will gain.

A key word in this issue is *perceived*. Unfortunately, what a person actually knows or how trustworthy he or she really is is not always as significant as how expert or trustworthy he or she is perceived to be. Many knowledgeable, trustworthy preachers are not regarded with the esteem they deserve, while some completely unscrupulous, ignorant preachers enjoy a reputation as real authorities of great character. This means that credibility can be counterfeit and spurious. Many ministers suffer extreme anguish watching unscrupulous preachers glorying in undeserved adulation from people who have been duped through various deceitful and manipulative tricks the preachers have used to appear expert and trustworthy.

But this should not prevent ethical ministers from examining their own expertness or trustworthiness, or the degree to which their congregations perceive them as such, to assess correctly their credibility in the community. Knowing about credibility factors, just as knowing about other elements in communication theory, does not imply unethical interests. On the contrary, it may mean removing obstacles that are causing the preacher to be a stumbling block in the communication of the gospel; or it may help him or her to eliminate the actual lack of expertness or trustworthiness discovered.

What do expertness and trustworthiness mean in the context of preaching? How can a minister be expert? What influences our congregation's perception of us as trustworthy?

Although no complete distinction is possible, expertness and trustworthiness roughly correspond in incarnational preaching with human existence and participation in the divine. Expertness means that as a human being, living among these people in this time and in this place, I must know something. I must understand the culture in which I live and the living needs of the people to whom I minister; and I must know how to interpret the word of God which speaks to them. This is my "expertness" as a preacher of the gospel.

But through the giving of myself to this task, which can only follow the giving of myself to Christ in his service, I become trustworthy and believable: "They which live should not henceforth live unto themselves . . ." (2 Cor. 5:15). Obviously no one is completely selfless, just as no one is completely informed, but to the degree that we "lose our lives for his sake," to that degree we allow the Word to become incarnate in our preached words. Let us examine the implications of this stance for the expertness and trustworthiness of the preacher of the Word.

EXPERTNESS

An expert in the pulpit is not an all-knowing, infallible source of information on all subjects in heaven and earth. If we try to pretend that, our lack of expertness will be soon discovered and our trustworthiness will drop accordingly. As J. Edgar Park once put it, "An expert is an ordinary man far away from home, and a saint's reputation too often depends upon the silence of his family."[2]

Credibility is badly damaged by attempts to bluff our way on subjects where we actually know less than nothing. Expertness does involve information, of course, though that is not the only factor. If we want to have our message received, we must be sure of our facts, as sure as we can be, and where we are uniformed say so or keep quiet. No one expects us to know everything on all subjects anyhow, but people do expect us not to claim divine right on misinformation that causes even grade-school children in congregations to giggle behind their hands.

Modern preachers who attribute the success of the long-antiquated "pulpit princes" merely to their times would do well to be as informed as they were. It was said that when Spurgeon spoke of grouse shooting you could be sure that he had read until he was expert on the subject, even if he made no more than a thirty-second reference to it. When Thomas Guthrie spoke on sailing, a man said, "He is an old sailor; at least, he was a while at sea!"; and when he spoke on medicine, someone said to another after the service, "If he stick [fail] the minister trade, the young man would make his bread as a surgeon!"[3] Phillips Brooks fired a shot that is still hitting targets today: "In many respects an ignorant clergy, however pious it may be, is worse than none at all. The more an empty head glows and burns, the more hollow and thin and dry it grows."[4]

Expertness for the ministry, however, involves more than mere information. It also involves understanding: understanding of people, understanding of the situation in which people find themselves, and understanding of the relation of the biblical witness to both. No preacher will be perceived as expert, no matter how extensive his or her mental file cabinet on facts biblical or secular, unless he or she has a kind of *relational intelligence;* that is, unless he or she has gained significant insight from reflection on our experiences with other persons.

Some preachers display dazzling factual competence and unbelievable relational ignorance. They are unable to pick up obvious signals transmitted from individuals or audiences, and they misread and mishandle what few impulses they do get. They cannot anticipate reactions, they cannot understand feelings, they cannot deal meaningfully with human needs. Nathaniel Judson Burton said in his Yale Lectures, "They [the people] do not like to be fired at by a glib expert who knows guns perfectly but does not know people . . ."[5]

Increasing one's sensitivity to people is far more difficult than adding facts to one's brain. If we realize that our relational ability is low, we must work hard to listen more and to read in areas where insight into personal factors can be improved. Perhaps we should also consider psychological consultation to gain insight into ourselves and our own lives. Most preachers who lack insight into the needs of others themselves suffer badly from confused personal relations.

Other factors in expertness—age, leadership, and similarity of social background—are either largely out of the minister's control or else can be enormously improved by a demonstration of increased factual knowledge and improved human understanding.

TRUSTWORTHINESS

If the minister cannot afford to be uninformed, he or she must be doubly certain of not being untrustworthy. An untrustworthy preacher of the word of God is unthinkable; and if people begin to think it, the credibility of the preacher is ruined. No amount of theological genius or biblical competence can save the preacher then.

Thielicke writes: "The fact is that a preacher is constantly betraying himself. When we meet a druggist, we do not necessarily note whether he loves or hates, whether he dispenses his pills with delight or whether he is eating his heart out in envy and care. . . . But with a preacher it soon comes out. . . . What the druggist thinks does not undermine the words with which he recommends this or that cough medicine, but the preacher, by the state of his soul, can belie the words which have been committed to him, no matter how well chosen they are as he utters them."[6]

In other words, the personal traits of preachers are far more involved in what they recommend than what druggists dispense. On the other hand, how would anyone react to a druggist who repeatedly pushed a cough remedy that he never used himself even though he owned stock in the company? His credibility would be exactly as low as those preachers who are manipulative for their own personal interest and inconsistent in their practice.

Let us examine briefly each of these three damaging elements in trustworthiness: personal motivation, manipulative methods, and inconsistent practice.

Personal motivation. A continuing liability to our credibility as preachers is our professional involvement in the Christian faith. Put bluntly, we are paid to advocate Christianity. For many people, this puts the sermon in the same category with a recommendation by ad people for a product they are paid to promote. God's laborers may be "worthy of their hire," but being hired doesn't help their credibility any.

The only chance for the paid Christian minister to maintain high credibility is to understand the difference between "hirelings" and faithful servants. Hirelings run away from the needs of the flock because they are hirelings, that is, because they are in it strictly for themselves and what they can get out of it. Faithful servants are also paid—but they care about their duties and love the flock, and they *risk themselves for them.* At that point they have nothing to gain for themselves. They will not earn a penny more for the risk they take or the extra pressure they subject themselves to. But they are faithful—trustworthy in the highest degree—because they are perceived as genuinely caring about the flock. "The good shepherd gives his life for the sheep" (John 10:11). It is not carrying things too far to say that the unequaled, centuries-long credibility of Jesus of Nazareth, even among non-Christians, is due to the completely selfless concern for others manifested in his life.

We must be committed to the same selfless service as our Lord. If we are perceived as pursuing a ministry for gain, either monetary or professional; if we seem to care for nothing more than ladder climbing and status seeking; if we say only what will please the galleries; if we pray loudly for "results" to build our reputations (and repeatedly insisting that "I just give God the glory" doesn't mean we are)—then we may be assured, whatever our own inflated self-images that our credibility is undermined by our obvious personal interests.

Manipulative methods. Persuasion is not manipulation. Persuasion is the attempt to influence others. Everyone in the Bible who ever attempted to accomplish the will of God, whether Abraham or Moses or the prophets or Paul or Jesus, was involved in persuasion. Persuasion is not morally wrong, nor is it morally right. The question is *what* someone is being persuaded to do, and *why*, and *how*.

Persuading a distraught woman not to leap to her death from an office building is good; persuading a child to try heroin is evil. In these cases, *what* is being urged is the key factor. *Why* something is being urged is also vital to the ethical appropriateness of persuasion. To attempt to persuade a businessman that the Christian church can be deeply meaningful to his life and the life of his family is good; but to attempt to persuade him to affiliate with the church to get him to lower his price on property the church needs is evil. *How* persuasion is done is likewise crucial. Persuasion that honestly and openly states all of the facts in a nonprejudicial way is fair and ethical, but persuasion that conceals or misrepresents facts is manipulative.

Manipulation, then, *may be defined as persuasion that is deliberately not in the best interest of the individual involved but is deceptively intended for the advantage of the persuader; or that attempts to get people to do something they would not do if they had the facts.*

Any preacher who cares about the commission of Christ to "go into all the world and make disciples," will find it impossible to avoid involvement in persuasive communication. But we should never resort to manipulation. Our motivation and methods should always be closely and repeatedly examined, and if in doubt, we should find out how our persuasive attempts are perceived by others.

When an audience suspects that the preacher has something personal to gain from persuasive efforts—more money, a larger pulpit, denominational status, popular acclaim—he or she is regarded as a manipulator. However, even if the end we seek is good, we are still manipulators if we uses deceitful means to accomplish it. For example, urging people to give money to carry out the work of the church might be a good thing both for the church and for the people, but promising that God will make them rich for so doing is manipulative. Such *specious promises* are often involved in religious manipulation.

Manipulation also *deliberately omits significant facts* from an argument. A church might well need a new building, but failing to mention that interest rates are at a ten-year high could be a damaging blow to the credibility of the argument. In such cases, potentially damaging facts should be discussed openly and dealt with. Then if the need is great enough to override them, persuasion has been accomplished without manipulation. If not, it is better to discover the problem sooner than later. Churches who later learn that they were manipulated by their pastors generally have rather severe reactions toward them. In fact, they may be persuaded (or manipulated) into going elsewhere.

One of the most unforgivable forms of manipulation is preaching a "cheap grace"—omitting the full demands of discipleship—to lure people into the membership of the church. Usually this hucksterism combines an oversimplified sales pitch with false promises of a carefree, God-will-give-you-whatever-you-want life.

This kind of sermon will promise anything to get "joiners" so that the "evangelist" can put another notch in his or her Bible (and these statistics, of course, will be modestly included in the next brochure).

Once people have been manipulated like that, they present a continuing problem for the church. If they do not drop out altogether in disillusionment, they frequently perpetuate the shallow, manipulative methods that attracted them in the first place.

Inconsistent Practice. Many preachers suffer from low trustworthiness because they are simple careless and inconsistent in their remarks. They are not deliberately manipulative, nor are they self-centered, but they are careless with facts. They express too many opinions on subjects where they are poorly informed. They cite half-remembered facts on the spur of the moment and someone catches them in an inaccurate statement.

Everyone makes this mistake at times, of course, frequently without ever realizing it. But if this kind of inaccuracy persists, the preacher is quickly labeled as uninformed, careless, and untrustworthy.

Sermon illustrations are a notorious field for inaccuracy and inconsistency. The expression "preacher stories" has become idiomatic for unbelievable assertions that are fanciful at best and downright dishonest at worst. Every illustration should be factually correct and carefully checked for accuracy. One unscientific science reference or one nonhistorical historical reference can seriously damage a preacher's credibility.

The primary issue at stake in trustworthiness, however, is usually not so much *factually incorrect* remarks as *exaggerated or untrue remarks,* such as illustrations that never happened at all, or that were told as if they happened to the speaker when in fact they did not. Some laity have heard several pastors in different churches tell the same anecdote as having happened to them.

Two Protestant bishops (who obviously had just returned from the same conference) began their chapel addresses on subsequent Sundays at a university with the same story, an incident that supposedly had happened to each of them the Sunday before as they greeted people on their way out of church. The second bishop, no more dishonest than the first, was hooted into silence, and his embarrassed host had to stand and explain to him the reason for the outburst. He never recovered, and the Christian cause almost didn't recover on that campus either.

If pastors were hooted down every time they were discovered in an untrue, exaggerated, or wildly inaccurate remark, we would have shorter sermons and more interesting worship services.

If a story sounds unbelievable—even if you personally trust the source of it—either be able to document it or don't tell it. No story is worth the loss of a congregation's trust, no matter how dramatic and appealing it may be.

Consider, for example, this story. It was Napoleon's genius to ignite the common soldier to fervid patriotism. To exemplify the French spirit, he used to tell this one:

Once he came upon an old soldier who had one arm and still wore his uniform, on which was displayed the Legion of Honor.

"Where did you lose your arm?" the emperor asked.

"At Austerlitz, sire," the soldier replied.

"And for that you were decorated?"

"Yes, sire. It is a small token to pay for the Legion of Honor."

"It seems to me," Napoleon said, "that you are the kind of man who regrets he didn't lose both arms for his country."

"What then might be my reward?" asked the old soldier.

"Oh, in that case I would have awarded you a double Legion of Honor."

With that, the old soldier drew his word and immediately cut off his other arm.

For years the story circulated and was accepted without question until one day someone asked, "How?"

Trustworthiness, perhaps more than any other characteristic, is expected of the preacher of the gospel. A congregation may be willing to forgive a lack of expertness, but if they perceive their preacher as untrustworthy, his or her credibility is destroyed. And no one in society should have greater credibility than the person who speaks for Christ.

CHARISMA: NOT THE COIN-IN-THE-FISH'S-MOUTH OF PREACHING

Closely related to credibility, and yet distinct from it, is the question of charisma. What is this mysterious element? Is it capable of analysis? If so, what significance, if any, does the concept have for the Christian preacher?

In communication theory, charisma has most often been associated with political leadership. Some public figures have been regarded as possessing mystical, almost magical powers of leadership and persuasion. Such persons are said to be charismatic, possessed of gifts that defy analysis. (The concept is closely related to Christian sources; in fact, the term "charismatic leadership" itself was borrowed by Max Weber from Rudolf Sohm's history of the church.)[7]

Charisma is neither intrinsically good or bad. Some leaders have used their charisma for good, others for evil: Mother Teresa, Winston Churchill, Franklin Roosevelt, Eva Peron, John F. Kennedy, Adolph Hitler, Eleanor Roosevelt, Mahatma Gandhi, and Mao Tse-Tung, among others, are widely regarded as charismatic figures.

Christianity is also fertile soil for charisma. Only politics can rival the church as a producer of charismatic leaders. A number of Christian preachers are particularly remembered as charismatic figures, among them Chrysostom, Francis of Assisi, Savonarola, Martin Luther, John Knox, William Booth, Phoebe Palmer, Studdert Kennedy, Martin Luther King, Jr., Fulton J. Sheen, and Billy Graham. Obviously this group is also a mixed bag of gifts, attitudes, and ministries. Is there anything in common among these people? Can charisma be attained or is it a pure gift, like one's height or the color of one's eyes? Is charisma the coin-in-the-fish's-mouth of preaching, something miraculously caught?

Until quite recently, only a very few serious studies, such as those of Max Weber in political science, have dealt with charisma. Many authorities on communication theory still continue to consider charisma as the result of a complex combination of many credibility factors or perhaps the possession of one of these to an extraordinary degree. One author of an excellent work on persuasive communication says of charismatic figures, "They remain as individuals whose effect on audiences and history is not explained by research literature."[8]

Continuing research, however, has begun to narrow the search for the key to charisma. Two basic characteristics seem to typify the charismatic relationship: first, *charismatic leaders are perceived as possessed by a purpose that is greater than themselves;* and second, *charismatic leadership requires a charismatic community.*

All of the charismatic leaders previously named definitely have one characteristic in common: they all were perceived as having given themselves in utter selflessness to a cause greater than themselves. People flocked to these leaders because they were able to project this sense of complete abandonment to the greater interest. In the case of Churchill, it was the defense of Britain; in the case of Hitler, it was the establishment of the Third Reich. But people gave fanatical allegiance to both because they believed these leaders to be totally dedicated to the common good rather than to personal interests. They may have been, or they may not have been. The essential fact is that they were perceived as absolutely absorbed in a cause greater than themselves.[9]

This means that unscrupulous politicians, or preachers, can counterfeit commitment and fraudulently lead. They may care nothing for a cause or for the people who fanatically follow them. They may care only for money or power or status. They may not be selfless at all but selfish, vain, and arrogant. Their only cause may be success, and the only people they care about may be themselves. But because they project the image of a selfless leader who has given up all personal ambition to serve the Great Cause, they are believed and followed.

Second, charismatic leadership requires a charismatic community. A definitive characteristic of the charismatic relationship is the unqualified belief in the leader and his or her mission by a group of followers.[10] That is, the purpose the leader projects must match the burning desire of a people. Francis of Assisi made himself poor for Italy's poor; Gandhi starved himself for India's starving. Unless the purpose of the leader matches that of the community, or unless he or she can arouse the people to his or her goals, the leader will have no charisma at all.

This means that no leader is perceived as charismatic by all communities. The same people who regarded John F. Kennedy as a magnetic leader would not feel the same about Adolf Hitler, nor was Martin Luther King charismatic for most members of the white community in the South. These leaders represented the dreams of the specific communities that followed them.

These are the two basic characteristics of the charismatic relationship, but *what are the personal traits* of the charismatic leader? At least eight such characteristics have been identified as common to charismatic figures: (1) exposure to varied environments and norms; (2) the ability to identify with, have empathy toward, and communicate with the plurality within the group they serve; (3) a high energy level, or an extraordinary degree of vitality; (4) presence of mind or composure under conditions of stress or challenge; (5) unswerving dedication to their goals; (6) the ability to project the impression of a powerful mind and range of knowledge; (7) a capacity for innovation and originality; (8) identification with the continuity of tradition, and the proclamation of the vision of a new and different order to come.[11]

There are many fascinating implications from this study for the Christian church and its preaching. To begin with, reread this list with Jesus of Nazareth in mind. It could scarcely describe him better. And if that is so, *this means that the follower of Christ, the one who is to be Christlike, will also be possessed of certain charismatic characteristics.* Even briefly touching on a few of these traits will suggest intriguing possibilities.

In the first place, if exposure to varied norms is an important experience for the charismatic leader, then our pluralistic age is not the detriment to charismatic leadership it is usually believed to be. Jesus lived in just such an age. And who should have more empathy toward this plurality—rich and poor, educated and uneducated, multiracial—than the Christian? Jesus could identify with these people and communicate with them. His disciples should be able to do the same. Likewise, the enthusiasm for life, the composure under stress, the dedication to goals, the understanding and innovation that typified Christ should also typify those he has claimed.

Perhaps most significant, the preacher of the historic faith should be able to identify with the continuity of tradition, as did Christ, but he or she must also proclaim the vision of a new and different order to come, as Jesus did. It is also interesting for the role of preaching that "the proclamation of his [the charismatic leader's] goal or mission may play no small part in initially generating the charismatic relationship."[12]

The very fact that charismatic traits can be identified means that charisma cannot be written off as magic. It is not absolutely mysterious, no matter how complex it is or how difficult to analyze in detail. It is not inherited. Some people may seem to be born with it, while others appear incapable of ever possessing it to the slightest degree. *But these are the exceptions.* If a person has minimal abilities in the areas described and, more important, if he or she can give himself or herself to a cause worthy of complete abandon and can project those feelings to a community of corresponding concern, that leader will be perceived as charismatic.

Few people may ever achieve the charisma of a Luther or a Gandhi or a Churchill—for one thing, few will stand at the intersection of time and need as they did, and few will possess their extraordinary communicative talents—but charisma is relative, and the gift of extraordinary leadership is not limited to a few charismatic geniuses.

Can the average preacher be charismatic? He or she can be and, to some extent, should be. Who should be more entitled to completely abandon himself or herself to a great cause than the minister of the gospel? Who, in more honesty, and with more integrity, should be better able to project this concern to people? Who should be more justified in urging a community to join in a common cause? Where should anyone expect to find a readier matching community of concern, a truly charismatic community, than in the Christian church?

If the church seems lacking in charismatic leadership, the blame must be shared. Perhaps it is true that its preachers have not been able to completely lose themselves in the Christian cause, or perhaps they have been timid and hesitant to project to others their genuine commitment to that cause. But perhaps it is also true that they have not found their concern matched by a corresponding charismatic community. Unless the church is equally committed to the common cause of Christ, unless the church is willing to lose itself for the sake of the world, and unless the church encourages its leaders by its equal devotion, it need not altogether blame the ministry. *Periods of great charismatic leadership in the church have been matched by great charismatic communities.* One encourages the other, and both are produced by obedience to the word of God.

Neither the church nor its preachers should seek after charisma. That would be self-serving and therefore ultimately self-defeating. "But seek ye first the kingdom of God, and God's righteousness; and all these things shall be added unto you also" (Matt. 6:33).

8. Impact, Communion, and Shock

The study of credibility and charisma in the person who preaches corresponds closely with another issue, the question of impact in the message preached. Is it possible for the disciple of the twentieth century after Christ to communicate with the same impact that characterized the preaching of the apostles of the first century? How can we shape the sermon so that our words allow the Word to strike with the fresh impact that always typifies the gospel?

Before we can answer these questions, we must first understand the relationship between impact, communion, and shock. This understanding is not only vital to the act of preaching but to the larger service of worship and, indeed, even to the total ministry of the preacher.

First, what is impact? Put most simply, impact is the effect a communication has upon its hearer. Translated for the preaching setting it means, "Does my sermon make a difference?" More specifically, "What, if anything, happens to people because of my preaching that would not happen without it?"

These questions immediately arouse emotions. Few preachers can reflect on them five seconds without experiencing a change in blood pressure. Some immediately become angry, or at least annoyed ("annoyed" being what an angry preacher is when not alone). This angry group is a curious mixture of left and right theologically and homiletically. Those on the right who see the preaching of the Word as an almost magical, or hypersacramental, and virtually objective reality resent the idea that "I" or "my" are involved in sermons at all. The preached word has impact. Period. Curiously, the left feels the same, but for totally different reasons.

Who am *I* to think that I have the right to change anybody? Isn't this the manipulative method of the huckster? And since when is it *my* business to care about whether I am effective or not?

Other preachers just feel depressed, or a little sad, at these questions. They are fairly sure that their sermons aren't making any difference. They have become resigned to preaching because they are still obliged to or because they have a dogged faith in preaching—if not in *their* preaching. For them, the answer to this question is simple: my preaching has no impact.

If preaching were a completely objective event, the preacher would not need to think about the possible impact, or lack of it, of his or her message. Impact would be guaranteed by the objective Word itself calling forth an irresistible response from its subjects.

But for that to be true, two things would have to change. First, the preacher's own involvement in the act of preaching would have to be overridden or abolished altogether; and second, the congregation's free human response would have to be destroyed and replaced by a programmed response to the message, a kind of divine posthypnotic suggestion. Since both of these conditions are obviously out of the question, the preacher cannot avoid the question of impact.

This is not to say that there cannot be an overemphasis on impact, on effect, on "results." There is an illegitimate concern involving impact. Whenever we make impact our primary concern, we are liable to all sorts of dangers. Even if we have scrupulously swept our homiletical houses free of indifferent preaching, we have made it all the more habitable for demons if our only care is for impact. Manipulative methods and a gallery-pleasing mentality are sure to occupy our preaching. Then we have betrayed the gospel by lapsing into a false subjectivity, an overeagerness to impress, to please, to excite.

On the other hand, only a false objectivism can ignore impact. People do matter. They are real. And they are really there, and the preacher is really one of them. As a person he or she was called of God to preach; as persons with distinct needs and hearing handicaps, the congregation sits before him or her. The human element is no less important in preaching than the divine element. The dangers on the people side of incarnational preaching cannot be overcome by denying the reality of the human element or ignoring it. You cannot make God more there by obliterating the humanity of the worshipers or their preacher.

With all of the dangers, then, that can result from a preoccupation with impact, nevertheless we cannot ignore it, the detriment of its absence or the power of its presence.

But just as the communication of the gospel stands at midpoint between the historical given and the existential given, so impact stands between communicative communion and communicative shock. To analyze impact correctly, we must begin with an understanding of communion as a function of communication; then we can observe the two factors that yield impact; and finally, we can see how an excess of these factors leads to communicative shock.

COMMUNION

To the right of impact stands communion. Technically, its true name is *phatic communion*. Phatic communion is presymbolic language. "Hello" is an example. In fact, all "hello" language—such as greetings, comments about the weather, and generalized inquiries ("How are you?")—is presymbolic, or communal, language.

Such language is presymbolic because it does not actually represent anything concrete but only serves to acknowledge mutual existence. It says I am here and you are there and I recognize our mutuality. Otherwise, these expressions don't mean anything. "Hello" is simply the greeting call of the American human (an interesting species); and "How are you?" is an empty inquiry that expects an equally empty reply—"Fine, thanks"—and one that is actually in mortal dread of anything more substantive.

As insignificant as these aimless niceties appear, they are really highly meaningful forms of communication. Phatic communion is an important language use because it creates bonds of understanding between people, and the small agreements that are reached

lead to the possibility of larger agreements later. Even more significant, recognizing the existence of other persons is the first step
toward community with them, and ignoring their existence is a
sure-fire way to destroy any possibility of it.

If you want to test this theorem, simply ask yourself how you
feel about the person who "never speaks," or how you feel when
someone passes you repeatedly and looks right through you as if
you were not there. Even if the oversight is completely innocent,
it is difficult not to develop feelings that later make true communication and friendship very difficult. A warm greeting and a genuine interest, however brief or passing, does exactly the opposite:
you think, "That's a person I'd like to know better."

Many a preacher has suffered from an innocent oversight in this
regard. As old Mrs. McGillicudy likes to tell it, "Pastor drove *right
by me* downtown today and never even spoke!" (The fact that the
pastor never spoke because he never even *saw* Mrs. McGillicudy
is beside the point.) Pastor Brown has committed an unpardonable
sin—he ignored her existence. Probably everyone knows Mrs.
McGillicudy and doesn't pay too much attention to her consistently offended manner. But Pastor Brown cannot afford for the
same to be said by the Smiths and Joneses of his congregation, too,
or he is in serious trouble. Then, "He doesn't care"—even if he
does. Communion is important, however trivial it may seem (it
usually doesn't appear trivial to *us*), and woe to the one who
ignores it.

This language exists because of a fact in human existence. Its
reality can no more be ruled out of the universe by "getting above
such trivia" than the law of gravity can be repealed by someone
with superior scientific understanding. The arrogant scientist who
steps off the twelve-story building will still hit the pavement, and
the superior theological thinker who ignores the need of people for
simple language communion will be dropped equally hard.

Greeting parishioners on the street, however, is not the only use
of communicative communion for the minister. At least as significant is our use of the familiar and the common in our preaching.

Language communication is only made possible through the

familiar. If "corpulent" is not in the listeners' vocabulary, then the speaker had better use "fat." The word may not be as delicate, but at least it's familiar—and therefore understandable. Likewise, you can read English, and likely not Arabic, because of your experience. (Unless, of course, you happen to be from Saudi Arabia, in which case, the reverse is true. But since you don't read English, my telling you so isn't of any use.) And because you and I have the English language in common, communication is possible.

The use of the familiar is also important to remind us of our common experience. The whole question of community, of oneness, of a sense of a "we-ness" and "us-ness" instead of a "you-ness" and "me-ness," is at stake. Without *anything* familiar, communication is literally impossible. Without *something* that is familiar, a sense of community is not possible.

There is a certain legitimacy for the longing on the part of the congregation for old hymns, familiar terms. These things establish identity with the common experience. They say, "We are a part of the same community." Without some of the familiar, at least, from a Christian's past worship experience, a sense of strangeness and even disorientation occurs.

That is why the young preacher is in serious trouble who goes out to his first rural pulpit and announces, "We aren't singing any more of those old hymns. I'm taking up the hymnals and passing out mimeographed sheets of meaningful hymns which my wife will play on the sitar. And though I don't expect you to understand it, for the first few weeks I will be sharing revolutionary insights with you from my advanced theological training to bring us to a mutual understanding." And they will likely come to one—the church will be looking for another preacher, and he will be looking for another pulpit.

Of course this preacher can console himself by telephoning his philosophical friends long distance and telling them that he has just proved his fidelity to the Cause by getting asked to leave his simple pulpit; but his friends—if better balanced—may suspect that all he has proved is his own poor judgment and perhaps his lack of Christian spirit. And he himself may secretly nurture a deep hurt and confusion at his rejection, which will likely grow into a bitter disillusionment with "what can be done" with the church. He may think he has championed the cause of truth and progress when quite likely what he has done is to refuse to say hello to the community, or even to have slapped people in the face when they stuck out their hands.

To those who insist, "But people aren't even *thinking* of the words of those old hymns," the only reply is, "You're right. They aren't." But the cognitive value in hymn singing isn't the only one. When the familiar notes are sounded and the familiar words are sung, there is a sense of unity, of this is what we are, this is what we've experienced, this is what we have in common. The same is true of familiar terms so long as they, as well as the hymns, are not theologically illegitimate or untrue to the Christian faith. Their age or familiarity alone cannot negate their value or meaningfulness to the spirit of community.

And it is more than a trifle inconsistent that some who most loudly insist on establishing true community are most offended by the familiar. (Often their own unpleasant early religious experiences are projected upon the attitudes of everyone else toward the familiar.) Frequently, if not invariably, those new and innovative methods, terms, hymns, or elements of worship that are regarded as meaningful eventually become locked into an invariable, repetitious pattern at least as predictable and ultimately as "meaningless"—except for the neocult, to whom they speak of the familiar —as the older ways so violently rejected.

The question that should be ultimately determinative, of course, is not whether terms or methods are old or new, traditional or innovative, but whether they best communicate the whole message of the gospel to the whole person. Communicative communion can play a valuable part in that.

But it is at this very point that the danger arises in the use of language as communion. The communication of the gospel can be forgotten entirely in an effort to establish commonality with the audience. We have all sat through almost unbearable services where absolutely nothing happened at all except mutual backslapping, endless "hello" saying, and vigorous head nodding. If an idea walked into the room, it would be voted down. In these services the highest good is imagined to be a group sitting in a friendship circle, holding hands, smiling vacuously, and singing "Blest Be the Tie That Binds."

People may become very enthusiastic after one of these services in which nothing was said that they did not already know and had not already heard a thousand times, particularly if it was what they wanted to hear and if it was said more fervently than usual. "Wasn't that great!" But if asked what was so "great" about it, they may become somewhat confused and reply, "I don't know— but wasn't that the best you ever heard?!" Oratory is born in this climate of striving to say nothing and to say it better than it has ever been said before.

It is this sort of perversion of true communion that causes people to become almost violent on the subject of the traditional. But cliché repeating and playing to the galleries, or "saying what they want to hear," is not honest communion in the Christian faith, but a base and often hypocritical pandering to the appetites of the crowd. Such "worship" soon becomes stereotyped and sterile.

In fact, about the only motivation produced by this consistent use of nonthink nonspeech is a fierce defensive rejection of anyone or anything that is different. The Bible may be quoted and the Holy Spirit may be invoked, but it is apparent that both are only used as familiar tools rather than heeded as dynamic challenges to an ongoing faith. Pharisaism of the lowest sort is only a step away, and the worst witch hunts and the most deadly cultic institutionalism alike have resulted from this language abuse.

Again, it is important to remember that no wing of the church has a monopoly on this kind of error. Normally, the "conservative" or right wing of the church is identified with traditional cliché language and cultic nonspeech. But the "liberal" or left wing of the church can be just as guilty. Whenever the gospel is forgotten in an effort to please, to conform to culture, to innovate for innovation's sake, a new language of Zion and deadening tradition are on the way. The innovative order of today soon becomes the expected routine of tomorrow, and the radically upbeat terminology that is so daring at first quickly sounds dated.

This aging process is inevitable and really is not so bad—if the innovations actually communicated the meaning of the faith better in the first place—but the accompanying mentality of antitraditionalism is usually as fiercely defensive of its own set routine and cultic language as the most ardent traditionalism.

Nevertheless, in spite of these dangers inherent in communal language, it is obvious that community of whatever sort, traditional or innovative, demands a certain degree of the common and the familiar. This does not need to be engineered into a communication method. It will occur naturally due to inherited or created tradition, unless prevented. On the other hand, excessive phatic communion leads to noncommunication and boredom because of an absence of impact.

The next question, therefore, involves impact. What factors result in impact for communication? And how can these be developed without destroying true communion or causing communicative shock?

IMPACT

Impact is the product of two forces, predictability and distance. Impact is in inverse proportion to both: the greater the predictability and distance of a communication, the less the impact.

Predictability. Impact is promoted by a lack of predictability. For example, if your little girl tells you that she is going to hide in the hall and whisper "Boo!" when you pass, it really isn't very scary and daddy or mommy has to work hard at looking frightened. But if not warned, that same simple act can make a normally unemotional person try to climb into the attic without benefit of stairs.

Much preaching lacks impact because of its absolute predictability. It begins the same; it ends the same. Its feeling level is the same; its volume level is the same. It is always flat, or it is always excited. Its order of arrangement is always the same, or nearly so. Its topics vary, but not much. Preachers change churches and churches change preachers in an effort to get some kind of variety into the preaching and worship experience.

Some preachers of integrity absolutely cannot understand why their messages have so little impact, while their lay people are frequently carried away (sometimes literally so) by another preacher or evangelist who is absolutely nothing but shallow and flamboyant. This kind of spiritual seven-year itch or religious middle-age crisis on the part of the laity may be regrettable, but it happens because impact in the church relationship has dropped to zero due to the utter boredom and absolute predictability of the experience.

The cure for the problem is not for the preacher to start telling deathbed stories or wearing loud clothes, anymore than buying a new wig or changing lipstick shades can really do much about a wife's problems with a restless husband. Some slight external changes in presentation, manner, or style may be called for, and within the limits of the preacher's own personality may help some. But the only real cure must take place at a deeper level. We must find within the Bible, within our congregations, within ourselves —within life itself—the authentic uniqueness of reality. Sameness plagues preaching, worship, and ministry when the incredible variety of life is blocked out and one facet of it is monotonously played and replayed.

The only predictability to which the preacher should be committed is the same predictability Jesus had, and that is a consistent devotion to the will of God. But since that devotion will involve him or her in ministry with all kinds of people in every imaginable setting in an ever-changing contemporary existence, as well as with the historical acts of God and the life of Christ in all of their incredible depth and richness, an authentic, unforced variety will be the inevitable result. As a matter of fact, boredom of minister and people is the surest sign of an inattention to the living Word in our midst and of a preoccupation with a few threadbare themes of our own.

In short, to increase impact, decrease predictability. Perhaps a simple varying of liturgy or sermon approach, or some other external adjustment is all that is needed. Likely, however, authentic unpredictability cannot be created so easily from the surface of things. But listening to the whole message of the whole Bible and broadening his or her ministry with people will give the preacher the same refreshingly different approach to life Jesus had.

Distance. The greater the distance in communication, the less the impact. Caesar had an often-quoted motto for his legions: "Shorten your swords and lengthen your boundaries." The same is true for communication: "Shorten the distance and increase your impact."

Sometimes actual spatial distance is a factor in impact. For example, if an airplane crashes in Bolivia, we scarcely notice the headlines—we should, but we usually don't. If one crashes in our backyard, however, we are not likely to stop talking about it for the rest of our lives.

It is not accidental that such powerful communicators as Spurgeon and Whitefield preferred to be surrounded by audiences. The actual physical distance between speaker and audience significantly affects impact. As much as is possible, the preacher should seek to be among the people as he or she speaks. Nothing worse ever happened to Christian proclamation than locating the pulpit at one end of long, bowling-alley shaped churches where at least fifty percent of the audience need opera glasses to see the platform.

Many of these problems cannot be overcome immediately, however; and even if they were, another kind of distance is far more significant than physical distance—psychological distance.

Continuing our analogy, that same airliner that went down in Bolivia will attract higher interest if people from your hometown were on it. If you knew some of those people personally, the impact is greater still. And if your spouse or family were among the passengers, your involvement would be acute. (Naturally if you yourself were on board, the impact would be absolute.) In each case, the physical distance remains the same, but the psychological distance is being progressively shortened.

All of us have had such experiences. Our own involvement with the people or the problem caused the distance to drop dramatically and the impact of the event to jump. While in Europe I caught fragments of a report of a bus wreck in New Mexico in which a number of people were killed. Later I learned it was a church bus loaded with young people going to a religious retreat sponsored by my denomination. Then I learned that the group was from a church where I had preached several times. Finally I was told that some people I knew had been among those killed. With each added level of personal involvement with the incident, the impact of the event upon me was radically heightened.

Preaching will lack impact unless the psychological distance between the message and the hearers is short. This means that preachers must talk about things that matter to listeners. Unless preachers are involved with the issues at stake, the psychological distance between them and the audience will be too great and the impact of the message will be low.

That is why doctrinal preaching is generally regarded as the most difficult preaching—not just because the doctrines themselves are profound, but because they are usually presented as abstract theological concepts that could only matter to a professional theologian. Unless a doctrine matters to people—and when correctly understood, they all do—then what is the use of preaching about it?

As in the case of predictability, shortening psychological distance does not call for artificial method adjustment. The preacher does not need to sit around craftily figuring the most personal, emotionally loaded subjects to fire at the congregation. What he or she *does* need to do is to really understand that "the sabbath was made for humankind, and not humankind for the sabbath" (Mark 2:27)—or in other words, that the words and ways of God were designed for *people,* for living, breathing, very human people, and not for themselves.

When we recognize the genuine human involvement in every line of Scripture, and when we realize that what people care about and need, at the deepest level of reality, is what the Bible talks about, then our preaching will bridge the psychological distance between the historical word and the contemporary world.

But when the predictability of the church is absolute and the distance between itself and people is infinite, is it any wonder that its impact is *null?* The words and deeds of Christ struck the world with incredible impact because their genuineness was so unpredictable and their involvement with life was so intimate. Those preachers who have the faith to become involved with the incarnate life of Christ in their own ministries to whatever degree— even that of a grain of mustard seed—will see the impact of their proclamation increase.

SHOCK

To the right of impact stands communion; to its left stands shock. Too much predictability and too much distance cause a message to have zero impact; but too little predictability at point-blank range can lead to communicative shock. And when hearers go into communicative shock, the death of communication is not far away.

Shock in communication means that the level of impact has been raised to intolerable levels. Listeners drop a barrier between themselves and the speaker to prevent further communication. Hearing is no longer possible. The message itself is lost because its impact stunned rather than motivated. Impact is not an absolute good, of which there can never be too much. If impact becomes the goal of preaching, rather than the communication of the gospel, positive harm can be done.

To understand the effect of communicative shock, let us examine another example. Physical shock can be caused either by physical impact or by psychological impact: a teenage boy went into shock and died after being struck in the chest by a rock thrown by a lawnmower; when told at the hospital of his death, the boy's mother also collapsed in shock. In both cases, impact was the cause of shock.

When we are *shocked,* in the psychological meaning of the word, it is always because we are surprised, startled, impacted by the unexpected. A certain distance factor is at work, too, because we

must be close to an event, either spatially or psychologically, before we can care enough to be shocked.

If this factor is projected into communication, it is not difficult
to understand how communicative shock can ensue. Whenever a
sermon—or for that matter, a worship service—becomes so different and unpredictable in its content or style that it is almost
disorienting to the congregation, shock may result. Or, if what is
dealt with in the sermon is so threatening and personally unendur-
able to the hearers that escape is the only alternative, then distance
has been reduced to the point that communicative shock is inevitable.

Obviously a delicate balance must be maintained between saying things so predictably and remotely that utter boredom results,
and shocking people so severely with the unpredictable and the
threatening that hearing is blocked or even killed. If the expectations of an audience for a sermon or a service are too badly frustrated, they may be disoriented and the message itself lost; on the
other hand, if their expectations are too closely met, they may be
left satisfied but unchallenged.

Again, the key to maintaining this balance is the focus of the
message. What is its purpose? To startle, to shock, to innovate for
the sake of novelty? Or to awaken complacency to the challenge
of the gospel, to speak plainly what must be heard, and more than
heard—accepted and acted upon?

But "speaking plainly" is not as easy as it sounds. What we
mean by a word-symbol may not be what the listener hears.
Understanding the *principle of contiguity* can help us at this point.
That is, the nearest meaning for a word or symbol in the mind of
the listener is the one that will be heard rather than a more distant
one. As we will see, this has important implications for the question of shock.

For example, if a preacher uses the word "myth" in the usual
context, listeners are more likely to take the word in its Greek
setting than in a theological one. The preacher may not intend in
the slightest to convey the fanciful imagery of the Greek legends,

but since that is the nearest-lying meaning for "myth" in people's minds, they will decode the word in that sense. Even if redefined, the connotative and emotive influences of the previous meaning may hang on to make the word suspect in spite of all efforts to the contrary.

The same holds true for symbols. In some circles the wearing of a robe by the preacher conveys a negative impression, while in others the absence of one does the same thing. In both cases, the near-lying meaning for clerical garb in the minds of the congregation dominates whatever the minister wishes to convey.

Contiguity cannot be ignored in communication. When it is, shock usually follows. No one could be expected to know all of the near-lying meanings for words and symbols in the minds of the congregation—in fact, these meanings vary from person to person—but deliberately ignoring conventional meanings for more esoteric ones is a tricky business in communication. If some preachers want to try, they should at least know what they are doing. Then if they decide the meaning transfer is worth the risk, they can make the effort more intelligently.

But word redemption for word redemption's sake is of dubious value. It is questionable whether some terms are worth redeeming, or whether they carry such an emotive load that the effort is questionable anyhow.

Obviously someone will always be going into communicative shock over something unfamiliar or distressing—in fact, psuedo-shock is a favorite pharisaic hobby—and the preacher cannot become verbally paralyzed in a hopeless effort to avoid the complaints of hypocrites, radicals, and cranks. But neither are we entitled to deliberately shock sincerely honest Christians to appear more theologically literate than they. It is true that we have been called to a redemptive ministry—but for persons, not for favorite terms.

Sometimes radical innovation and shocking content in preaching and worship are nothing more than a desire on the part of preachers to punish, to strike back, sometimes at people long dead or times long gone. If so, they should not be surprised when people strike back or refuse to allow them to work out their problems on them, nor should they deceive themselves that they are martyrs for the truth.

The progress of the kingdom has likely been as often hindered by meaningless innovation as by meaningless tradition. "Giving people what they want" is cheap and base, and the preacher who is afraid to struggle against traditional culture that holds the Word captive is unworthy of his or her calling. But "giving people what they *don't* want" is equally mean and low when that means putting the desire to punish above the desire to proclaim.

When the gospel is lost in a senseless struggle over cultural tastes, then the true progress of the cause of Christ in the community is often set back a dozen years. Worse, the people may become permanently confused over what the real point of the gospel is—some deciding to defend tradition forever with others committing themselves to a lifelong crusade for constant change, whatever it is. Most people have past religious experiences that cause them to lean one way or the other. If encouraged by a misguided preacher—whether a dogged defender of tradition or a dedicated iconoclast—a church can be totally torn apart and almost permanently misled.

Impact, then, must result from the eternal Word encountering the contemporary person. If committed to hearing and declaring the still unheard and ever-radical word of God, we as preachers can never be so bound to tradition that noncommunication and boredom ensue; nor can we be so committed to overturning everything familiar that we drive people into communicative shock and actually prevent the progress we profess to love. When attached to the proper basis, communion is an essential feature of Christian communication. The deep trust it builds encourages people to open themselves to the true impact of the gospel. Understanding the functions of communion, impact, and shock can prevent needless tedium and bloodshed in the church and save the preacher from wasting his or her ministry in mindless wars on the cultural periphery.

Having briefly examined the interworkings of these three concepts, we must now see how the form of the sermon and the language of the sermon influence the communication of the gospel and produce either impact, boredom, or shock.

III. THE SHAPE OF THE SERMON

9. The Word Becomes Flesh

The ultimate test for incarnational preaching comes at that moment when proclamation ceases to be theoretical and takes on flesh and blood as the sermon. When preaching dwells among us, then we know whether it really is what it gives itself out to be. We only know preaching as the sermons we have heard, not as a pure, disembodied ideal. This means that preaching cannot avoid the crucial and difficult question of the form of the sermon.

If incarnational preaching is not to remain an abstract ideal, we are faced with the necessity of finding a form that allows it to become a living reality. Whatever the shape of this kind of preaching, it is evident that it must take seriously both the historic revelation and the contemporary situation. But these two poles are never more powerful in their attraction than in the influence each of them wields over the possible shape of the sermon. A cluster of methods has gathered about each pole, and each has attracted equally prominent and serious exponents.

For example, those preachers whose confessional tradition or theological positions have primarily attracted them to the *historic given* of proclamation favor forms that suit that emphasis. Since the text of the Scripture is greatly emphasized, they tend toward expository preaching and often toward deductive stances. The homily is frequently the form of choice. They believe that the Bible is the only proper starting place for the sermon. And since the proper order is always God to persons, a heavy downward movement is evident in the structure of these sermons. Frequently such "human devices" as illustrations, introductions, and topical themes are downgraded.

Karl Barth is the classic example of this emphasis. He insists that the preacher must be faithful both to the text and to life, but "it is always better to keep too close to the text" if a choice must be made.[1] Again, "the movement does not consist so much in going toward men as in coming from Christ to meet them. Preaching therefore proceeds downward."[2]

On the other hand, those preachers who are naturally attracted to the *contemporary given* of the preaching task favor person-centered, life-situation, inductive preaching forms. This emphasis frequently magnifies the use of literature, innovative forms, illustrations, contemporary applications, and involvement with current issues.

Historically, Harry Emerson Fosdick probably comes to mind first, but he has a crowd of others around him who believe that the contemporary post of the hermeneutical arch is the proper end of the bridge from which to begin. Fosdick definitely believed in the use of the Bible in his preaching (and he specifically repudiated topical preaching[3]), but he believed that the proper starting place for the sermon was the problems of people. In his famous article, "What's the Matter with Preaching?" in *Harper's Magazine,* July, 1928, he wrote: "Start with a life issue, a real problem, personal or social, perplexing the mind or disturbing the conscience; face that problem fairly, deal with it honestly, and throw such light on it from the spirit of Christ, that people will be able to think more clearly and live more nobly because of that sermon."

Both of these positions have enthusiastic, sometimes even fierce, defenders. I would not question for a moment the earnestness of these convictions (I haven't got the courage!), nor the validity of many of their insights. Nevertheless, I must insist that any attempt at resolving the tension in proclamation between the historic and the contemporary will prove unsatisfactory.

Both of these efforts are attempts to guarantee that Christian proclamation will occur because of an approach. But that is impossible. *No homiletical hedge about the gospel can ensure the contact between the human and the divine.* There is no form that can guarantee proclamational correctness. The homily cannot do it; expository preaching cannot do it. The devil had his mouth full of Scripture when he tempted Jesus in the wilderness, but he never spoke the truth. Nor can life-situation preaching, or dialogical preaching, or inductive preaching guarantee proclamation. These approaches may interest, intrigue, or involve the listener—but in what? Is interesting preaching, even shared preaching, always relevant preaching? Can relevance be guaranteed by form?

Any sermon form that ignores either the historic revelation or the contemporary situation violates the incarnational nature of proclamation.

Even when one of these approaches does not ignore the Bible or the people, but only places its dominant focus upon one or the other, it still cannot be regarded as *the* answer to sermon form. Since none of these approaches—inductive or deductive, life situation or expository—*defines* preaching, none of them can *equal* preaching. Depending on the preacher, the text, and the congregation, any number of approaches might be preferred. But since preaching cannot be equated with any one method, no one method can dictate the form of the sermon.

Preachers have been partly intimidated by terminology, most of which is utterly meaningless to them in the first place. They hears of "expository" preaching, "textual" preaching, "topical" preaching—but what does that mean? How much text does it take to turn a "textual" sermon into an "expository" sermon? How little text to turn a "textual" sermon into a "topical" sermon? Can "expository" sermons have topics? Can "topical" sermons have texts? What is an "expository" sermon? Is it how much attention the preacher gives the text? If so, then how much attention, and what kind, does it take to qualify a sermon as "expository"? Or how little, before it is merely (perish the thought!) "topical"? Or is it *what kind* of attention the preacher gives the text? If he or she parses all the words in fifty-four verses of Scripture, is it an "expository" sermon? Must the verses be presented in order? What if there is a unifying theme or, to use an ugly word, a subject? No wonder some preachers have become altogether cynical about sermon form!

Even more intimidating than "expository preaching" is the more recent term "biblical preaching" ("I am of Apollos; I am of Cephas; but I am of Christ!" [1 Cor. 1:12]). But what is *biblical* preaching?

Is that something different from expository preaching?

But isn't that exactly the problem? Isn't "biblical preaching" redundant? In fact, is it not true that there is no "biblical preaching," there is only *preaching?* Can there be any preaching that is not biblical? That is, preaching that is ultimately independent of the historic revelation? Or for that matter, can there be any preaching that is not life-centered? Obviously there can be addresses from the pulpit that are one or the other, or neither, but is this *preaching?*

Preaching is an applied word, a term that in the Christian setting sustains the closest possible relationship with the content of its message and is therefore one that cannot be separated from that message without losing its meaning altogether. Nor can Christian preaching be separated from life and made abstract, remote, impersonal. The nature of the Christian message itself demands that.

All of which simply means that limiting modifiers on the word *preaching,* such as "biblical" or "life-situation," may be necessary at times as correctives on the practice of Christian preaching, but *they do not really add to its meaning.* Nor should they be understood as *limiting* the sermon; as if "biblical" preaching should ignore the human setting or "life-situation" preaching should ignore the Bible.

When preaching seems to forget the Good News it has to tell, then perhaps it needs to hear of "biblical" preaching; and similarly, when preaching forgets that it must minister to the changing, complex problems of contemporary people, then perhaps it needs to hear of "life-situation" preaching. But neither alters the intrinsic nature of preaching. Likewise, "incarnational" preaching adds nothing to the nature of Christian proclamation; this expression is merely another attempt to call our attention to the true nature of preaching itself.

Each of the clusters of methods that have gathered about the historical pole and the contemporary pole have worthy insights. Those on the historical side recognize the importance of the Christian message and the necessity of working carefully with the biblical text; those on the contemporary side recognize the necessity for grappling with the flesh-and-blood problems of real people. As a result, the specific approaches to preaching suggested by each emphasis should be regarded as useful *methods* rather than exclusive, definitive statements on preaching. Any of these approaches to sermon development—inductive or deductive, life-situation preaching or expository preaching, the rhetorical sermon or the homily—can be useful forms for Christian preaching, so long as their emphases do not become so one-sided that they do violence to the nature of preaching itself.

What then, if anything, can the preacher do to ensure his or her preaching at this point? If no particular form of the sermon can guarantee Christian proclamation, is the preacher left without any guidelines at all? What principles can he or she follow in developing fresh forms for preaching?

Two elements affect the nature of the sermon: the substance of the message and the shape of the message. Let us examine some principles that are basic to each.

THE MESSAGE: SUBSTANCE

First, we may state two basic principles that regulate the content of the sermon: (1) the sermon must not be separated from the historic revelation; (2) the sermon must not be separated from the contemporary situation. In fact, since the historic revelation and the contemporary situation are inherent to preaching itself, we might go so far as to say that preaching *cannot* be separated from these things and still remain preaching. Let us see what implications these principles have for the nature of the sermon.

1. *Preaching must not be separated from the historic revelation.* If preaching becomes separated from the historic revelation of God, what is the norm for the Christian message? Are all utterances Christian? What is to determine a Christian message from a non-Christian message? Like it or not, the Christian preacher is inescapably bound to the Bible. If the spirit that speaks to us does not say what Jesus said, it is not his Spirit (John 14:26; 15:26). We preach not ourselves, but Christ. And the Christ we preach is defined by the historical Jesus of Nazareth.

With all of the difficulties and problems of hermeneutical effort, there is no escaping that struggle. It is just as wrong for preachers to absolutely abandon any attempt at interpreting the meaning of the historical Christ for us as it is for them to believe that a particular interpretative system can objectively capture his Spirit. Therefore Christian preaching has been, and ought to continue to be, connected with original language studies and exegesis. Bonhoeffer and Bultmann are as emphatic at that point as is Barth.

Again, this does not mean that taking a text ensures Christian proclamation. Many a sermon "takes a text, departs therefrom, and returns not thereunto." That is one reason so many people have only the vaguest notion what Christianity is all about, like the old woman who always cried whenever she heard the word "Mesopotamia." A sermon may be full of texts but empty of the gospel. Every cult and heresy from the first century on has been long on proof-texts and short on authentic interpretation. Meaningful preaching must speak the vital, lively message of the Bible rather than using its texts as a pack of spiritual tarot cards for Christian fortune-telling.

Spurgeon said it well: "I know a minister whose shoe latchet I am unworthy to unloose, whose preaching is often little better than sacred miniature painting—I might almost say holy trifling. He is great upon the ten toes of the beast, the four faces of the cherubim, the mystical meaning of badgers' skins, and the typical bearings of the staves of the ark, and the windows of Solomon's temple: but the sins of business men, the temptations of the times, and the needs of the age, he scarcely ever touches upon. Such preaching reminds me of a lion engaged in mouse-hunting."[4] "Holy trifling" does nothing to impress the importance of the Bible upon the congregation; in fact, this insignificant handling of the Scripture actually diminishes the significance of the word of God for the real problems of real people.

Conversely, it is possible for preaching to occur without the reading of a text. Bonhoeffer insisted that Luther often preached without a text, yet nevertheless biblically. If the message that is delivered is informed by the authentic message of the Bible or the true spirit of Christ himself—not any Christ, but *Jesus* Christ—then preaching has occurred. But even then, the revealed Word has resulted in the spoken word, if indirectly. We continue to affirm the actions of God.

For example, when Fosdick "took his text from Broadway," why did he choose to examine one particular line from a play over the others he had heard? It was because the note of reality it struck echoed the note of biblical revelation. But if brought into question, every message must be able to establish itself as gospel. And therefore, whether immediately or ultimately, preaching can never be separated from the historic revelation.

2. *Preaching must not be separated from the contemporary situation.* Because there is a human factor in the preaching equation, the sermon must confront the personal and corporate problems people face. The sermon must involve itself with analysis of the human situation, illustration of the principles of the gospel in terms of contemporary life, and application of the word of God to the specific situations. Therefore psychology and sociology can serve as useful tools in the exegesis of the human situation just as critical methodology serves as a useful tool in the exegesis of the text. Our understanding of the human condition facilitates analysis of the living situation and the application of the gospel to life.

We may agree with Ott when he says that this interpretation must be done without the sermon "deteriorating into a simple amplification of human self-judgments on the basis of moral, sociological, psycho-analytic criteria and such like"; yet these sciences may help us to do what Ott suggests: "The picture must be drawn concretely, with reference to the daily life of men just as it is. . . . It must be brought home to him in concrete illustration, that he may accept it."[5]

Our sermons cannot reflect profound knowledge of the first century and abysmal ignorance of the twentieth century. No one can be true to the biblical text and ignore the congregation. The biblical word is never a word in abstraction. It is always a specific word to a specific situation. Jesus used concrete language from his contemporary situation to incarnate his ultimate revelation. However it is done, "applying to life" is essential to proclamation.

This becomes increasingly difficult for the preacher as life becomes more complex and as provincialism becomes less acceptable. Fifty years ago H. V. Kaltenborn, managing editor of the Brooklyn *Eagle,* had a sign on his desk that said that a dogfight in Brooklyn was more important than a revolution in China. That was never true, but the ridiculousness of the statement becomes more evident every day.

But how can the pastor be specific in preaching? How can the church speak the commandments, as Bonhoeffer has urged? Can the preacher "know" about the school board, the UN, the police force, the local housing and zoning ordinances, the water and sewage system, the Congress and the Supreme Court? Maybe; a little; and no. Obviously he or she cannot be an authority on all subjects. What then?

The church must be specific, but what does that mean—doctrinaire pronouncements on everything, whether ignorant or not? Or should the sermon be forced into vagueness, withdrawal, and eventual silence?

If preaching is to be truly incarnational, then we who preach must be involved with human life; and to the degree that we are, our sermons will be also. Our preaching must be specific enough to incarnate the Word in the contemporary, but it must also understand that it cannot play guru to the world. The principles of the gospel must not be left in abstraction, but neither can the pastor apply texts like Band-Aids to every specific dilemma of every member of the congregation.

Concretely illustrating and specifically applying the gospel to life, however, translates the gospel from the idiom of the first century to the idiom of the twentieth century. By so doing, application assists in the interpretation of the Word. Faith is then made possible, since "faith cometh by hearing, and hearing by the word of God" (Rom. 10:17).

And through faith-action on the part of the church—the believing people of God—specific application of the gospel by the congregation can occur in countless situations the pastor could not even know about, much less comprehend. *This is the true concretion of the message.*

Must specific problems be discussed in detail in every sermon for preaching not to be separated from the contemporary situation? No, I think we must take some recognition of the emphatic insistence of both Barth and Bonhoeffer that the word of God provides a concrete application in itself. Just as a text must not always be quoted directly for a sermon to be Christian proclamation, so a sermon may be intimately connected with human life without analyzing particulars of the contemporary setting.

But I think we need to realize that both of these statements merely set the outer limits for Christian proclamation; they are not normative for it. There is no need for seeing how near the edge we can drive the sermon without falling off. Preaching without reference to Scripture is a dubious practice, and so is preaching without reference to the human situation. The most enthusiastic advocates of either textual explanation or analysis of the human situation rarely resorted to these extremes. For example, Barth's sermons consistently included references to the contemporary situation and illustrations as well, and Fosdick's sermons averaged about a dozen references to the Bible.[6]

The determinative question for Christian preaching is not *how much* biblical reference is made, nor *how much* contemporary reference, but whether the circuit is closed between the Word of God and the human situation. Preaching must commit itself to both, realizing that *when the living Word touches the living situation, the preaching event occurs.* Any approach to the sermon that does not separate itself from one or the other permits the possibility of preaching.

THE MESSAGE: SHAPE

These two principles speak to the content of the sermon. But content is not the only influence on the nature of the sermon. The arrangement of these materials, the order—or lack of it—in which the presentation is made, determines the shape of the sermon. Four basic principles may help the preacher to arrive at a form that facilitates preaching: communication requires form; the form employed must be capable of conveying a message; the message demands a dynamic rather than a static form; and the dynamic form of the sermon requires the oral medium.

1. *Communication requires form.* Without organization, communication is impossible. This is true of the message as a whole, or of a sentence, or even a single word. For example, the letters T-R-E-E, in that order, communicate an image, but E-E-T-R communicates nothing. And what is true of a single word is also true of the arrangement of words within a sentence, or of thoughts within a sermon.

Because of the difficulty of arriving at satisfactory organization, the preacher is tempted toward formlessness. The freedom that is within the gospel and within the person struggles against form. But whether the form chosen is innovative or traditional, the message that is within the preacher must assume some form of expression or it cannot be communicated at all.

Form is essential to freedom. A certain humility is required of the artist who must limit herself or himself to a particular medium, to the particularization of a vision in a given form on canvas or in clay or stone. But as limited as that expression may be, without it the artist cannot communicate at all. There is no music without sound, no poetry without words, no art without shape. These forms set the vision free by giving expression to it. Without the sculpture, Michelangelo's *David* would be more trapped in the artist's mind than it was in the stone.

2. *The form employed must be capable of conveying a message.* Preaching is declaring the Good News. Not all forms of communication are equally adapted to this end. In his examination of those forms best suited to the expression of the Christian message, Paul Tillich prefers Expressionism, rather than Impressionism or Romanticism, since "that which is expressed is not the subjectivity of the artist in the sense of the subjective element which is predominant in Impressionism and Romanticism."[7] The gospel confronts us with reality, and the form of the sermon must be suited to the communication of that reality; Romanticism idealizes it too much, and

Impressionism makes it too arbitrarily subjective.

On the other hand, Realism also fails as a form because it merely repeats without interpreting. Expressing the reality of the gospel does not imply a mere parroting of words—which may explain why *keryx,* or "herald," is almost never used as the word for "preacher" in the New Testament; the ancient herald was widely regarded as nothing more than a paid parrot. Preachers, however, must be involved with the message they bear and the people to whom they bear it. Not merely repetition, but interpretation is required to communicate the reality of the Christian message.

Nonetheless, it is not *any* message, but a certain message which we have to communicate. In defending certain experimental sermons against the charge that "they go too far and in some instances actually alter the original message of Christianity," John Killinger correctly reminds us that we must not commit the fallacy of focusing too closely on the dogmatic formulations of the Christian gospel and miss the total meaning and spirit of that message. But if it is true that the human being is "a free spirit and must not be indentured to any system," it is only the message of the gospel that liberates us. "If you continue in my word, then are you my disciples indeed; and you shall know the truth, and the truth shall make you free" (John 8:31–32). Indeed, it is "God, in Christ," and God alone, who has "called us out from all totalitarian superstructures"; therefore we must question whether "our first obligation now is to our own centers of freedom."[8]

What is freedom? Rudolf Bultmann insists that "genuine freedom is not subjective arbitrariness. It is freedom in obedience. . . . Genuine freedom is freedom from the motivation of the moment; it is freedom which withstands the clamor and pressure of momentary motivations." Likewise, he reminds us that this idea of freedom, constituted by law, was well known to both ancient Greek philosophy and Christianity, but that "in modern times, however, this conception vanished and was replaced by the illusory idea of freedom as subjective arbitrariness which does not acknowledge a norm, a law from beyond. There ensues a relativism which does not acknowledge absolute ethical demands and absolute truth. The end of this development is nihilism."[9]

This leads us to question also whether language in preaching can become so open-ended and playful that it is "committed to the game, not to the end in view. . . . It does not manifest high control needs, but abandons itself to the activity and to whatever outcome eventuates."[10] But is "whatever outcome eventuates" invariably the gospel? And are we in fact manifesting "high control needs" if we use language "to reach certain goals which we already had in mind when we began"?[11] If so, are there *any* sermon forms that communicate but have no end in view and therefore are nonpurposive, *especially* experimental sermon forms, which usually demand the mastery of art forms such as poetry or drama and in fact require more careful planning and structured use of language than the traditional forms?

I think it is true that we must allow language "to lead us along paths where knowledge is uncertain, revealing new worlds to us in the process."[12] This is indeed highly important. I will attempt to suggest an approach to preparation that facilitates this process. But creativity and absolute spontaneity are evidently not synonymous.

In any event, the form chosen for the sermon—whether experimental or traditional—should not become identified with purposeless speech or subjective arbitrariness, but it must be capable of conveying the Christian message.

3. *The message demands a dynamic rather than a static form.* To insist upon meaningful form for the sermon is not to insist upon a rigid shape for the message. Some forms are dynamic and fluid; others are static and lifeless.

A brick and a flame both have form, but there is reason why a brick is not as interesting to watch as a flame. The brick is static, it has no movement, but the flame is lively, changing, intriguing. That is the reason we watch the flames in the fireplace on long winter evenings rather than the bricks around it. Nevertheless, fire has form; combustion is as specific a reality as stone.

Preaching must be constantly in search of dynamic forms to express the dynamic reality of the gospel. All traditional methods of preaching were once new and innovative, and communication demands a spirit of inventiveness: "Real communication is not static; it can seldom be accomplished for very long without experimentation and innovation."[13]

Unfortunately, seminary training in preaching merely furnished many preachers with a set of homiletical cookie cutters which they routinely mash down upon the dough of the text, and presto! out pops a little star, or a tree, or a gingerbread man (a five-pointed sermon? an organic sermon? a life-situation sermon?). No matter that the text doesn't want to go into these forms; the poor thing is mashed and tortured until it is made to say things it never intended to say.

There is nothing wrong with any of these forms in themselves; the crime is the dully mechanical and arbitrary way in which they are imposed upon the text. As much as possible, the shape of the reality encountered in the gospel should determine the shape of the sermon. At times traditional forms may best express that reality, but, depending upon the preacher, the text, and the congregation, innovative approaches might well be demanded.

The redeeming principle, however, is neither innovation nor traditionalism, but *that we shape the sermon in a living form that brings to expression the living reality of the gospel.*

4. *The dynamic form of the sermon requires the oral medium.* Nothing so facilitates the dynamic nature of preaching as the oral medium. Even experimental forms, if written into fixed sentence formulation, can become static. And nothing so lulls a congregation into passivity as the "whoosh" of the opening of a canned, hermetically sealed sermon—whether traditional or not. Unless the oral medium is taken seriously, the most innovative sermon forms with the most profound sermon content will be static. And as such, they violate the essential nature of preaching itself as personal encounter.

To a greater or lesser degree, preaching theories have generally recognized the historic revelation and the contemporary situation as essential to the sermon. But the recognition of preaching as word-event, and particularly as an *acoustic* event, has been much slower in coming. Preaching is not merely a *verbal* event, it is an *oral* event. Verbal communication may be either written or oral; but as we have seen, in the history of Israel and in the preaching of the early church there is no mistaking the preferred method of communication.

Nor was that incidental. Oral communication permits dynamic personal encounter, and that is not at all incidental to preaching. And it does so to a degree far above written communication because of its immediacy. Of course all sermons are spoken, but as we shall see, not all sermons are really constructed to fit the oral medium.

Since the sermon is spoken, it must be shaped to suit the oral medium. That is as essential to the communication of the gospel as the correct interpretation of the biblical text or the contemporary situation. First preaching learned that it must take the text seriously; then it learned that it must take the people seriously; now it must learn that it must take the medium seriously.

10. Out of the Gutenberg Galaxy

Following the nineteenth century and the advent of popular literacy, the sermon was steadily transformed from its original oral medium into a literary, written medium. This change was partly due to the impact of printing as a medium for communication and partly due to the sensational success of the "comets in the Gutenberg galaxy"—to play with McLuhan's term—the literary preachers to that literary age.

The influence of these preachers upon the form of the modern sermon is incalculable. The sermons of Robertson, Spurgeon, and others were printed and distributed to millions. Homileticians subsequently used those written sermons as models of excellence for their preaching classes. And although this approach unquestionably produced many good results, it also had one unfortunate effect upon the sermon. Students were encouraged, directly or indirectly, to *write* sermons like the ones they were reading.

As a result, the sermon was increasingly prepared for the eye rather than the ear. Devices suited for reading—paragraphing, formal syntax, tightly fitted logical arguments, complex outlines, literary language—were superimposed upon the sermon. Of course the sermon continued to be delivered orally, but increasingly from a manuscript really prepared for reading.

Like a satellite trapped within the gravitational pull of a planet, preaching has been locked into the Gutenberg galaxy. The sermon must break out of this orbit if it is to be able to communicate within its own medium.

The methods of the nineteenth-century preachers were largely effective for their age, but they have become increasingly less so as culture has shifted its interest. This is the reason many preachers sound sadly Victorian, or like chaplains to a literary society. What has happened to the sermon is what McLuhan also describes —*the lively communication medium for one generation has become the art form for the next generation.*

McLuhan's theories, like his writings, are often more suggestive than logical, but they may help us to explain the situation in which preaching finds itself. For example, McLuhan says that as we develop new media for communication our relationship to the old media changes. The new environment created by the new media causes the old media to become art forms.

Many questions could be raised about McLuhan's division of civilization into three ages, the Preliterate or Tribal, the Gutenberg or Individual, and the Electric or Retribalized, and the order in which each of the senses became dominant—first the ear, hearing; then the eye, seeing; now the central nervous system, total sensory experience. Nevertheless, according to this system, speaking was the dominant medium of communication in the aural, or Preliterate, age; printing was the dominant medium during the visual, or the Gutenberg, age; and telegraph, telephone, and television have become the dominant media during the Electronic age.

Obviously this explanation tends to be simplistic; the use of our senses is not so neatly layered, nor is the function of the media. But like most of McLuhan's themes these suggestions are stimulating and provocative, and it is interesting to pursue their implications for the development of communication in the church.

Let us accept for a moment these two suppositions—that various senses become dominant in various ages and produce a dominant medium of communication and that the dominant communication medium of one age becomes the art form of the next age. What does this theory suggest for preaching?

Speaking was the dominant communication medium in the Hebrew-Christian tradition in the biblical centuries. The art form for that age was the Temple ritual, the Passover celebration, and other liturgical acts that celebrated the past events of that tradition. As printing became the new dominant medium for communication in succeeding ages, speaking was changed from a medium of communication to an art form—oratory. At first the church was intimidated by printing. But soon that changed, and preachers began to capitalize upon it with the result that the sermon was increasingly prepared with the eye in mind rather than the ear, that is, with the thought of possible publication.

At first that was a realistic option, both in England and in the early American colonies. A staple diet of the colonial press was pamphlet sermons, and more than 40 percent of the entries in Evan's *American Bibliography* were sermons.[1] But as the electronic media came into being, consumption of printed sermons dropped radically. Soon the only consumers of sermons were those who sat and listened to the spoken sermon. *Then the manuscripted sermon, prepared according to the rules of writing to suit the printing medium, became the art form of preaching.*

Even today, when the possibilities for publication of any one Sunday's sermon are infinitely small, preachers continue to prepare their messages for one medium and deliver them in another. It is not incidental that the manuscript is widely regarded as the final product of the preacher's *art.* If today's preaching is not regarded as a lively form of communication, part of the blame at least must be attached to the manuscripted sermon—the art form of homiletics.

This would not be true if the principles for written and oral communication were alike. But they are not. For example, everyone has noticed that even the finest oral communications generally look horrible when transcribed. John Broadus preached an excellent series of sermons at Calvary Church in New York; he was urged to publish them, but when he saw the stenographer's transcription of them he was so horrified that he called off the project. Many of us have had similar experiences, but does this mean that the sermon was done poorly in the first place? Not at all. It simply means that what suits the ear does not suit the eye.

What about the corollary of that law? Has it ever occurred to us that if spoken speeches look bad when transcribed, the opposite might also be true—*that written speeches sound bad when heard?* There are really no exceptions to this law although we've all heard sermons from manuscripts that seem to be. But in those cases, the manuscript has been forced to make radical concessions to the spoken medium.

What are the major differences between oral and written style? Even a partial listing should help us to understand the problem.[2]

In the first place, the primary difference is that one style is intended for the eye and the other for the ear. Readers have time to ponder, reread, and even look up words if necessary; hearers must understand the message as it comes or not at all. Readers may proceed at their own pace; listeners go at the pace of the speaker. If writing does not proceed in linear style, readers get bored; but if a speaker avoids repetition, listeners get lost if concentration is broken even for a moment.

Furthermore, written style is arranged according to the needs of the eye. It uses paragraphing and formal syntax. Paragraphs are useful to the eye, but they have no meaning to the ear. Written style needs formal syntax to avoid confusion. Until the age of printing, punctuation was used for nothing more than an opportunity for a speaker to take a breath. But printing necessitated the use of commas and periods to set off clauses for the eye, and McLuhan says that the curse of English grammar is a direct consequence of the printing press.[3]

Even more decisive for preaching, McLuhan points out that when words are printed they become visual, static elements and lose much of the dynamism that characterizes the auditory world. They lose much of the personal element in the emotional overtones and emphases of the spoken word.[4] In oral communication the speaker and the listener are in interreaction within the situation, but writing prevents such a response.[5]

It is also interesting to note that McLuhan suggests that Jesus did not commit his teachings to writing because "the kind of interplay of life that is in teaching is not possible by means of writing."[6] And he quotes Thomas Aquinas as saying, "Therefore it is fitting that Christ, as the most excellent teacher, should adapt that manner of teaching whereby his doctrine would be imprinted on the hearts of his hearers."[7]

But do listeners know the difference between "oral" and "normal" sermons? They do. An audience can successfully label a speech as being "oral" or "nonoral" in style even though they only hear the nonoral version of the speech, or the oral, and when they are not given a definition of what constitutes an oral style.[8] Furthermore, listeners find oral speeches to be more understandable, more interesting, more informative, and superior in style.

To overcome these difficulties, teachers of preaching have long advocated "writing like you speak." But that is a hybrid art that nobody teaches. Learning to speak and learning to write are difficult enough in themselves without learning to hybridize the two. And why do it anyway? Why not prepare for the oral medium in the first place?

Preachers should realize that their problems don't stop once they have written a manuscript; in fact, they have just begun— now they *really* have a problem. What do they *do* with the manuscript? They have three alternatives—all bad. First, they can read the manuscript; nobody recommends that, for obvious reasons. Second, they can memorize it; nobody recommends that either. And third, they can get as familiar as possible with it in the study and then try to do without it as much as possible in the pulpit. This third alternative is the method generally recommended, but it still leaves preachers with plenty of problems.

When preachers try to follow a manuscript mentally in the pulpit without having it with them, they present a curious sight. When they are successful in recalling the sermon, they sound polished and look poised—sometimes too polished and too poised, like a child delivering a piece learned for school. On the other hand, when they are unsuccessful, their word choice and syntax are radically different. They may also get a vacant look on their faces as they rummage around in their mental attics trying to remember all those beautiful phrases they wrote and rewrote in the study.

Meanwhile, of course, their mouths have to go on working. But since they aren't too happy about it, they may look slightly irritated, which in turn may cause the audience to wonder what they have done to offend their pastor. Nevertheless, there is nothing to do but plunge on, and so they proceed on to the next section of material. But then they may remember those well-written phrases they needed five minutes earlier. Unless the manuscript preacher is an unusual person, he or she will give in to the temptation to go ahead and say them anyway, in place or not, causing the audience to wonder how in the world the pastor got back on *that* subject. The whole procedure gives the preaching a curious, disjointed effect.

As for those preachers who take their manuscript into the pulpit and try not to look at it, they usually look like preachers trying not to look at a manuscript. They may struggle valiantly to look the audience in the eye, but it is apparent that their hearts are not in it, and they keep sneaking furtive glances at the pages beneath their fingers. If they are bold enough to go ahead and look anyway, they often give the impression of a kiwi bird going to water: now the head is up, now the head is down. Meanwhile the audience sits respectfully listening, as though hearing a sermon required great politeness—which in this case, it does. Active mental dialogue and personal encounter give way to polite listening.

I know that some preachers can master the use of a manuscript so that their delivery is smooth and natural. Many of the finest preachers in Christian history preached exclusively from manuscripts. I know that. But that doesn't eliminate the problems I have described. They are still there, and the manuscript preachers who excel do so in spite of their manuscripts, not because of them.

For years preachers have been intimidated by the "ideal" of these great preachers and their polished manuscripts. They have been asked, "Isn't preaching worth the effort? Can we afford to go into the pulpit half-prepared?" Karl Barth has even warned darkly that we will be held accountable for every idle word in the day of judgment and used this scripture (Matt. 12:36) as a proof-text for the absolute necessity of a manuscript.[9] (We will not take this as a typical example of the great exegete.) Naturally he equates anything else with a lack of preparation.

But are these really the alternatives? Is it preparation versus unpreparation, the careful manuscript versus the offhanded talk? Is there no other approach that can prepare us as carefully and as thoroughly as the manuscript, or more so, and that connects us more directly with the true oral medium for the sermon?

THE ORAL MANUSCRIPT

Let me suggest a method that I believe to be superior to the writing of a manuscript. I know that all preachers are not alike, and there is no method that is best for everyone. In spite of what ought to be true, some people might be helpless without a manuscript. But I don't believe that it is the best method for most preachers. Those who use a manuscript should realize that they are not merely using a crutch, they are putting a brace on a healthy leg.

I am convinced that much of the stiffness and impersonality of our preaching, the boredom and lack of interest of our hearers, and the feeling of nonparticipation and disinvolvement of our congregations are due to the manuscript method of preaching. (It would be ridiculous to attribute these problems to manuscript preparation alone; but to my knowledge, it has scarcely been pointed out as any part of the problem at all, and I believe it is much more to blame methodologically for our troubles than the often ridiculed, "three-point," traditional organization.) Recent works on homiletics have increasingly underscored the importance of the sermon as an oral product that needs to be produced orally. Fred Craddock says, "Much of the awkwardness and discontinuity created by writing and then oralizing a text can be relieved by preparing orally from the outset," and he recommends that the preacher "mentally talk through a message." [10] Eugene Lowry says, "Prepare sermons out loud."[11]

I repeat: in those cases where the method has been mastered and preachers have been able to communicate intimately and directly with their congregation, they have done so in spite of their manuscripts and in the face of overwhelming odds against them. On the other hand, I am equally well aware of the disastrous effects of nonpreparation. There is nothing more deadly to preaching than the person who can say nothing for thirty minutes, and knows it. If forced to choose between listening to this preacher with the rotary jaw, to use Spurgeon's term, or to the poor reading of a well-prepared manuscript, I'd choose the manuscript every time. If the preacher had to choose between doing without careful sermon preparation and doing without direct contact with the audience, I suppose he or she should do without direct contact with the audience. But that's like deciding which eye to see with. You don't have to make that choice.

In looking for a better procedure, where do we begin? (At this point, perhaps I had better warn you that we are only going to look at the overall process for the sake of clarity; the details of mechanics will come later.)

Initial Study. The oral preparation method begins exactly like the manuscript method. First, the preacher should make a careful study of the text—which involves both exegetical and meditative study—and establish a tentative plan for the sermon in rough notes. This plan includes no more at this time than the unifying concern, or direction, or theme of the sermon, and a tentative arrangement of the basic directional sentences or steps in the development of this theme.

To this point, the preparation of the sermon is a matter of thought, but beyond this early stage it should be a matter of speech. The tentative direction of the sermon that thought has suggested should be made definite through speaking. We begin with the rough oral draft.

The Rough Oral Draft. Put each of the tentative directional sentences, or major movements, in the theme on a separate sheet of paper. Then preach aloud on each of them as long as ideas suggest themselves, using free association. Make no effort to hinder the free flow of ideas or to arrange them in order at this time. But keep a pen in hand and pause in speaking only long enough to note briefly the key directional phrases or sentences that emerge.

Each of these sentences should introduce a *thought block* that has really struck the heart of the concern of the text or of the people. These phrases correspond with the topic sentence of the paragraphs in a manuscript. But in this case they do not introduce a paragraph—no one speaks in paragraphs—but a thought block, "something I want to talk about," which may represent one or more minutes of oral development.

This stage corresponds exactly with the writing of the rough draft of the manuscript—*except that it is being done in the medium that will eventually be used.* The composition is oral, not written, and the difference can be plainly heard in the final product. Verbal fluency will jump dramatically using this method. And rather than practicing on your audience, you are practicing on yourself.

Furthermore, we can speak at least five to ten times faster than we can write. A written rough draft of the number of words used in the oral process would take just that much longer; a two-hour oral session would require at least a ten-hour written session. This means valuable time saved, and a more efficient use of sermon preparation time with this approach.

It is important to remember that the initial arrangement of the basic directional sentences, or even your understanding of the sermon theme itself, will very likely be altered as the speaking process unfolds. These ideas are highly tentative; they serve only as a starting point for the sermon. You will often discover that your initial impression has been clarified and refined in the speaking process. Don't hesitate to alter the pieces to say what you want to say. Many of us have been trapped by "logical" outlines that would not let us speak the gospel as we understand it.

In this rough draft stage, you will not know what to say first— should I start with the biblical situation or with the contemporary situation?—or whether some pictorial, illustrative material should be used before either is introduced. But talking it out allows you to *hear it, try it,* and then decide.

Sometimes you may preach aloud for fifteen minutes or more on each of the major movements in the theme before you say anything worth saying. (At least you will find that out in the study rather than in the pulpit! How often preachers practice on their congregations—and learn five minutes before the end of the sermon what they should have said in the first place!) It will be a common experience to realize suddenly, *"That's* what I've been trying to say!" Not only the organization, but the very meaning of the message is being discovered in the speaking process.

Once the basic content of the sermon is set, decide how to begin —the introduction—and how to stop—the conclusion. Then when you have finished this process of preparation, the rough draft of the oral manuscript is completed.

The Final Oral Manuscript. At this point, what do you have? A few lines to begin; perhaps a few to conclude. A few basic directional sentences, if these are necessary to move the sermon through the meaning of the message. Under these principal movements several key sentences that introduce thought blocks, some which deal with the biblical situation, some which deal with the contemporary situation, and some which may also indicate the use of pictorial, illustrative material, or the need for it.

Then what? Examine your notes. Rearrange the key sentences, and perhaps even the main movements themselves, into the order that seemed called for by the speaking process. For example, on the first run you may discover that the second directional sentence should have been first; or that it really said the same thing as the first and therefore is not needed at all. Or within the first movement, you began with a narrative based on the text and led into a contemporary narrative; but it quickly becomes apparent that this order is awkward and should be reversed. Or, as the rough oral draft unfolds, you may jot down a dozen sentences under the first movement that seemed to introduce promising areas of thought, only three or four of which actually prove to be worth keeping. In other words, having heard your sermon, you are now able to revise it.

If you are reasonably satisfied that this revised arrangement permits the gospel to be heard, then preach aloud once more. *This is the final draft of the oral manuscript.* Obviously you will continue to revise if necessary, but this time you are attempting to preach in as near final form as possible. Sharpen the focus and the language of the message. Try to preach without reference to the material before you, but if necessary, refer to it. If your development is simple and accurate, it will not be hard to recall; if you cannot work through it easily, quite likely there is some problem with the movement of the sermon.

THE SERMON BRIEF

You will discover that this oral process has produced an instrument for you to retain and refer to—not a sermon outline, not a sermon manuscript, but a *sermon brief*. What does the final product look like?

If there are no divisions in the sermon as in more contemporary sermon forms, the brief will simply be a page or a page and a half, likely not more, of basic directional sentences, each of which introduces a thought block of oral discussion. But if the sermon has divisions ("points"), as in traditional sermon forms, the form of the sermon brief will be slightly different.

First, there will be a *grouping* of three to five sentences that indicate the beginning of the sermon. Then the basic "divisions" follow, each stated as a directional sentence—something that can be *said*, rather than a "point," which generally cannot be spoken as written. Underline these sentences for clarity.

Under each of these statements, indented somewhat, follow the other key sentences that discuss the biblical situation and the contemporary situation. (Not more than six to ten sentences at most. Remember that each of these sentences is merely a springboard to launch you into a body of thought you want to discuss.) Finally, if a conclusion is called for, it will consist of a few sentences in a block grouping, just like the introduction. A diagram may help to illustrate this form.

Use spacing, underlining, and indenting to make the sermon brief as simple and uncluttered as possible. A good sermon brief should be easy to visualize during preaching. The exact form of this instrument is not as critical as the form of a manuscript because it serves simply as a reminder of the oral preparation, which is really the form of the sermon. But a clean, simply arranged,

SERMON BRIEF

_____
_____ .

3–5
sentences

Introduction: _____ .

_____
_____ .

Basic Directional Sentence (Division)

_____
_____ .

_____
_____
_____ .

_____ .

6–10
sentences

_____ .

_____
_____ .

_____
_____ .

Key sentences, each
introducing its own
thought block of
discussion. (Exploring
the biblical material
and the contemporary
situation; presenting
pictorial, illustrative
material, etc.)

Basic Directional Sentence (Division)
(etc.)

_____.

_____
_____ .

3–5
sentences

Conclusion: _____
_____.

easily visualized brief will help the unity and movement of the message.

The sermon brief, then, is more than an outline and less than a manuscript, but in my opinion, it is superior to either. It has many *advantages.*

1. For one thing, the sermon has produced the instrument rather than the instrument producing the sermon, as in the case with the manuscript.

2. Furthermore, it is truer to the nature of conversation because it is less rigid, less fixed, more fluid, and therefore more adaptable to the living encounter of the sermon event.

3. The sermon brief does not tie the preacher to the wording of a manuscript. It allows that freedom of creation and spontaneity of response that are essential if preaching is to be an event in the worship service. Something *happens* between preacher and congregation; everything has not already happened in the study. The manuscript gives the impression of a report on an event rather than being an event itself.

4. On the other hand, because it provides more specific direction for the sermon than a bare outline, the sermon brief does not give the impression of unpreparedness, vagueness, or aimless wandering. The preacher is not as surprised as the audience to hear what pops out of his or her mouth, as is often the case with the purely extemporaneous method, nor does he or she chase rabbits through brambles for thirty minutes.

5. Finally, and most decisive, the oral process of preparation results in an oral product for the oral medium of preaching. Neither of the other methods does.

The naturalness, directness, and freedom that preachers will enjoy in the pulpit as a result of this method will delight both themselves and their congregations. I am convinced that this is more important to allow preaching to be itself—a living encounter of the living Word with the living situation—than either polished phrases or innovative forms.

At least two *objections* are often raised against this approach. Some preachers are convinced that they will lose all freshness and enthusiasm if they speak their sermons beforehand. I have never forgotten that comment from a student who had struggled painfully to say something, *anything,* in his first sermon to his small congregation. After seven agonizing minutes, he sat down. (But no one objected—it *seemed* like an hour!) When he asked how anyone learned to talk conversationally with an audience, I suggested oral preparation. "What!" he said. "You actually say your sermon before you preach?" I assured him I did. "Why! If I did that, I'd lose all my fire!"

On the contrary, the assurance that oral preparation gives allows us to enter deeply into meaningful, exciting dialogue with our hearers. It sets us free to concentrate on the real meaning of the Word for the real people who sit before us. For the first time, perhaps, we will actually *see* people and talk *with* people, rather than looking *at* our ideas and talking *about* a subject.

Another objection might be raised. Some preachers may feel that they cannot "remember what to say" with no more than a handful of directional sentences produced by speaking. Wouldn't it help at least to tape the oral draft and play it back to remember it?

Surprisingly, perhaps, the preacher will soon discover that just the opposite is true. The problem is forgetting what you said initially in the rough oral draft and decided to eliminate in the final oral draft. Speaking makes an amazing impression on the memory. If you recorded the first oral draft, you would lock yourself into that pattern and revision would be extremely difficult.

But if you will simply note the key sentences that emerge in speaking, rearrange these into the order that seems most natural and repreach the sermon in that form, you will know what you wants to say and how to say it. Only the basic pattern for the development of the sermon is to be set; during delivery variations will occur naturally in the exact wording within the thought blocks. *But these variations are essential for naturalness and freshness of expression.*

I would suggest allowing a day or so between the rough oral draft and the final oral manuscript. Give the sermon time to grow a bit in your experience. Usually if the first draft is finished early in the week, by Wednesday at least, then Friday is a good time to talk through the material again. And even on Sunday morning before the service, you would do well to mentally "preach aloud" your sermon. Creation, revision, and rearrangement really never stop—not even in the pulpit.

After this kind of oral preparation, many preachers do not need to take the sermon brief into the pulpit with them. But if you feel ill at ease without it, particularly in your first few experiences with this approach, the brief will not interfere badly with your presentation. Naturally you will be freer without it, and in time you can easily learn to do without it. To prepare yourself to do so, you should ask yourself the following questions prior to your final oral preparation: (1) What is the main concern of this sermon (its purpose; theme; subject)? (2) What do I want to say about that (order; movement; main divisions; "points")? (3) How do I begin (opening movement)? (4) How do I proceed within the first movement, the second, etc. (mental review of the order of basic directional sentences)? (5) How do I conclude (final thought block)?

When you can move through each of these in your mind, you are ready to speak your sermon without notes. You will never recall every sentence, but that doesn't matter. What little you lose in polished phrases or content—and it will be very little, if you have prepared orally—you will gain in intimate, direct communication with your congregation.

I am aware that a great many traditional homiletical questions so far remain unanswered, and it is now time to hear what they are asking.

11. From the Study to the Pulpit

At this point a number of practical questions clamor for attention. What about the traditional parts of the sermon—introduction, conclusion, titles, outlines, points, and subpoints? How do I do these things—or should I? (The following two chapters will look at narrative/story sermon issues.)

Even more basic, how do I find something to preach on? Where can I get ideas and material for the sermon? How do I get from a text to a sermon? And how can I deal with contemporary issues that have no direct biblical precedent? Finally, and perhaps most critically, how do I *do* it? How can I find time in the week to prepare? And how do I plan ahead for a preaching program?

No one could feel homiletically messianic enough to answer all these questions. But in many pastor's conferences on preaching, these are the issues that always come up. Frankly, I don't believe them to be as desperately critical as we make them out to be. A solid approach to the Bible and to life, careful work habits, and a willingness to grow and learn will take care of most of them. In fact, no one can really answer any of these specifics for anyone else. But I am glad to express my own approach to them for whatever it is worth. It may be of some help in some areas to someone. It also may not be.

Books have been written on each of these questions. I will only touch briefly on a few of these issues to put them in perspective within this approach, and to illustrate the possibility of cohesion between a theory of proclamation and the most practical matters of sermon preparation.

I am aware that I will leave open far more packages than I will tie up with neat bows. Good. Use these methods if you can; step on them going on somewhere better if you can't.

IT'S MONDAY: OR, NOT AGAIN!

Getting started has to be one of the preacher's biggest headaches. Sunday has just ended—for better or worse—and the pastor feels he or she deserves a vacation. But whether he or she takes a day off or not, Monday will still be Monday, and only preachers know what "a month of Sundays" means: everytime they look around, here comes Sunday—and another sermon (if not two!). Then what?

Here are some rapid responses to typical questions.

How Do I Find Something to Preach About?

Year in and year out, this has got to be the question that plagues the preacher the most. What do I do when the barrel is empty?

As always, prevention is better than cure. Regular, careful listening to the Word and the people—to the historic revelation and the contemporary situation—will provide more than adequate sermon ideas and content. Learn to exegete both the Bible and the congregation. Inspiration for sermon ideas may come from either direction. This is the fundamental, long-term answer to this perennial question.

But what if you feel you have *already* been aware of both of these resources and yet you still feel "dry" of sermonic inspiration? A few practical suggestions may help you to diagnose your own methodological needs in each area.

Biblical Sources

Actually, the Bible is not a bad place to look for sermons. (But don't let that out, or everybody will get in on it.)

Study the Bible in many translations. Most of us have heard the King James so long that we don't see a third of the freshness of the biblical text. New translations show us things we've overlooked before. And read widely in the Bible. Most of us never preach from vast areas of biblical literature.

Underline the provocative expressions that stop your eye. These arresting phrases unlock doors of sermonic thought. Be sure to preach the *meaning* of those phrases in context, however, not clever essays on catchy phrases. Move from meaning to meaning, not from phrase to phrase.

Do the same with the text in original languages. Cutting corners here wastes time later. Barth said he could always tell if a preacher had studied the original texts. But be sure to truly *translate,* not transliterate, the biblical message—the *piel* and the *aorist* yield precious little preaching by themselves.

Listen long enough until you hear. Most sermons are empty because the preacher has not listened long enough before he or she started talking. There is nothing harder than coining proverbs every Sunday or in playing revelational guru week by week from your own philosophy or experience. It's tough enough letting God be God and trying to interpret what that means in a contemporary setting, without trying to be Abraham, Moses, Paul, and the Oracle of Delphi for your church.

Nobody invents the telephone all over again before making a call, but some preachers feel obligated to invent the whole religious world before breakfast every morning. Don't be ashamed to listen to the testimony of the Christian community of the past, both biblical and postbiblical witness. Others have already sought to interpret the biblical revelation. They can help. Hear them too.

Hold these textual ideas until maturity. Some of these biblical expressions will leap full grown into sermons. Most won't. Don't preach green sermons. Let the original intriguing idea develop as you turn it over in your mind. Sometimes this may take months.

A good program of biblical study will yield many ideas, however, most of which are not so obscure. Make a note card on each of these texts and your initial impressions about them, and keep them for future use. (Personally, for these textual idea cards, and illustrative material cards also, I prefer a very sophisticated filing system known as the "Messy Drawer Filing System"! Put a rubber band around them and drop them into a drawer. That's it. Go through them when you need them.)

Realistically, no contemporary preacher can spend months maturing every sermon idea. We must use more of a hothouse culture system. And if every sermon is not absolutely finished—and which one is?—give the congregation credit for being able to take a solid concept and work out the maturing of it in their own experience. But "be not deceived, God is not mocked," and neither is a contemporary church, by flashy phrases that are apparently profound and actually empty.

Contemporary Sources

Either the Bible or the contemporary situation may lead to sermons. Some preachers feel it is illegitimate to "get an idea and go find a text to match it." Not at all—providing that the idea has arisen from the need of people and providing that the text is *listened to* once it is found. We must always be ready to be taught by the Word or even to stand corrected by it if necessary. Our contemporary experience in Christ and the historic revelation of the Word must always be in dynamic interplay. In that sense, listening to the word about us also opens doors for sermonic thought, just as it did for Jesus in his earthy, practical, pictorial preaching.

Observe your environment. That's what Jesus did. Keep up. Study life, people, the news, yourself. Be alert, aware, alive.

Stretch yourself. Get involved with a variety of interests. Don't preoccupy yourself with your own tastes. Every church has both chess players and football fans. You don't have to be both, but you *do* have to appreciate both. "I am become all things . . ." (1 Cor. 9:22). That's why children wanted to listen to Jesus. We will not have any trouble speaking to various age groups or special interest groups if we are interested in the interests of others and show it.

Develop a regular reading plan. No one can experience everything—and we shouldn't. Reading allows an extension of experience. Without it, don't ask why you have trouble finding ideas, or why you only preach "the same old things."

But where in the world do you start? Personally I follow and recommend a sixfold reading plan, or "The Noble Sixfold Path to Reading." Rather than reading from one book one week and from another book another week, you will read wider and more satisfactorily if you read from six sources simultaneously.

Here's how it works. Select six books from six different categories of literature. Read a while from each book every week. Bracket those passages you want typed out. Drop in a note card at that page, and keep on reading. Type out these excerpts, or give the books to your secretary to type once a week. Put the cards in a drawer and scan through the stack when sermon writing. They will speak for themselves to your specific needs. (I like this method better than indexing since one illustration can fit many topics. File or index these cards after preaching, either by topic or with the sermon itself.)

What are the six categories? They are arbitrary. Suit yourself. I would include novels; historical material (fiction and nonfiction); biography (such as *The Public Years*, Baruch; *From Pagan to Christian*, Lin Yutang); diaries and journals *(Markings,* Dag Hammerskjold; *Notebooks,* Camus; Whitefields and Wesley's journals); poetry (separate volumes and anthologies; *One Hundred Modern Poems; A Treasury of Christian Verse).* The sixth I leave open for any miscellaneous work that comes to my attention. You may fill it with a special interest, such as drama or science. (Maybe it shouldn't be, but I consider it mandatory to schedule definite time for reading theology. Either add it as a category, or schedule a separate time to read those books and journals.)

When I finish a book in any category, I replace it with one of the same category. In that way my reading can be comprehensive and planned, yet varied. I read in any book I like, as long as I like.

A program of this sort will prove to be one of the most rewarding things you can do. It will provide a practical way for you to get the help literature can provide: it will aid your understanding of life, in and of itself, which is primary; and it will serve as a communication tool to help others understand the Christian message.

How Do I Get from a Text to a Sermon? From an Idea to a Text?

This is the other tough question about starting a sermon. Assuming I've located a text, how do I get to a sermon? Or if I've got an idea, what do I do about the Bible?

It's the middle ground that kills us. That is, we have learned how to exegete texts and likely also how to analyze contemporary psychological and ethical situations—but how do you get the two together? How do you move from one to the other? The process is really circular; so we could begin at either point, but I'll start with the traditional movement, text to sermon.

From Text to Sermon

Assuming that we know how to study a biblical text historically and critically and that we are keenly aware of our contemporary setting for ministry, we may still have trouble. We may either use a text as a kind of underwriter's label of spiritual safety on a clever contemporary essay, or we may do a first-century travelogue on manners and customs of Bible lands. Depending on our training and theology, we may have trouble one way or another in authentically involving the Bible in the sermon.

Three suggestions may help us to move through the middle ground between the historical and the contemporary. Ask these questions of a text:

Where does God encounter the human situation in this text? What human issues, problems, and concerns are illumined by this passage? What does God reveal about our common lives in the ancient narrative? List every reason you can see for this word to have been retained as revelation: what does it tell us about ourselves? About one another? About God? What insights does it provide, what truths, about our specific contemporary situation? Determine the basic concern that strikes you from the text. The theme and structure of the sermon will eventually emerge from this inquiry.

What difference would it make if we all heard this word? How would life be affected if we all were willing to hear the word of this revelation? What changes would come to our lives if we would believe it, act on it? Listing these possible effects gives point and purpose to the sermon. They clearly establish the need for our specific human response to God's initiative.

What homiletical focuses are possible within this text? People, sayings, events, or the setting of the text itself? In the healing of the boy following the transfiguration (Mark 9:14–29), for example, a sermon might focus on one or more of the *people* involved: the boy, the father; the disciples; the crowd; Jesus. Or on the *sayings:* "Why could not we cast him out?" (9:28); "Lord, I believe; help thou mine unbelief" (9:24). Or on the *events:* the healing; the questioning of the scribes; the failure of the disciples. Or on the *setting:* the contrast of this experience following the transfiguration events.

Even if all of these elements were used in a sermon, one of them would likely provide the principal focus on the text and the remaining incidents would be a part of the peripheral vision of the sermon. And if only one or two verses out of the pericope actually form the actual text (*textus,* fabric) of the sermon, the remaining verses form the context.

When these three questions have been examined, the preacher has taken concrete steps in the middle ground—that is, practical hermeneutics—between text and today.

From Idea to Text

Obviously many of the sermons of Jesus arose from his encounters with people and their needs. The same will be true for any minister for Christ. Daily ministry and observation of life will call for Christian proclamation. Many of these ideas will readily identify with Scripture; some will not. What procedure is possible in these situations?

In all cases, exegete the basic principle underlying the contemporary situation. It is possible to preach on many subjects that have no specific biblical precedent; for example, the modern drug culture. If any contemporary issue is troubling or challenging to the life of the congregation—either immediately or ultimately—then analyze the life principle of the question. What is its basic issue? The accuracy of the pastor's exegesis of the contemporary scene in this case is a key to the worth of the sermon it produces, exactly, in fact, as sermons that begin from a text must correctly exegete the historical scene to be Christian proclamation.

Compare and contrast the contemporary approach to this principle with the Christian message. Several years ago I heard a sermon on the so-called hippie communities in California. The speaker identified their concept of love as the distinguishing principle of that culture and compared and contrasted the views of that group on love with the biblical principle. In this case, the sermon was actually about love, the text was on love, and the hippie experiment became a running illustration, pro and con, throughout the sermon.

Be careful to be fair both to the contemporary issue and to the text. Don't fight straw people. If you don't really have the facts on an issue, or if you can't be fair to it, then you are not ready to preach on it. Likewise, if you don't really intend to listen to the Bible when you get there, don't use it as a motto on your own personal battle flag. Cultural religion is always promoted by this abuse.

"AND THE SERMON WAS WITHOUT FORM AND VOID, AND DARKNESS WAS UPON THE FACE OF THE DEEP"

A second cluster of practical questions surrounds the form of the sermon. How can the preacher find a procedure that implements the principles previously described? How do the traditional sermon parts relate to this theology of proclamation? Or do they?

All sermon preparation goes through three phases. In *phase one,* the sermon is without form and void and darkness is upon the face of the deep. This is the stage of creative chaos, but it is a necessary phase in sermon preparation.

In *phase two,* "Let all things be done decently and in order." No sermon talks about everything, in just any fashion—or it shouldn't. The basic unity and movement of the sermon are established in this second phase. Simplicity, strength, and cleanness of design should typify the sermon at this stage.

But this is not the final step. Some preachers go into the pulpit in chaos, and others preach in neat, rigid structures, but neither is the proper final state of the sermon. *Phase three* involves making the sermon an oral product, something *sayable*—"and they listened the more willingly . . ." It is this phase that is most often neglected, and yet it is the one most readily apparent to the congregation. They know the sermon is an acoustic event, even if the preacher does not. For this reason, I have already stressed the necessity for oral preparation.

But what practical structural suggestions might facilitate this process?

Is an Outline Necessary, Evil, or a Necessary Evil?

First, we must understand the difference between neoscholastic preaching and what we may refer to as gestaltic preaching. In neoscholastic preaching, "points" are overemphasized; the point gets lost in the points. In gestaltic preaching, the whole is greater than the sum of its parts. The what of the sermon, its message and mood, the whole dominates in gestaltic preaching. Some suggestions toward holistic sermons:

1. Unity and movement are the only indispensable elements in structure. Outlines may help that, but only if they are natural rather than forced. Natural outlines are called forth by the material; forced outlines are superimposed on the material.

Nevertheless, in every case a sermon must have a basic *unity* of theme, or message, or mood if it is to be understood. (If you wish to communicate chaos or confusion as a message—for whatever reason—then disorder and non sequiturs are appropriate.) *Movement* is also essential. A sermon must start somewhere and go somewhere. "Points" are only ways of indicating movement.

If the whole of the theme must be divided for clarity, the parts must equal the whole. (Or, in other words, if you can't eat a whole apple in one bite, slice it into pieces; but the pieces, if put back together, must equal an apple, not a hybrid apple-lemon.) Otherwise, no unity is present and no movement is possible.

That is, if the whole message cannot be heard in one basic thematic statement, which is first stated, then explained, described, and illustrated (as in a "one-point" sermon), then divide it into basic directional sentences ("points") that provide understandable movement for the theme.

2. Use no subdivisions at all. Subdivisions are a sure way to confusion and reflect an overemphasis on "points" and ideas. A "three-point" sermon, each with three subpoints, is a nine-point (idea) sermon. All any of us can do with a sermon like that is talk ourselves to death trying to explain so many ideas.

I would suggest this as a basic rule: only subdivide if forced to by the text. Do so only for textual clarity and fidelity, to set forth the basic concern of the text, never for random listing of additional explanatory ideas.

3. Allow the development within the sermon to proceed functionally. That is, allow the *interpretation of the text* and the *statement of the human situation* to put flesh and blood on the bones of the key ideas.

In other words, in developing your basic theme, you should deal with two functional elements: the *historical given* (declaration of the gospel; presentation of the historical revelation; narration of the text) and the *contemporary given* (description of the present situation; relation of the scripture to contemporary life), rather than abstractly subdividing and subsubdividing thematic inferences that probably get away from both.

Do not rely upon endless subdividing of ideas, in neoscholastic fashion, to provide the content of the sermon. Many preachers trained in this art have wound up with an elaborately complex outline and still had no idea what on earth to *say* once they stood up to speak.

Two principles may help this process:

(a) Remember that pictorial, illustrative material may help to clarify either of these functional elements. Use *alternative repetition:* alternate more abstract idea language with picture language. People cannot listen long to abstraction without description. (Better yet, let the description/narration come first and result in the reflection/abstraction.)

(b) Remember also another basic law: *compaction increases density.*

The more terse and epigrammatic your sentences, the greater their sectional density. Eventually they become steel-jacketed bullets that fire right through your audience with zero impact. (Another problem of a tightly written manuscript.)

4. Use transitional sentences to facilitate movement. In more traditional sermon forms, these are linking sentences, sentences that move the sermon from one key thought to another. Between the introduction and the first division, a transitional sentence tells us that the whole concern of the sermon also involves a specific thought; between each of the divisions, a transitional sentence tells us that there is more to come.

There are three basic kinds of transitions: the fully stated, partly stated, and fully suggested.

(a) *Fully stated.* Both the previous idea and the subsequent idea are stated: "So the resurrection of Christ speaks of God's victory, but it also speaks of our victory." The formula for the fully stated transition is X, X: content on both sides of the link.

(b) *Partly stated.* Either the previous idea or the subsequent idea is stated, and the other suggested. Two formulas are possible: X, ?; or ?, X. Content is present on only one side of the equation. For example: "The resurrection of Christ speaks of God's victory, but is that all it says to us?" (X, ?.) Or, "This is one meaning of the resurrection; but it also speaks of our victory as well. (?, X.) In the first example, where we have been in the sermon is stated and where we are going is implied; in the second, where we have been is implied and where we are going is stated.

(c) *Fully suggested.* Neither the previous idea nor the subsequent one is stated; both are implied. The formula is *?, ?.* No specific content is present at all. For example, "The resurrection assures us of one victory. But there is another." Or, quite simply, "But is that all?" In this case, "that" points backward, "all" points ahead.

How do we know which of these transitions to use? The oral manuscript itself will lead toward one or the other. For example, if a division closes explicitly with the key idea, then it would be ridiculous to immediately repeat that idea in a fully stated transitional sentence. Either a partly stated or fully suggested transition would better establish the unity and facilitate the movement of the sermon. But if a division has not explicitly stated its point, then a fully stated transition may be appropriate. Oral practice will soon lead to logical and natural transition sentences.

5. Remember that creative forms for sermon presentation result from sound principles.

Fosdick described his three basic forms as the box sermon (three points, or so, nailed up in parallel fashion like boards in a box— which form he said he liked least but did most); the river sermon (one point, winding around many turns but staying within the banks of the same river); and the tree sermon (organic development, with growth and interrelationships shown: "it begins with this; it leads to this; it results in this").

Luccock described countless special forms: the chase technique (idea pursued: "is it; is it; is it?"), the classification sermon ("some do this; some do that; and others do thus and so"), the ladder sermon (one idea builds upon another), and so on. Contemporary homileticians have favored forms from the arts, use of varied media, talk-back styles, narrative forms (telling a story), and countless other creative innovations. Which is best?

If a form suits the meaning and message of the sermon, if it follows meaningful methods appropriate to good theology of proclamation, and if it is the form that allows the historic revelation to speak most distinctly to its contemporary congregation— it is good structure, whatever its arrangement.

WHAT ABOUT INTRODUCTIONS, CONCLUSIONS, TITLES?

At this point we are ready to deal with these traditional sermon parts. Obviously they have had a place in traditional homiletics. Are they essential to all sermon forms?

Introductions

Not all sermons must have introductions, but all sermons must begin. And however the sermon develops, the same two principles hold true for the beginning of every sermon: *it must be concrete rather than abstract* and *it must plainly set the direction for the sermon.* I prefer to start with something that can be photographed—something tangible and tactile rather than abstract and theoretical. Begin as close to reality as language can manage. After all, we are speaking to people, not about subjects.

When is it appropriate to create an introduction in the traditional sense of a distinct sermon part? If the sermon has divisions, one is generally needed. Why? Because the congregation may become confused otherwise. They may lose the point in the points. They will not know what "point one" is a division of.

A traditional introduction typically does three things for the sermon: it reveals the basic concern of the message; it makes contact with the people; and it establishes contact with the text. (I say "typically," because the direct use of a text, for example, may not occur in the introduction, though it frequently will.) That is, an introduction will *create interest for the theme from the text.* These three elements are on a lateral plane; each arises out of and relates to the other. They may occur in any order.

But it is important that every sermon begin *concretely, specifically,* rather than theoretically or abstractly. If the text is a graphic, colorful narrative, the sermon may well open with it. But if it is a weighty, difficult Pauline section, for example, or an obscure bit of Hebrew history, then perhaps the sermon should begin with a description of events in the contemporary situation that will arouse interest in the text. Try some arrangement of these elements aloud; revise it if it doesn't provide the necessary unity and movement.

Regardless of which comes where, however, be sure that the beginning of the sermon plainly reveals the concern of the sermon, the theme of the sermon, the *what* of the sermon; and that it arouses interest in that, rather than in one of the lesser divisions of the sermon.

A frequent fault is using the beginning of the sermon to introduce the first point rather than the whole of the sermon. Another mistake is failing to subordinate interest-arousing material to the concern of the sermon as a whole, so that the congregation may be quite interested in some colorful piece of material but is distracted from, rather than attracted to, the larger purpose of the message.

May a sermon do without an introduction? (Barth would ask if one *may* have an introduction.) Definitely. If the order of the sermon as a whole proceeds functionally—that is, without idea divisions at all—then a formal introduction is not required. The sermon simply unfolds inductively, explaining and applying its single, undivided concern as it proceeds.

Conclusions

What has been said about introductions may also be said for the conclusion of the sermon. Not all sermons have conclusions, but all sermons must conclude. Like the introduction, the conclusion must be specific and pointed rather than vague and abstract. With or without a formal conclusion, this principle holds true for the end of the sermon.

If the final movement of the sermon has brought the message to a conclusive climax, tacking on a formal part called a conclusion is pointless. But if it is important to the message to tie together the lines of thought that have been opened, an explicit conclusion can make plain the concern of the sermon. This may be done by summary, challenge, or appeal.

Titles

A subject and a title are not the same. A subject is what the sermon is about; a title is what you call it. Titles are not really very important, relatively speaking. A good one creates interest and helps make specific the subject. But no one should make a fetish out of catchy title building.

After all, how can a title really be used? In the newspaper, church program, billboard? Perhaps. If a title is used in the sermon itself, it must be introduced naturally, that is, said in a normal sentence. *Not,* "If I had a title today, I suppose I should call it . . ." Of course you've got one—otherwise, you wouldn't be saying that in the first place! If it can't be said naturally, forget it.

Titles traditionally have been classified as descriptive or poetic, more analytic or more suggestive. But any title should do some of both: indicate the sermon direction and arouse interest. Titles may take the form of sentences, questions, exclamations, or phrases with limiting or descriptive words. One rule: when in doubt, don't. That is, use good taste and be plain rather than strange.

Remember two things: First, the greatest value of a title is in clarifying your own vision of the sermon. Second, your title should focus on *us*—what this means for *people*—rather than on *it* (biblical or contemporary topics—"Paul's Hard Trip," "Essentials of Good Stewardship").

OF TIME AND THE RIVER

The final practical question concerning sermon building is in some ways the most important one. How do I do it? What kind of a schedule will allow me to do my other work and still preach effectively? Must I obey Fosdick's Law: an hour in the study for each minute in the pulpit? (Or shall I resign now?)

How Do I Do It?

Naturally nobody can set up a weekly schedule for anyone else. Here are a few principles that may help:

1. Forget about "an hour for a minute." That is a contemporary impossibility. Some of us preach two or three times a week (like it or not!). And anyway, that would give a disproportionate place to sermons in the total task of ministry. If you can allocate fifteen solid hours a week to the preparation of the total sermon and Bible-teaching duties, you're doing well. And that's an outside figure. (I'm not counting every possible minute at home or on the street that the sermon may be working in your mind.)

2. Try to reserve morning for study. At least, all but the last hour (11:00 A.M.– 12:00 noon). Realistically, you will have to return calls, answer mail, hold conferences. But try to guard the fresh hours for mind work. Start early. Use afternoons for outside calling, hospital ministries, and so on.

3. Arrange the week to help the process. Monday ought to be

Low Motivation day (if you work at all). Do whatever does not call for the highest motivation. Traditionally, preachers haven't exactly raced into next Sunday's sermon on Monday. (If you can, congratulations. Your prize is on the way.)

Personally I arrange my sermonic week this way: Monday is my morning for reading (do something else if that kills you to think about it); Tuesday I do devotional study, preliminary exegesis, and attempt a tentative sermon structure; Wednesday I do Bible study (from one Old Testament and one New Testament book; one feeds my midweek Bible study, the other my Sunday evening sermon); Thursday I do my first oral manuscript; Friday I do my final oral manuscript, or Saturday, depending on time demands; and on one or the other, I complete my Sunday night oral preparation. (I try to do homilies, or Bible studies, on Sunday night to provide variety in worship and simplicity of sermon preparation. It also seems to suit the mood of the hour better.)

Arrange the week to suit your own needs. But recognize the limitations on your time, get started early (in the day, and in the week), and keep up your contact with the Bible and with contemporary life.

How Far Ahead Should I Plan? And How?

Those who always follow the lectionary do not face this problem. Others have more flexibility but face serious choices. However, some preachers can work out a year's plan in advance, complete with titles and texts. They don't need my help. I need theirs.

I do believe that planning as specifically as that a quarter ahead is good. In my opinion, however, a general, open plan for a full year is more helpful. Here are some principles:

1. Block off on a calendar all holidays and church holy days (Christmas, Easter, etc.). Plan to preach sermons that will deal with these high days, or perhaps a series to lead up to them.

2. Select some local and denominational church emphases to be observed (Christian Home Week, Mission Week, Stewardship Sunday, etc.—you couldn't preach on all of them unless you spent all day at church every Sunday).

3. For the remaining weeks, indicate month by month (more or less), portions of the Bible to be covered, sermon objectives to be pursued, special sermon types to be used, or sermon series to be followed. These may be indicated on the calendar singly or in combination.

For example, in the first quarter of the year you might choose to preach from the minor Prophets and the pastoral Epistles; or, in the evenings, devotional sermons from the Psalms; in the second quarter, ethical messages on the home and family for several weeks, and dialogue sessions in the evenings on the morning sermons. And so on. Endless permutations and combinations of these very general, basic elements are possible and provide at least some security and comprehensiveness in your preaching program.

4. At any rate, try to set out a plan that will help you, not get in your way or become artificial. Change it if you need to; never let it interfere with a real need. A good general plan, however, will prove useful by preventing monochromatic preaching and pet-theme pursuit and by promoting broad use of the Scripture and a variety of approaches.

Beyond this point, we're all on our own. Perhaps my approach-for-now may have helped to add an idea or so to your personal program. I hope so. If not, don't complain; send help.

In recent homiletical thinking, one approach to the sermon has become so prominent that it bids to sweep the field. That form is narrative, "telling the story." Because of its significant contributions to preaching theory, as well as its prominence in homiletical literature, we must now focus on that specific form alone.

Is it the answer to the many troubling issues raised by the structure of the sermon? Can narrative return preaching to its original dynamic?

12. Once upon a Time . . .

A funny thing happened to preaching on its way toward consensus: agreement broke down. Perhaps a story could tell it best.

Once upon a time there was great unrest in the land of preaching. No one could agree on which sermon form should reign over the pulpit. Forever and ever—at least as long as anyone living could remember—discursive, rational argument had held sway over the sermon. Preachers *knew* how to arrange their sermons: points, subpoints, and subsubpoints, from Roman numeral I to triple subscript "i" in parenthesis, all following one tightly reasoned argument and sprinkled lightly (very lightly) with a few good illustrations made a very nice sermon indeed.

But the natives became restless. Suddenly in church one day a woman stood up, right in the middle of the sermon, and screamed, "I hate *points!*" Of course this woke everyone up, which disturbed them, and the noise disturbed the preacher. Soon almost every head was nodding in agreement, and the preacher left the pulpit baffled and discouraged.

Meanwhile, high in their ivory tower, the homileticians, the Valiant-for-Truth's of the preaching world, those legendary authorities on the subject of the sermon (the legend was that they *were* authorities) were greatly troubled. And well they should have been. For down below, now completely encircling their sacred tower, thousands and thousands of preachers shook their fists in helpless rage toward the skies.

"No one likes our preaching," cried one. "They go to sleep before the introduction is over!"

"Right!" cried another. "If it were not for the illustrations, nobody would remember anything at all!"

At first the homileticians didn't know what to do. There had been complaints before, of course, but never anything like this.

They scanned their ancient books and manuscripts. They searched for other formulas. They argued violently with one another (using thesis, antithesis, and synthesis of course). They even sent messengers out into the countryside to see what preachers in more remote provinces were doing.

Finally the answer came: we must use story. Yes, that's it, they said. We must use story. That's how Israel began, telling stories around its campfires. That's the way the prophets gained the attention of their listeners. That's how Jesus preached at Nazareth, and that's how he taught—in parables. That's also how the apostles and early disciples preached, in historical recital of the deeds of Yahweh and the life of Christ. Why didn't we see it sooner? they asked themselves. No longer would preaching be deductive arguments, but inductive stories. No longer would preaching be ruled by ideas, but by experience. No longer would preaching be arranged in space, but arranged in time.

And down below, the smiles of the preachers matched the smiles of the homileticians, and the preachers all marched back over the hill smiling and waving to the happy homileticians who crowded the one window in the ivory tower. And they all went back to their pulpits to preach happily ever after. The End.

Not quite. For one day, while narrating a story that had no points (and no point either, so far as anyone could discern), the same preacher was startled to see the same woman stand up in her pew and scream, "I don't understand your stories! What are you trying to tell us?" But the preacher only smiled enigmatically, thinking that the "brighter ones out there would understand it," exactly as he and all of his preacher friends had thought for hundreds of years when people complained about following complicated outlines.

But deep in his soul there were again the stirrings of unrest, and when these tidings reached the homileticians, they also cast about in their minds wondering what these things could mean. Have we not yet found the Holy Grail? they asked. Is there to be no Camelot?

To be continued . . .

A STRONG CASE FOR STORY

For those readers who do not completely understand our little fable, a few words about its context may help. The turbulence of the 1960s was also a time of turbulence for preaching. Pastors and laypeople alike reported widespread discontent with preaching. Soon preachers and homileticians entered into the search for more effective methods for communicating the gospel.

As is usually the case in the early stages of such exploration, many experimental sermon forms—some of them bizarre—were attempted, but few succeeded. The values of dialogue were recognized and entered into the question, and for some time it appeared to many that the traditional "monological" sermon was finished. For reasons probably not fully known either to those who practiced dialogue sermons or to those who refused to, however, the method never captured the field. It remains today as an alternative sermon form for some preachers, while its reminder of the values of dialogical address made a larger contribution to preaching and continues to inform the nature of contemporary preaching.

The emergence of story or narrative, however, as a vehicle for preaching—if not *the* vehicle for preaching—found a more enthusiastic reception. "Recent interest in story," says Richard Lischer, "as a form of religious discourse has spread across the breadth of theology and church life with the result that no discipline or activity remains untouched by the vocabulary of story, storytelling, narrative, or narration."[1] Many books by homileticians instructed us in the possibilities of narrative preaching.[2] Other homileticians such as Eugene Lowry in *The Homiletical Plot* and *Doing Time in the Pulpit* and those represented by Don Wardlaw in *Preaching Biblically* sought to extend the concept of sermon as story, though not without some modifications. Likewise, Fred Craddock made two highly significant contributions to our understanding of inductive preaching in *As One Without Authority* and *Overhearing the Gospel*.[3]

Biblical scholars, particularly those working in the area of parables, also gave strong endorsement to narrative, especially Dan O. Via, John Dominic Crossan, Sallie McFague TeSelle, and Robert W. Funk.[4] Structuralism likewise caused considerable excitement —both positive and negative—with its promise of meaning inherent in the structure of the text itself. These efforts were led by Daniel and Aline Patte, Roland Barthes, Northrop Frye, E. D. Hirsch, and others.[5]

Frustrated with the "scientific" efforts of historical criticism to discern the background of the text—which sometimes was guilty of the fallacy that having arrived at the genesis of the text, it had gained the significance of the text—structuralism sought to find the significance of the verbal form of the text for expressing its content.[6] However, in spite of its lengthy studies with extensive use of diagrams, structuralism remained opaque to many, if not most, who studied it. It was likewise criticized for also seeking to "go behind" the text by seeking its "deep meanings" and for yielding little exegetical results, at least for the present.

Other sources were more profitable for the advocates of story. In an article that has been highly influential, Stephen Crites wrote on the "Narrative Quality of Experience," in which he argued for the narrative structure of human experience itself and suggested that memory is the inner form of experience. Therefore experience can derive a specific sense of its own temporal course in the world only through the narrative of what he terms "sacred and mundane story."[7]

Another important work that has been much referred to with reference to narrative is Frank Kermode's *The Sense of an Ending,* in which the literary critic emphasizes plots as organized time that moves toward "end stress," or final resolution.[8] Strong assistance also came from certain quarters of linguistics, particularly in some of the remarks of Paul Ricoeur, such as, "The history of human experience can be brought to language only as narrativity."[9] Furthermore, we were urged to use less "ideational" language and more "tensive" language. "Tensive" is a word used by Philip Wheelwright to suggest language that is alive with conflict, elasticity, suggestion, and plurality of meaning.[10] (I well remember when I first began using the term "oral manuscript" and a distinguished professor at another university shot back, "Oral manuscript? What a perfectly stupid phrase! They aren't oral—that's why they're called manuscripts." It may have been stupid, but it was also an example of tensive language, language that seeks to move us from one place to another.)

Furthermore, the entire movement of narrative theology added additional impetus to narrative, as in works such as Gabriel Fackre's *The Christian Story,* Wesley Kort's *Narrative Elements and Religious Meaning,* James B. Wiggins's *Religion as Story,* and Brian Wicker's *The Story-Shaped World.* [11]

Likewise, black preaching asserted with abundant evidence that "the black tradition has excelled in this art form," both in the past and in the present, so much so that Henry Mitchell asserts that no other form ought to be used in preference to a good story: "When one uses an intellectual argument or essay form, it ought to be either an adjunct to a shorter story or a choice growing out of the fact that one has no story suitable for that particular gospel idea. It is no accident that black preachers ask of another preacher, 'Can he tell the story?' "[12]

Finally—as if all of the above were not enough—the efforts of canonical criticism, particularly the works of Brevard S. Childs and James A. Sanders, added further fuel to an already blazing fire.[13] It is no wonder that homileticians quickly seized this new initiative to see if it could finally be what Lischer called "the perfect glass slipper of form," by which "not only the sermon would be transformed into a beautiful princess, but we ourselves would also be transformed."[14]

How could we summarize the many advantages claimed for narrative, story, or plotting? The answers differ, of course, from writer to writer; by no means is there complete agreement on what is meant by these things. Nevertheless, some advantages are held in more or less general agreement.

First among these would be *the claim that the nature of life itself is narrative.* Since narrative best corresponds to life and, indeed, since memory is "the inner form of experience," there is an identification and response by the listeners to narrative that is not possible in any other way.[15] People will listen to a story with more sustained attention because narrative is the nature of life itself. Craddock says, "The form fits," and quotes Barbara Hardy: "We dream in narrative, daydream in narrative, remember, anticipate, hope, despair, believe, doubt, plan, revise, criticize, construct, gossip, learn, hate, and love by narrative."[16]

Second, *some biblical studies suggest the event-nature of the texts themselves:* "A text of oral origin does not have for its foundation an intellectual structure but a structure that inheres in events. It represents in itself the sequence of events in which it arose and which have passed into the life of human beings."[17]

Third, *plots in sermons are regarded as superior to outlines.* Lowry defines a plot as the moving suspense of story, from disequilibrium to resolution: "Its typical stages are (1) opening disequilibrium, gaining complication toward (2) escalated ambiguity, climaxing into (3) reversal, and moving out into (4) denouement. This is the plot of a typical story as a narrator tells it and surely the shape of a sermon, which orders experience as a preacher proclaims it."[18]

Thomas Long defines plotting somewhat differently: "In summary, then, the process of 'plotting' a sermon involves interpreting a biblical text, allowing its claim upon us to form the aim—or denouement—of the sermon; ascertaining the cognitive, emotional, and behavioral issues that need to be heard (these become, in effect, the *elements* of the sermon plot); and arranging those elements according to the preacher's sense of their communicational connection into a sequence that anticipates and progresses toward the denouement."[19] The biblical text is regarded as an embodiment of experience rather than as a container for truth, "like a plastic cup is the container of a milkshake,"[20] and a plot is believed to accomplish that arrangement in a sermon better than an outline.

These recent developments in narrative understanding clearly seem to have gained some ground for the sermon. How much ground has been gained—and, more importantly, whether any ground has also been lost—remains a question, as we shall see.

Nevertheless, the claims of narrative are impressive, and its divergence from older sermon forms appears almost absolute. The accompanying chart might make clearer those differences.[21]

Elements	Narrative Sermon	Traditional Sermon
Style:	Narration	Argument
Focus:	Events	Theme
Form:	Process	Structure
Arrangement:	Plot	Outline
Approach:	Inductive	Deductive
Method:	Orders experience	Orders ideas
Means:	Ambiguity, suspense	Logic, clarity
Language:	Tensive	Stenic (ideational)[22]
Goal:	Happening; participation	Understanding; agreement

THE PLOT THICKENS . . .

The triumph of narrative or story would seem to be complete. But not quite. For within the writings on homiletics many questions have been raised about the nature of this new sermon.

What does it mean, in fact, to "tell a story" in a sermon, even more *as* a sermon? Must a story always be told in every sermon? And shall it be a recital of the biblical story or the creation of a contemporary story? Shall these be interpreted or uninterpreted stories, stories with or without reflection? May narrative preaching be used regardless of the biblical literature that underlies it? What about letting the shape of the scripture influence the shape of the sermon? What is to be done with nonnarrative biblical literature, such as the Pauline Epistles, the Psalms and other Wisdom literature, and countless other passages? If we are talking about "plotting" a sermon instead of "telling a story," does that rule out any consideration of a unified theme or does it not in fact require it? Finally, and most significantly, if the newer sermon forms are to be truly superior to the older, can they validate their claim of being arranged on solid biblical-theological grounds rather than on rhetorical grounds?[23]

But it is at precisely this point that the strongest objections to the narrative sermon as the final word in sermon form have been raised. "Even so universal a genre as story, it will be argued, has its limits of usefulness whose transgression involves both theology and preaching in a reduced or distorted rendering of human life and human revelation." According to Richard Lischer, those limits are aesthetic, ontological, theological, and sociopolitical.[24]

Theologians and critics such as Fuchs, Crossan, Via, and others have sought to recapture biblical narrative as an *aesthetic* object that, like the parables of Jesus, may legitimately be isolated from its context because it bears its meaning in itself. Lischer challenges that assumption, asking, "What story lifted from its background still *works* on any but the moralistic or universalizing levels?" He adds, "In a time when the 'background' of most congregations is deficient, is it the preacher's task to jettison what remains of it?"[25] Mary Ann Tolbert likewise concludes that "for a full elaboration of their meaning the parables are *dependent on their context.* Hence every different context into which they are placed will result in a different interpretation."[26]

Furthermore, the aesthetic approach to story appears to Lischer to rest on several critical mistakes: an assumption of the supreme importance of plot among the several components of stories; a naive estimation of the simplicity of storytelling that grossly underestimates the hermeneutical distance between *the* story and *my* story; and a belief in the power of such aesthetic vehicles as parables to subvert or change our world "nonreferentially" (independent of their background in the traditions).[27]

Second, while "the essential relationship between story and experience cannot be seriously doubted," that does not mean that an absolute *ontological* argument on behalf of story can be assumed. Such an assertion falsifies those vast and deep nonnarrative domains of human life."[28] Since a story is a plot the episodes and complications of which are directed toward resolution, such a shape is not always true to the way things are but "mercifully— or arrogantly—imposes a pattern on the disorder and anarchy of life as it is." This "fictive concord" is an attempt to make tolerable the middle ground between life's beginning and its ending.[29] This is seen as another attempt to bring rhetoric in line with a contemporary anthropology.

That is, as our understanding of human experience changes, we search for a rhetorical form that best explains our own identity. The older sermon form of divisions and subdivisions stressed the rationality of person and message in correspondence with the perceived orderliness of society and, indeed, the cosmos itself. Since that sense of order is no longer adequate to explain who we think we are, homiletics turns instead to a story or a series of personal anecdotes to provide that missing order.[30] "Any story that moves from complication to resolution can be an act of faith in the orderliness of things—a way of keeping the wolf of chaos from the door."[31] It may also provide a way to flee into either the artificial and less threatening objectivity of ancient history or into the more gratifying, less authoritarian-sounding realm of personal, interiorized religion. Both escapes are in sharp distinction to the biblical word of prophetic challenge, "This day is this scripture fulfilled in your ears" (Luke 4:21).

Closely related to this criticism of story are the questions raised regarding story's ability to perform the *sociopolitical* and *eschatological* dimensions of preaching. The cross-resurrection event points first to the brokenness of life, the interruption of story, and bids us to sit where the storyless, forgotten people sit and then proclaim the eschatological hope of deliverance in the resurrection event of Jesus Christ. But in so doing, preaching ceases to be historical recital and becomes theology. Likewise, just as the eschatological nature of the Christian faith could not be limited to a strictly narrative form of exposition, so the sociopolitical implications of the gospel demand that the story be interpreted. As we have said earlier, the sermon of Jesus at Nazareth did not shock or scandalize the congregation so long as he was involved in historical recital. But when he moved from narrative to theology, from uninterpreted to interpreted story—through his example of God's favor coming to the widow of Sidon and to Naaman the Syrian when Israel was full of widows and lepers—they rioted (Luke 4:14–30).

It is at this same point that Sallie McFague TeSelle says that she sees "a storm brewing" because of the challenges posed to the traditional reliance of the Christian tradition on *realistic narrative forms* by the very different assumptions of the writers and artists of the post-Christian era. These writers give little attention to the "sacred constituents" of plot, linear time, character development, the hero, resolutions, beginnings and endings. "When much of experience mirrors chaos and disorder, not exclusively but particularly visible in Third World oppression, then many of our assumptions must be questioned: 'Is personal development sequential and linear? Is the story of a people, not of an individual, the story we should tell (as black and feminist theology is suggesting)? Are there any heroes or should there be? Are 'resolutions' ever achieved?' "[32]

Finally, the sufficiency of narrative-only forms of preaching has been challenged as a vehicle for communicating effectively. Wardlaw warns: "While some preachers show sufficient skill with narrative sermons to need little or no reflective passages to aid the sermon's impact, many other preachers who attempt narrative-only sermons too often leave their hearers stranded in the story line for lack of clarity about the sermon's intent"; he therefore suggests that we resist "the more recent temptation to baptize narrative itself as sufficient vehicle for the Word in Scripture without some attendant reflection."[33]

THE LINES CONVERGE

Fortunately, upon closer examination the differences among homileticians regarding narrative sermon forms, while substantial, are not absolute. In fact, a careful reading of their writings reveals surprising correspondence at key points.

For example, Lischer says, "Although they cannot be resolved, the essential relationship between story and experience cannot be seriously doubted."[34] Story continues to play an important part for theology as theology's generalizations "continue to call attention to and rely upon the foundational stories. And it is the stories, with which theology never falls out of dialogue, that help shape the community's identity. We become what our stories tell us we are."[35] Story thus becomes not only the "raw material" of theology but also the raw material of faith: "Faith appropriates Israel's past, scans the ways in which that history has or has not been operative in an individual's or the community's past, and applies all the data as a down payment on the future."[36]

Narrative likewise has significance for the future promise in preaching: "Preaching that would conform to the eschatological hope has something to learn from the narrative thrust of the biblical witness and from the historical and pilgrimlike quality of the people of God." On the other hand, that future promise is obscured by argumentative styles of preaching: "The rhetoric of thesis, propositions, subpoints, and proofs underwrites the bondage of the promise. Such rhetoric establishes truths at the expense of possibilities." In contrast, "preaching-as-promise is not neat or buttoned down."[37] Although Lischer insists that preaching whose content "enlivens hearers to the presence and the future of Jesus Christ" cannot be accomplished by filling sermons with stories, it does require "unfolding the promise with a *narrative logic,* to the end that the truth is not pronounced but arrived at"[emphasis mine].[38].

Likewise, the emphasis of Eugene Lowry on "plotted" sermons is not as negative toward theme as it would appear on the surface. In contrast to Lischer, and even Craddock, both of whom have good words to say for the concept of a sermon theme or thesis sentence, Lowry is not complimentary about one-sentence sermon summaries.[39] But at times he does use language that indicates that the sermon should have one specific theme or issue: "It is important then to select what appears the most problematic issue raised in or by the text and to wrestle with determination for considerable time—but allowing no final conclusion to be reached."[40] Again, he emphasizes the importance of talking to someone about "the gestating sermon idea or text—long before a sermon begins to take shape," and says, "One should talk the sermon ideas out loud. . . ."[41]

None of this, however, should be taken to mean that these

homileticians have, in fact, backtracked and ended their revolutionary sermon theories with quite traditional methodological suggestions. For example, Lowry's *sermon idea* is intended to evolve through a process rather than an outline, and Craddock's *theme,* "the governing idea of the sermon," is not to be referred to as a "proposition" since that might lead to an argumentative sermon form.[42]

But this does illustrate an important if not crucial point. So far as I am able to tell, these writers are not advocating sermons that are so exclusively narrative in their form that there is no place for theological reflection—the sermonic "idea" or ideas—or even, properly understood, for drawing propositional inferences from the text. In other words, they allow for an *interpreted* rather than an uninterpreted story.[43]

For example, in explaining what he means by "narrative structure" for promoting inductive preaching, or "generating the dynamics of overhearing," Craddock explains what he does and does not mean relative to "narrative" and "story." First, he does not mean that "narrative is to replace rational argument in Christian discourse. . . . We need always to be warned against the use of narratives and stories to avoid the issues of doctrine, history, and theological reflection." He reminds us of those who read Kierkegaard and "become enamored of his stories and forget his insistence that Christianity can be conceptualized."[44] He also does not mean by narrative form the exegesis of texts of secular literature, "ferreting out religious meanings" for preaching; nor does he mean merely "reading or reciting long narrative portions of Scripture verbatim." Finally, he is not proposing that the sermon be merely a long story or a series of stories or illustrations: "While such may actually be the form used for a given message, it is not necessary in order to be narrative."[45]

Then Craddock delineates what he means by "narrativelike" communication as over against strict narrative:

To be narrativelike means to have the scope that ties it to the life of a larger community; it means the message has memory and hope; it means to be life-size in the sense of touching all the keys on the board rather than only intellectual or emotional or volitional: it means conveying the sense of movement *from* one place *to* another; it means having this movement on its own, as though the presence of the listeners were not essential to its process; it means thinking alongside the hearers.[46]

Dan Via's modifications to the narrative concept are likewise critical to our understanding of "story" in the sermon. Although he calls the plot of parables "the controlling form to which all else is related" and asserts that the basic speech mode in the Bible is the story, "a narration of action in time"—so much so that "in the biblical view life itself is of the nature of a dramatic plot"— nonetheless he emphasizes the importance of theme in narrative literature: "Our emphasis on plot, however, should not make us forget that *all narrative literature contains both plot and theme or thought in some relationship* [emphasis mine]. In fact they are two sides of the same formal principle with plot being theme in movement and theme being plot at a standstill." For some works, Via says, plot is more important while in others theme is, but "the decision about which one is more prominent will often be a matter of interpretive emphasis. Of plot we ask 'How will it turn out?' and of theme 'What is the point?' "[47]

These converging lines of reflective theme and narrative plot at least point us toward a new direction for the sermon.

THE CONTEXTUAL SERMON: THE GREAT GULF FIXED

How can the practicing preacher derive the gains won by the advocates of story without ignoring the crucial objections to that method as raised by others? Can a meaningful synthesis be achieved?

I believe that it can. What I propose to do is to take the concept of "contextual preaching"[48] and enlarge upon it to see if it cannot, indeed, comprise an adequate design for the practical development of "narrativelike" sermons within the theology of proclamation I have called incarnational preaching. I begin with two presuppositions:

1. *There is no one form that is exclusively ideal for the organization of the sermon.* One has never yet been found, and we will not find one now. In fact, you can be sure that you are off to a partial or distorted concept of preaching if you are practicing one rhetorical form as *the* form for the sermon: "Beware of Greeks (rhetoric) bearing gifts." The content of the kerygma shapes the form of our preaching, not the form the kerygma. "Indeed the surest clue to the reign of the subject matter by the religious classic [such as the biblical writings] can be witnessed by the relative inadequacy of any religious form for communicating its meaning." That should not be surprising, says David Tracy. "If, in fact, our realized experience of the religious classic is a recognition of the event-character of a true manifestation of the whole, how can we expect a fully adequate form, genre or style to express *that?*"[49] And what is true of those greater proclamations, such as the Gospels, will also be true of lesser proclamations, such as our sermons.

2. *Determinations of form must be made on a biblical-theological basis, not on rhetorical foundations.* Our answers, if any, are already contained in the nature of the kerygma itself. All other foundational approaches are inadequate and deceiving. The God of the past is also the God of the present, and it is that God who proclaims to us the promise of the future. The form of the sermon is determined by the contexts of the gospel: the *historical context* of our faith must unite with the *present context* of human need and point to the *future context* of the hope in Christ. Preaching therefore that is "necessary, edifying, and constitutive for the church" will come when a man or woman is "totally exposed, if not shattered, by two voices: the cry of despair and want resounding from today's situation and the voice of God that cannot be muted."[50] Those voices, united, and those voices alone, shape the structure of the sermon.

With these presuppositions in mind, let us look at the problem the distance between the context of the biblical world and the contemporary world poses for preaching. As I see it, that problem is best stated by Paul Ricoeur, and I will attempt to briefly summarize his analysis and enlarge upon it for our understanding of the place of narrative in sermon.[51]

Christianity presents itself as a kerygma—an announcement, proclamation, message, or what Ricoeur calls "a discourse addressed to."[52] Of course, that proclamation comes from an entirely different context than ours. The question is, how can we communicate the meaning of the kerygma in a comprehensible discourse? "How can we make ours something to which we have become strangers."[53] Our problem is to return to contemporary discourse a language that does not pertain to the same cultural circle as ours. We are not faced simply with the problem of *explaining* text but of *interpreting* text. Explanation is understanding what the text meant in its historical setting; interpretation is so translating the text that it is allowed to interpret our situation in our day, confronting us with categories of meaning we have avoided or long since forgotten.[54]

The hermeneutical task, therefore, is always to overcome a cultural distance. The task of the proclamation of the gospel is, like all interpretation, to "conquer a remoteness," that distance between the past culture to which the text belongs and the present culture to which we belong. This search is not merely to understand the ancient past. The primary result of such interpretation is *self-understanding through understanding the other.*[55] The interpreter accomplishes this overcoming of distance by making himself or herself contemporary with the text, insofar as that is possible. This is necessary because it is not only the language of the text that has become remote to us. Indeed, the radical questions of the text, with their demands and promise, have become even more foreign to our culture.

This has another significance for the preacher of the gospel. By "transferring ourselves into another universe of meaning," we put ourselves at a kind of distance from our own understandings, the conventional wisdom of our time. Therefore in addition to *approaching* the world of the text, we must also become involved in a process of *distancing,* a "de-construction of the assurances of modern man." This de-construction, however, will be a positive one, because it will become a "de-construction of what destroys."[56] We must enter the world of the text with a suspicion with regard to ourselves and the certitude of our own culture.

Furthermore, this entire process of approaching the text and distancing ourselves from the text must be brought to language. We can only do this by becoming broadly involved in the *context* of the kerygma; we become involved in "contextual dependence at the level of the message." Even the simplest message in the text takes its actual meaning from its connection with a given context and a given audience against the background of a given situation. Our interpretation through preaching, therefore, is a process by which we use "all the available contextual determinants to grasp the actual meaning of a given message in a given situation." By context we do not mean only the linguistic context of the actual words themselves, but "the speaker's and the hearer's behavior, the situation common to both, and finally the horizon of reality surrounding the speech situation."[57]

This *"horizon"* of the text represents the *potential* present in it, its *drawing power* toward worlds unknown to us, its *promise of reality.* The discourse of the text is the interpretation of reality, and our proclamation, like that of the biblical writer, must also be an interpretation of reality. We must realize that we are not speaking merely of the *situations* of the text but of the possible *worlds* of the text. Unlike animals, human beings have a world as well as a situation. The duty of preaching is to so present the text that a new world of possibilities is opened to the hearers. We must always beware of reducing preaching to merely explaining the historical situation, or what Jürgen Moltmann calls nothing more than "situation illumination," a key fault, he believes, that results from "staring at the results of historical exegesis." In fact, he says that the present great gulf fixed between exegesis and proclamation arose with the beginning of historical exegesis and its presuppositions.[58] The danger is that we will not preach the text but the situation of the text, comparing it with present situations. Rather, says Moltmann, *we must ask what the text has made necessary,* the promise and the hope that has challenged their situation and must challenge our situation.[59]

That is, preaching must open its hearers to possible ways of being in the world beyond their situation and even the author's situation that the text reveals before them. This implies that the hermeneutical circle is not a circle between two subjectivities, the preacher/listener of today and the speaker/author of the biblical text; we cannot transfer ourselves into the spiritual life of other speakers or writers to discern their psychology or intent. But what we can do is to "follow the dynamics of the work, its movement from what it says to that about which it speaks."[60] Preaching is the bringing to language of a *world,* not merely the recognition of another person. It is not our business to attempt to discern something behind the text but rather to present ourselves *before* the text; we must "let the work and its world enlarge the horizon of my own self-understanding."[61]

Interpretation, then, is "the process by which the disclosure of new modes of *being*— or, if you prefer Wittgenstein to Heidegger, of new 'forms of life'—gives to the subject a new capacity for knowing himself." At the same time, we must avoid "the fallacy of the absolute text," or of the text-in-a-vacuum. This error reacts to the text as if it were not made by human hands at all, forgetting that "a text remains a discourse told by somebody, said by someone to someone else about something."[62] A constant dialectic must occur between event and meaning.

In this sense, Scripture functions as a lens through which the world is viewed rather than being seen as an object of study whose significant meaning is located outside itself. So the Reformers resisted allegorizing and emphasized what George Lindbeck calls "intratextuality," which "heightened the emphasis on proclamation, on the preached word." What does this imply for our preaching? "In the intratextual context, this emphasis on the living word involves applying the language, concepts, and categories of Scripture to contemporary realities," and it "redescribes reality within the scriptural framework rather than translating Scripture into extrascriptural categories. It is the text, so to speak, which absorbs the world, rather than the world the text." Believers, therefore, do not "find their stories in the Bible, but rather . . . they make the story of the Bible their story."[63]

CONTEXT: PAST, PRESENT, AND FUTURE

Our contemporary preaching of the gospel must, therefore, if it is to be preaching at all, be involved with the past, present, and future of the text. These three contexts must be engaged in the sermon for the kerygma of the text to be heard.

The *past of the text* must be explored to gain access to the world of the text. We need not discard the valuable tools of critical research simply because the results of that study have sometimes dead-ended in "a collection of lifeless facts."[64] As Craddock says, "We could no more return to precritical biblical study then we can live as though this were the eighteenth century, but neither is the text honored or the church served by regarding historical criticism as the last and only word in Biblical study."[65] The overemphasis on historical "fact" has led to obliteration of some of the most profound biblical insights—the battle over the book of Genesis is a prime case in point. Craddock says, "Imagine one person tossing out Shakespeare's *Othello* because there is no historical evidence that there ever was a Moorish general in the service of Venice, while another person embraces it as 'true' because a rare footnote in an ancient history of Italy proved a Moor once so served."[66]

In the three elements of the fundamental context of the Old Testament—narration, words of God, words addressed to God— both the sequence of events and the human response to them determine the character of the Old Testament and "make the study of Israel a condition preliminary to all exegesis."[67] We are directed toward this use of past context by the biblical writers themselves. In the Old Testament, for example, the various writers from diverse communities constantly harken back to the earlier context of their faith. But they regarded no word as complete and finished within itself; rather, it held forth a larger promise for the future. Von Rad says, "Here nothing bears its last meaning in itself, but it is a down payment of yet greater wonders."[68] Likewise Moltmann says, "The facts are never seen as completed incidents which have had their time, but rather as moments in the process of Promise-history."[69] In their use of the past, the Old Testament writers looked to the future.

Then the New Testament, of course, makes abundant use of the Old Testament in its preaching. Many of the texts we employ from the New Testament are themselves interpretations of texts from the Old Testament. For example, Luke "employs form as well as content to assure the reader that the story you are about to read concerning Jesus and the church is continuous with the story of Israel. In other words, the writer uses Scripture to create a world in which the account is to be heard, thereby weaving the fabric of trust essential for communication." So Craddock concludes, "Prophets in the Old Testament and the New, and prophets today, know and make abundant use of the tradition commonly shared with the listeners."[70] Therefore we use the Bible as a "book of precedents," not to transplant ourselves or our listeners into bygone epochs, but as evidence that God is living and that God's message still has meaning for us today.[71]

In summary, we must encounter the past world of the text insofar as that is possible. This encounter must include the world of the community that preserved and preached these words as well as the world of the events that underlie them. Since words and even events may signify meanings for us today that are different from their original meanings, the preacher must serve as translator and guide on this journey. Only when we have heard the message of the text along with its original listeners are we ready to hear it as its contemporary listeners.

However, just as my little fable of preaching at the beginning of this chapter needed added contextual information for those who were not familiar with it, so the context of a biblical story may need explanation for understanding. Obviously words and even situations can have different meanings now from their meanings in the biblical text. We cannot pick up an expression from the Bible and move across to the same expression in popular usage today and understand its meaning, much less exegete it out of the dictionary as is the custom in so many Sunday School devotionals: "Webster says . . ." The preacher must serve as a guide through this terrain.

For example, after the reading of the Gospel, Ernesto Cardenal encouraged his congregation in Solentiname, a community on an island in a Lake Nicaragua composed mostly of fishermen and their wives, to discuss the lesson for the day. Their observations show remarkable insights into the gospel, but it is also evident that Cardenal found it necessary to explain the setting of the text or, in some cases, their thinking would run far afield of the text. But with a simple clarification of the textual setting, their interpretation yielded profound results. For example, after explaining that the complicated Jewish dietary laws, particularly concerning pork, were given because God was concerned about the health of the people, Cardenal asked what meaning that could have for them, in a small village where the raising of a few pigs provided them with their only source of meat. A woman said, "You said God gave these rules so they could be healthy. So in our village it would mean, Eat pigs."

On another occasion, Cardenal led them in a study of the Good Samaritan in Luke 10. They had great difficulty understanding that the determining question in Luke 10:36 was who "proved neighbor" to the man who fell among robbers:

One answered: "The man without religion was the neighbor."
"It wasn't the wounded man?" [an earlier impression, dying hard]
"It wasn't the wounded man. . . ."
Filipe: "It seems that instead it's the one who serves that's the neighbor."[72]

The insight came, but the pastor had to guide through an ancient context.

The *present of the text* is the second major context of Scripture. Strangely, it is somehow easier to think of a text as having a past context and perhaps even a future context, than a present context. Yet with the reading of any text, the recounting of any biblical narrative, the description of any Pauline reformulation, the text immediately has a present as well as a past. Markus Barth says that Scripture itself is a "conversation" of various witness and we are invited to participate.[73] The ultimate concern of the writers of the text was a restatement of the original oral tradition with which they wished to have conversation, and that had far-ranging effects. The new textuality, or written nature of the Scripture, has had an unfortunate effect on our way of hearing the words of the Bible: "We treat words primarily as records in need of interpretation, neglecting all too often a rather different hermeneutic, deeply rooted in biblical language that proclaims words as an *act inviting participation"* (emphasis mine].[74]

With every change of setting, of preacher and congregation, whether in the biblical age or in our own times, the new narration of a text takes on new meaning. For example, in the telling of the parables, Werner Kelber says that "no single telling of a parable is quite like any other"; because of their "hermeneutical open-endedness," parables are "peculiarly dependent on oral, social contextuality."[75] So Kelber concludes, contrary to modern aesthetics of literature, that "parable is first and foremost a speech act delivered by a speaker to hearers," and therefore "of all synoptic speech forms, the parable is the least capable of functioning as an autonomous linguistic object." As a result, "parables cry out for interpretation due to their metaphorical quality."[76] These new insights into the orality of the biblical materials, including even the writings of Paul, shed new light on the importance of the present for the context of the kerygma.

At one time, Christian proclamation enjoyed a much greater unity with its tradition than it does today. Again, one of the unfortunate by-products of the work of historical criticism was the division of the Story into *their* world and *our* world. Instead of preaching the biblical story as those who participate in its tradition —and indeed continue it—we tend to study it, preach it, and hear it as *their* story; and it is only with great difficulty heard as our story.[77] We have suffered what Hans Frei calls the "eclipse of biblical narrative."[78] A proper stance relative to the present context of the kerygma is essential for recovering the immediate voice of the gospel.

This stance requires one other consideration. It is not enough to recognize the present context of our sermon text; in the sermon we must also create the present context of the listener. Hermann Diem writes, "The ideal requirement of Christian speech consists of this: ... It must not only talk *about* the listener's situation between the twin possibilities of offense and faith, but must place [the listener] in that situation—and in order to do this it must first create that situation."[79] The present world, the world we share in common context with our listeners, must be so recreated that they will say, "That's the way it is. I have thought about those things myself, but I never knew anyone else thought about them." Not that this reconstruction is simply a psychological or sociological description on the surface of things. Far from it. But when I, as a preacher of the gospel, stand as a living, contemporary being before the world of the text, that text then so illumines my experience as a member of this community that I am able to reflect that illumination into the secret places of other hearts as well.

Yet there is still danger here. We may so individualize the text, so limit it to "our" situation—one that does not extend much beyond the boundaries of our neighborhood provincialism—that we do not truly recreate *"our,"* for *our* situation is the situation of the world, the entire world of today as it is before God. Theologians such as Justo and Catherine Gonzales have reminded us that our larger context is not that of a largely white, well-to-do world. The overwhelmingly larger part of our world is neither white nor well-to-do, but multiracial, poor, and for the most part oppressed. It also contains women who struggle for equality and the old who struggle for dignity. *Indeed, when we speak of "minority groups" we are speaking of ourselves.* These absent ones must also be brought into our comfortable morning worship, with all of their disruptive energies, or we cannot hear the gospel at all. "The absent powerless must be brought into our midst by consciously asking 'how would this biblical text be heard and applied authentically by someone in a radically different political and social setting?' "[80]

For example, the average American has difficulty accepting the fairness of the pay scale in the parable of the workers in the vineyard who are paid the same even though they worked different amounts of time (Matt. 20:1–16). But to migrant workers who have waited all day for a job and who, through no fault of their own, were not hired until late, the parable does not speak of unfairness but rather of the generosity of God. It speaks, in fact, of the same scandalous grace that is God's trumpet call in the New Testament and of the "loving-kindness," the *chesed*, God's continuing mercifulness in the Old Testament. In fact, to correctly participate in the real world of the Bible, the "then" of proclamation, is to correctly participate in the real world of today, the "now" of proclamation.

But this understanding of the biblical world by the contemporary interpreter implies what Juan Luis Segundo terms an "ideological suspicion." That is, we must recognize that no interpreter is without bias, even the great exegetes of the past. We all approach the Bible as human sinners, those who find it hard to shed the cultural robes about us; we prefer our own kind, our own race, our own gender, our own country, our own ways of making money, our own ways of defending our own interests. Struggle as we might, no interpreter is ever completely free from pushing biblical interpretation through the grid of his or her personal culture.

It may not seem so to those of us who are in the majority tradition of mainstream Western theology, but it is so; and the experience of countless Christians of other races, social classes, political ideologies, and even genders around the world tell us ever more loudly that it is so as a continuing reality in their daily experience. As Segundo describes the movement from suspicion to faith:

Firstly, there is our way of experiencing reality, which leads us to ideological suspicion.

Secondly, there is the application of our ideological suspicion to the whole ideological superstructure in general and to theology in particular.

Thirdly, there comes a new way of experiencing theological reality that leads us to exegetical suspicion, that is, to the suspicion that the prevailing interpretation of the Bible has not taken important pieces of data into account.

Fourthly, we have our new hermeneutic, that is, our new way of interpreting the fountainhead of our faith (i.e., Scripture) with the new elements at our disposal.[81]

Like the disciples of old, we must acquire new ears for hearing and new eyes for seeing. Just as the radical religion of Jesus intruded upon the comfortable world of disciples as well as that of scribes and Pharisees, so the ever-revolutionary gospel must intrude upon the comfortable world of today's preachers and listeners. That is the present context the kerygma demands.

The future context of preaching extends the promise of the past and the promise of the present into the promise of the future. The God who *has* delivered and *is* delivering, *will* deliver. The narrating of the Old Testament saga in Israel was not so much intended as a rehearsal of a dead past but as a prologue to a living future. Likewise, the New Testament trumpets the hope of Jesus Christ, "who is and who was and who is to come, the Almighty" (Rev. 1:8). The ultimate paradigm of the future hope of the gospel is the resurrection in the event of Jesus Christ. The kerygmatic story is not locked up in the past; the resurrection announces that it is open to the future.

The rabbis noticed in the Genesis account of creation that each day had a morning and an evening except the sabbath, which had no evening. So they announced in a beautiful parable that God's sabbath had not ended and was therefore open even today. Likewise, the writer of Hebrews tells us that "an offer of God's rest" remains open even unto us (Heb. 4).

A fundamental duty of preaching, then, is to bring about an awakening to promise, to the call and claim of God upon the future as well as the past, an awakening of what Ricoeur calls "the imagination of the possible."[82] The faithful God who delivered Israel and who raised Jesus Christ from the dead is the God of the possibilities of our worlds, both private and public, both personal and corporate. We cannot end any preaching of the gospel with the facts of the past or the demands of the present; every sermon must end with the future of the promise and the promise of the future. As Kierkegaard said, "We must make room for God to come."[83]

In summary, the *past, present, and future contexts* of the kerygma itself demand full participation in our preaching. As preachers we are to uncover the abiding promise in every historical witness, a promise that brings "the dawning of the future" into our present. The goal of all our historical exegesis will then consist not only in illuminating the "situation" of a text but much more in seeking the "horizon of a text in its promise-history."[84] That will enable us to answer the most important question for preaching: not how *can* I preach this text, but why *must* I preach this text?

The promise of God that was seen by Israel in its historical experiences, and those promises of God in the life of Christ and the experiences of the early church now press their claims and their blessing on us. The eschatological promise of this future was opened through the experience of the resurrection of Jesus and, as Moltmann says, that promise requires nothing less than its proclamation through preaching and mission:

For a sermon does not refer to the dead past, but rather it proclaims the future which has been opened and made certain through the coming of Jesus Christ. The faith which this preaching creates is not a historic certification but a confirmation of the promise which is present in these events and it is likewise a judgment which proclaims that every entity will be overthrown which does not yet correspond to the promise. . . . Even as the New Testament texts, so also the sermon must contain both: gospel *(euangelion)* and promise *(epangelia)*. Without the gospel from the event of Jesus Christ, the promise loses its character of certainty. Without the promise, the gospel loses its character of hope. . . . The more we are successful at saying both together—in narrating the remembered history so that with its telling the future is proclaimed, and in proclaiming the future by remembering the event of the resurrection—the better the sermon is. History and proclamation converge in this promise-history, for that which makes both text and sermon necessary lies in the promise. In it is held the experience of reality as history."[85]

But how can preaching perform this high task given it by the kerygma? Then, more specifically, we shall have to answer how an individual sermon can be structured to unite the past, present, and future of the promise and thus fulfill itself as preaching.

13. Worldly Preaching: From This-World to Real-World

We have now returned to the point from which we began. We have raised the question of the meaningfulness of narrative or story for Christian proclamation. We have briefly traced its influence upon contemporary Christian thinking and noted objections to its dominance as a preaching method. We have noted areas of disagreement among homileticians and we have noted areas of mutual concession and concord. We have taken a clue from the concept of "context" and expanded it to suggest that contextual preaching might offer a more inclusive framework for kerygmatic preaching than narrative or story, which may be included methodologically within it.

I would like to examine next a threefold movement that, I believe, can maximize the benefits of narrative insight for preaching and direct us toward a narrativelike form for the sermon. (We are again indebted to Paul Ricoeur and his work on "the language of faith" for the theories that underlie the first two of our movements.)[1] First, there must be a movement toward the kerygma of the text; second, there must be a movement away from the kerygma of our world; third, there must be a return to our world with the kerygma of the gospel, through what I will choose to call "worldly preaching," by which these two worlds are made one. Finally, when we have understood the meaning of "worldly preaching" for proclamation, we must turn to the implications of this approach for the shape of the sermon itself.

FROM THIS-WORLD TO REAL-WORLD

THE MOVEMENT TOWARD THE TEXT

As we have already seen, each of us stands at a considerable distance from the ancient biblical text. Its language is foreign to us. More especially, its thought world and culture are foreign to us, and to many its questions and concerns are likewise foreign. How may we move toward this world? How can we overcome the distance of ourselves and our hearers from the kerygma of the Scripture?

Ricoeur suggests an often-quoted triple movement toward the text: first, we approach it with an initial naiveté, allowing its story to stimulate all our senses and responses; second, we approach it with a critical examination of its own cultural expressions, discerning the true scandal of the text from the false scandal of its ancient world view; third, we reapproach the text in a second naiveté, wherein we allow the world of the text to address us with its narrative and present us with its claims and promises.[2]

But why is our world at such a distance from the biblical text? Is it merely a matter of the terminology of its ancient worldview, of its four-cornered earth and its "seven-dayed" creation? No, the alienation is much deeper than that. We have forgotten the radical questions conveyed in the event of Jesus Christ. At the same time, we in our world are convinced of the rationality of all levels of reality. We believe that the world and all that is in it are objects susceptible of being explained and that we have become autonomous agents of our own history. We might call this a belief in the *universally explainable.*

A second belief accompanies the first, which further explains our distance from the biblical kerygma. Ricoeur terms it a belief in the *"universally available."*[3] Through technology, everything has become available to us, from the world of things to the world of human possibilities. Only immortality escapes us, and we attempt to evade the reality of death by every deception possible. We "use" the world, and for that matter persons in the world as well.

Our technology extends beyond the scientific; it includes our management and even manipulation of the sociological and the psychological.

The result of all this is a "hollowness of our existence," a kind of "existential senselessness," a life on the surface of things. "It is not, therefore, *against* this given of culture, but in its very heart that we have to rediscover the question of 'to be lost' or 'to be saved.' "[4] It is the duty of the sermon, through the preacher's understanding of the world of the text and his or her interpretation of the kerygmatic event, to make a world available to the hearers, even the world of the new potential of the gospel.

THE MOVEMENT AWAY FROM THE WORLD

Because of the distance of our world from the text, it then becomes necessary for a *disorientation* to occur as well as an orientation. We must call in question this process of secularization that separates us from the values of the kerygma itself. Ricoeur suggests three possible directions as a means for calling into question the presuppositions of the modern mind.[5]

First, a description of human existence, of the human condition, may help distance us from the conventional wisdom of our age. We must illuminate the difference between our world's mastery of objective knowledge and its mastery of "the condition of existing."[6] The more we yield ourselves to the deceit of the scientific and the technological as adequate means of existence, the more the true nature of existence hides itself from us. Everything that awakens consideration of our "birth-death-existence-decision-communication with others"[7] calls into question the smug certitude of our culture.

At this point, however, a word of warning is in order. We must not lapse into the fallacy of challenging people only at the boundaries of their experience—life-and-death threats to their existence —with religion's only domain as the mysterious beyond. We must take seriously Bonhoeffer's warning that that is unworthy of the Christian message and in fact falsifies it. That is, it seems to me, exactly our temptation when science and technology claim the world for themselves. But we must not confront men and women at the point of their weakness but, indeed, at the very point of their strength. When the church has preyed on the fears of the world, the world may have yielded, but eventually it hated the church, not loved it. We must seek to press the claims of the gospel upon our highest and our best selves, not merely on our lowest and our worst. Grace must continue to be operative even in the illumination of the emptiness of secular life; the word of reconciliation must always speak louder than the word of judgment. The positive image of the life of Jesus Christ among us shows far more the distance between our existence and true life than all of the negative boundary threats we can imagine.

Second, everything that enlarges our vision of the world may also increase this distance. All of us are far more parochial than we acknowledge. Our worlds generally do not extend much beyond the boundaries of our neighborhoods. We love our families, our friends, our clubs, our way of making money, our country, our race. Whatever makes me more aware of the others in my world, those who struggle with limitations caused by their gender or by their race or by their poverty or by their age or by their powerlessness, helps open me up to another world. The inclusiveness of the love of God as manifested in Israel and in the life of Jesus deconstructs a part of my world, even as it reconstructs the possibility of another world. Indeed, I must be led to see that it is not really *my* world, but *our* world; therefore radical individualism in religion must give way to a larger gospel that will change economic, cultural, and political structures as well as personal attitudes. We must challenge the church "to pursue a historical adventure in a humanity that seeks to become whole."[8]

Third, others can be opened to the possibilities of faith if we address them in kerygmatic language. Our world speaks essentially in three languages: ordinary language, scientific language, and technological language. Ordinary language is the language of the everyday event. Scientific language is language that objectifies and describes. Technological language is use-language, language that consumes and disposes of. This latter language is the language of availability, including some uses of psychological and sociological language.

But preaching must speak in yet a fourth language: kerygmatic language, the language of promise. This language is the language of *being,* which in contrast to scientific language *understands* and in contrast to technological language *awakens possibilities.* [9]

In the declaring of the kerygma there is indissoluably bound the message of hope: the narrating of the deliverance of the children of Israel announces also the possibility of deliverance from all bondage; the eschatological announcement of the resurrection of Jesus opens the possibility of a future for all humankind. To hear this language is to stand before a world of possibilities, to partake of a truer existence, to imagine a higher order.

In these three strategies, therefore, there is the possibility of gaining distance from the false kerygma of This-World, a true "City of Destruction," as in Bunyan's metaphor. And every movement away from This-World is a movement toward Real-World, the world envisioned and proclaimed by the Suffering Servant, the One for Others, the Christ of God.

THE RETURN WITH WORLDLY PREACHING

A final movement is necessary in the strategy of contextual preaching. We have moved toward the kerygma of Scripture; we have moved away from the kerygma of the world; we must then return to our world with the kerygma of the gospel.

Certain uses of historical criticism brought about the unfortunate division of "their" (biblical) world and "our" (contemporary) world—an interruption that caused us to stop preaching as those *within* the Tradition and to begin preaching as ones looking *at* the text, even as ones outside the Tradition. But a far worse development had already taken place. The world was divided into "sacred" and "secular," and preaching quickly aligned itself one way or the other. Paul's concept of "worldliness"—the world insofar as it did not conform to the will of God—was soon transformed into a negation of the physical, so that everything "worldly" must be avoided. (Money, however, somehow seemed to be excluded from the ban.) "Sacred" was then increasingly institutionalized, particularly within the precincts of the church, so that preaching beat a hasty retreat from the world, pausing only occasionally in its flight to fire a few quick shots over its shoulder at what it perceived to be the enemy.

That was one direction preaching took. But others, recognizing that this cloistered view of life limited preaching's appeal to only the hardiest pilgrims, soon found other routes of march. To avoid the loss of power by this retreat into the "sacred," they surrendered the gospel to the world. By promising either physical or psychological gifts to their followers as a result of faithfulness—particularly faithfulness to their institutions—religion thus became merely a "sacred" means to a secular end.

Both "sacred" and "secular" ploys in preaching, however, lose the gospel and surrender the world. We must now see how the languages of preaching can either promote this division or restore the unity of Word and world. These languages may be described as it-preaching, I-preaching, and we-preaching.

It-preaching. Under the stress of tension between the Word and the world, much of preaching moved toward "it-language." Impressed by the gains of philosophy and science, with their corresponding mastery of a world once ruled by religion, preaching ceased from its human declaring of the Story and lapsed into it-language. This was the language of abstraction, of objectivism, of a deductive rationalism. Like science, this theology ("science of God") abstracted faith until the very lifeblood had gone from it. For some, this language gave preaching a cool detachment, an "objective" distance that was appealing; for others, it gave preaching a hot-blooded, argumentative, proof-text mentality that was equally appealing. In either case, Scripture became an object, not a subject, a legal brief, not a letter of love. In both cases these wielders of the objectified gospel regained power in the world, the power of dogma and doctrine, the power of legalism and law, the power of punishment and praise.

This it-preaching is a clear case of proclamation adopting scientific language to maintain the place of religion in the world.

I-preaching. On the other side, an equally fierce struggle was going on. "I-preaching" began to assert itself. This preaching rejected the abstraction of the gospel and insisted instead on the interiorization of the gospel. Rather than the language of science, I-preaching adopted the language of psychology. Faith became private territory. And the more the text was historicized and atomized by "scientific" preaching, the more it became spiritualized and interiorized by psychological preaching.

Yet this preaching, seemingly so personal and even so "spiritual," is only the religious equivalent of technological language. For this preaching also emphasizes acquisition, the acquisition of psychological benefits and personal adjustment. "Possibility thinking" is pure technological language, for it does not speak of the possibilities *for a world* when the children of God act like children of God and transform This-World, that God's will might be done on earth as well as in heaven. Rather, it clearly speaks of possibilities *for the individual* from This-World and in This-World, of personal success and technological mastery of the "universally available"—only now the technological language has a religious accent. Even so, it is still involved with consumption, use, and disposal.

Both it-preaching and I-preaching are exclusionary. It-preaching is obsessed with rules, laws, facts, ideas. Persons are buried beneath the system. I-preaching is also exclusionary; it plays to the needs of the cult, with little reference to the larger world. Here creation is buried beneath the ego of the individual.

It-preaching is preoccupied with structure, with "points" and outlines. I-preaching is preoccupied with anecdote, with triumphal stories of successful businesses and well-adjusted families. Instead of going out into "Jerusalem, Judea, and the uttermost parts of the earth," the map of I-preaching's terrain is limited to the interior of the psyche.

We-preaching. Both I-preaching and it-preaching are extensions of the first-century understandings of "Word" as understood by Greek Stoicism and Jewish rabbinicism. The Stoics, if you will remember, saw the word as "truth-for-me"—I-language; the rabbis saw it as the eternal Law—it-language. Both of these concepts were contradicted by the prologue to John's Gospel. There *Word takes on flesh and dwells among us—"we-language":* thus our concept of *incarnational preaching,* Word that keeps on taking on flesh even in the form of human words in the proclamation of the gospel.

The liberating language for preaching, then, is *we-preaching,* preaching that partakes fully of the entire context of the kerygma. "I" stands at one end of an arc; "it" stands at the other end. At the top of the arc, in the center between the two, stands "we." "It" recognizes objects/facts; "I" recognizes feelings/individuals; "we" recognizes the complete human experience under God. We-preaching stands resolutely in the *past* of the faith, the Tradition of the faith; it embraces the *present* reality of life and of faith; and it reaches into the eschatological *future* of faith to claim its promise and be claimed by it.

We-preaching is inclusive preaching. Its world extends geographically to countries other than its own; its world extends sociologically to races and classes other than its own. Because of its inclusive faith it must announce the claims of Christ upon every structure that does not honor those claims of equity and justice; because of its inclusive grace it must announce the forgiving, reconciling love of God for all estranged from God and from one another.

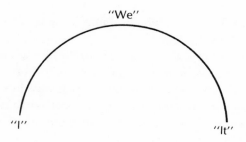

This is *theological preaching,* preaching that encompasses the dimensions of world and person but that preeminently takes its cues from the nature of God. It shapes its proclamation according to the shape of the kerygma, not according to any foundational principles of psychology or rhetoric. It permits whatever form will permit the kerygma to be heard. It only prohibits what would prevent the kerygma from being heard.

This is truly *worldly preaching:* not that it embraces secularity, but that it confronts *the world as it is* with the *gospel as it is.* It is worldly preaching because it is truly realistic preaching, true to the nature of creation and true to the nature of humanity. It is worldly preaching because it calls the world to be what it should be before God, and it refuses to allow the world to make another religion out of itself. It is worldly preaching, most of all, because it refuses to acknowledge two worlds, the world of the "secular" and the world of the "sacred." It proclaims one world—Real-World—the world of our Lord and its Savior, Jesus Christ. It is worldly preaching because, in Bonhoeffer's terms, it "places the church again in the center of the village"—not in the old sense of the ecclesiastical domination of society, but in the sense of the new community of God extending its inclusiveness to the whole world. And that is not only "worldly" preaching—that is preaching.

THE NARRATIVE SUGGESTION AND THE SERMON

But we have still to translate this vision of preaching into a sermon. Unless the "narrative suggestion" moves beyond generalized insight into specific shape, its real value for preaching is questionable. What are the practical implications of this approach for the form of the sermon?

To seek to answer this question, I would like to approach the subject in two ways: first, by a personal reflection on my own experience with this kind of contextual/narrativelike preaching; and second, by a summation of principles I believe to be useful for this kind of sermon from my own thinking and that of others who have written on this subject.

My first explorations into this field began when I attempted to analyze "nontypical" sermons. Certain sermons by Dietrich Bonhoeffer, Reinhold Niebuhr, some by Harry Emerson Fosdick, the later sermons of Paul Scherer, and particularly the almost expressionistic sermons of G. A. Studdert Kennedy seemed to defy the laws of homiletics as the standard texts described them. Others with whom I discussed these sermons regarded them as triumphs of talent over theory or, in the case of Fosdick, the popularity of a new psychology-oriented method of problem solving through preaching.

My own examination of these sermons suggested otherwise. I noticed several things in common among them, varying of course from sermon to sermon but with enough consistency to suggest a pattern.

First, they seemed to follow a structure I could only describe as "knotting the problem" (later I probably would have used other terminology, but at the time that was how I saw it). They began by raising a question of human existence, posing it in a way that one could scarcely imagine it being done better by anyone, showing a dilemma so profound that the fiercest critic of Christianity could not have said it better. And they added to their acute observation of the contemporary world an equally acute theological perspective, one that deepened the significance of the matter until at times it seemed scarcely bearable, much less solvable.

Then, at the moment at which all seemed darkest, they introduced the tiniest glimmer of light. Perhaps it would be, at first, an insight from the best of humanity; or it might be the faintest glimmer of hope from an ancient and forgotten lore, even the tradition of the Christian faith. But only a glimmer, nothing more: no flooding searchlight of truth, no blinding illumination from above of the scarred landscape of the earth; no triumphant shout of deliverance for beleagered humankind. Only a glimmer, nothing more.

Then that glimmer itself would be questioned, closely examined, covered, at times, with every objecting hand possible. Nonetheless, it continued to flicker in the darkness, until finally its faint light turned into a gleam of hope, its rays suddenly catching one facet of life now here, then there, until at last the radiance of that light extended over the troubled plain of our existence. And if these sermons did not provide complete solutions for every problem, there was in them the sense of a vast and overarching hope, a promise that invaded even our history. There were times, particularly when I listened to the sermons of Fosdick, when I could imagine no solution to the human dilemma described, and when the gospel's resolution was described, I could not imagine why I had been so concerned in the first place.

I also discovered a second characteristic in common among these sermons. *Each of them, in its own different way, moved back and forth between an ancient world and this modern one,* addressing our world with their questions and presenting our questions before their world. Again, there were times—particularly in the sermons of Bonhoeffer— when I would not know if I were standing there with Gideon in a dead world suddenly come to life or whether he was standing with me in the midst of my existence and my struggles. These studies were enlightening and suggestive, but it would be much later before I understood, I believe, the internal nature of this preaching.

My second personal experience with contextual preaching came after reading some of the earliest writing on narrative and preaching. Although I appreciated these theories, I still remained perplexed about their meaning for the practice of the sermon. By that time I had begun what became a seven-year return to the pastorate, and so I decided to commit myself to narrative preaching— whatever that meant—for one year. I put myself into texts that lent themselves to narrative, and I began a series entitled, "From the Advent to the Ascension."

My experience with those sermons was so favorable that I continued into the book of Acts, something I had never intended and certainly would not have anticipated with a great deal of relish, since I consider Acts rather more difficult preaching terrain. My experience there again was so profitable that later I began an ambitious series in the Old Testament, this one entitled "From the Patriarchs to the Prophets" (there was obviously a great deal of eschatological hope in undertaking that one!). As it turned out, I got as far as Solomon—whatever that says to you—and then went off to serve as president of the International Baptist Seminary in Ruschlikon/Zurich, Switzerland. What had begun as a one-year experiment had turned into a four-year adventure.

What I offer next, then, as practical suggestions for developing contextual sermons comes from this personal experience with narrative preaching, my reflection on the writings of others in the field, and the subsequent analysis of sermons of those who advocate some form of narrative/story/contextual sermon.

Remember that plot always involves theme, and theme always involves plot. Stories without themes are wandering stars, and themes without plots are motionless structures. Strictly speaking, there cannot be a plot, or a story, without a theme:

A story, too, must be more than just an enumeration of events in serial order; it must organize them into an intelligible whole, of a sort such that we can always ask what is the "thought" of this story. *In short, emplotment is the operation that draws a configuration out of a simple succession* [emphasis mine].

Furthermore, emplotment brings together factors as heterogeneous as agents, goals, means, interactions, circumstances, unexpected results. . . . This configurational arrangement transforms the succession of events into one meaningful whole which is the correlate of the act of assembling the events together and which makes the story followable. Thanks to this reflective act, *the entire plot can be translated into one "thought" which is nothing other than its "point" or "theme"* [emphasis mine].[10]

Ricoeur thus indicates the thematic nature of any story. Of course themes can be pursued in other, more analytical ways. For the most part, however, I believe the kerygma is best served and communication is best received when the sermon material is organized according to the "logic of narrative," which I understand to be more descriptive than analytic.

Nonetheless, even though this preaching is largely descriptive, that does not mean that it cannot powerfully affect those who hear it. Robert Coles, Harvard professor and child psychiatrist, says of his landmark work in the study of children:

I am not a survey social scientist. I claim no definitive conclusions about what any "group" feels or thinks. . . . One can only insist on being as tentative as possible, claiming only impressions, observations, thoughts, reflections, surmizes, speculations, and in the end, a *"way of seeing."* . . . In this study I aim essentially to evoke, to suggest rather than to pursue a more cognitive approach or a psychopathological orientation."[11]

Yet Coles's work has been far more powerful in its influence than many surveys and quantitative analyses.

One must realize that highly analytical and therefore "objective" preaching is in radical discontinuity with the kerygma. Even the most abstract Pauline formulations participate in the Story more than the abstracted and dessicated sermons of neoscholasticism. Again, this does not mean than any sort of deduction in the sermon form is a violation of true preaching. To the contrary, there may be times, places, and situations when such an analysis, even such an argument, may be appropriate. Nevertheless, this should not be the norm for Christian preaching. Whether in the Gospels or the Epistles, human beings are working within a human situation and because of that we must seek to locate our sermons within the narrative of life.

The question is, how is this to be done? Just as there is no one form for the sermon, so there is no one prescription for arriving at a sermon that truly proclaims the gospel. No doubt somewhere in the Christian tradition a sermon could be found that does everything "wrong" and yet does everything brilliantly "right." (However, when Spurgeon was once attacked for criticizing the methods of certain evangelists, being told that "they do much good," he replied, "Only the gospel which they preach does much good; the rest does much harm.") The principles that follow may help to make more specific an understanding of sermons structured according to our "narrative logic."

Limit the focus of the sermon. This suggestion follows the *principle of contraction.* No story talks about everything; no novel covers heaven and earth. You also cannot preach on everything, not even on all the "everything" in the text. Bonhoeffer says that each text does have a center of understanding, but that any sermon is true to that text so long as it preaches accurately from any segment of the circle about that center. If this were not true, there could not be multiple sermons preached from the same text, each bearing true witness to the text.

But I would add to that observation that this "segment" of the circle then becomes the center of the focus of the text; the rest of the circle provides background and context for the sermon. *Subordination* is a great art in preaching. Do not march all characters to center stage; do not have everyone speaking at once; do not try to explain every historical nuance of every phrase in the text, and certainly not of all the texts suggested in the lectionary.

We must see *something,* not everything. *We must learn to work larger on a smaller canvas.* Our preaching should not be so global. (By that I do not mean that it should not have the larger focus of the world beyond our neighborhood, only that its inventory of ideas should be limited.) This is one of the virtues of narrative/story sermons and generally the trouble with thematic sermons, that try to analyze truth comprehensively with subpoints or "sure steps to success."

The contextual sermon should present a limited scene, one manageable within the scope of sermon time, held together as a manageable rhetorical unit by the biblical depiction of the event, or person, or situation. Likewise, if proceeding from contemporary life, there must also be a limited focus, such as "images of prototypal situations," as Richard Lischer terms them—single, striking incidents—as used to great advantage by Frederick Buechner.[12] These are not "stories," narratives as such, but the explication of a single incident from contemporary experience woven into the larger context of the gospel and life.

Robert Coles has done monumental work on the life of children in contemporary society by listening to the individual and narrating the telling incident. Instead of relying on studies that survey thousands of children, Coles relies on "clinical field studies" of individual children, which "do more than risk the subjective; they embrace it." By going for these smaller truths, Coles has revealed larger, more striking truths than those of many surveys. He does so by contributing "those details, those anecdotes, those revealing incidents, those puzzling, confusing moments which can offer their own instruction to us—the muffled ring of the small truth which brings us closer to some of life's ironies and ambiguities."[13] A limited focus, in that sense, does not limit understanding—it extends it.

Seek insight into a world. Remember that God intended only one world, not two (our/their world, sacred/secular world), Real-World, as intended in creation for persons and creatures; indeed, "the whole of creation has been groaning together," as it "waits with eager longing for the revealing of the children of God" (Rom. 8:22, 19). Seek insight into that world from both the past and the present. *From the past,* ask, "Where does God encounter the human situation in this text?" That is the intersection of the Story with the world. Ask, "Where is the promise in this episode of the Story? Where is the claim of the gospel upon us?" Or, if initially struck by some contemporary incident, by some note of guilt or grace *in the present human experience,* seek its place within the Story. Ask, "Where is the hand of God revealed at work today?" Know that God, who was active in the past Story, in such pain or in such beauty then, is also active in our world through the Spirit, writing new episodes to the old Story.

This kind of insight into our world requires "in-seeing." In a fascinating study, the monks of New Skete, New York, have written of their life's work in caring for and training dogs, mostly the great German shepherds. At the beginning of the training, each monk is assigned one dog, and that dog sits beside him when he eats, goes with him in training through the day, and sleeps beside his bed at night. The monks have learned that there is a difference between having "oversight" of an animal and having "insight" into the animal. (The term "in-seeing" was adopted from the writings of Rainer Maria Rilke, where he contrasts "Einsicht" and "Durchsicht.")[14] They try to practice "in-seeing," seeing the world through the eyes of another. They believe that no one can truly understand an animal or train it unless care and love have enabled that person, at least to some degree, to see the world through the eyes of the animal, to see the frustrations and demands of life as the animal sees them.[15]

We must practice "in-seeing" also before observation of our contemporary world will yield insight for preaching. We must seek to "sit where they sit," to see through the eyes of the other, to take our place among the oppressed—not as sympathetic, paternalistic "understanders" of the less fortunate, but those who know themselves to be oppressors who are also the oppressed. Or, in studying the Bible, we must seek to hear the text as it was preached (and they all were preached, either in their early oral or later written form), to hear with the ears of the first congregations to whom these messages were addressed.

This leads to a word of caution: in preaching narrative texts, the preacher needs to avoid psychologizing the text through its characters or even through attempting to discern the intentionality of the writer of the text. Both of these searches lead to blind alleys. Contemporary writers as well have warned against attempting to read multileveled symbolic meanings into texts by discerning some hidden, allegorical meaning on the part of the writer. William Golding, author of the contemporary classic *Lord of the Flies,* became repeatedly angry when so many mystical meanings were thrust upon his text. He said that he wrote the work following World War II when it became apparent to him how cruel human beings could be to one another, and that was the source of his story —period. When Georgia O'Keefe was questioned about the symbolism hidden in her pictures, she said (when she said anything!), "I paint what I see." Earlier, Tennyson was questioned about his enigmatic poetic expression, "God made himself an awful rose of dawn." Some interpreters believed that expression referred to hope, others to judgment. When Tennyson was finally asked, he said "the power to compose such concentrated forms of expression is other than that of interpreting them." And with that enigmatic statement, he left his poem wrapped in enigmatic beauty.

We must look at the world of the text, not at the imagined psychology of an author, for our insight. It is this "in-seeing" through the experiences of others, both past and present, that yields insight for the sermon, the end toward which the sermon will eventually move. And as we allow ourselves to be led deeper into both the past event and the present experience, the scattered and meaningless incidents of This-World become united as insight into Real-World.

Allow theological reflection to unite the "then" of the gospel with the "now" of experience. This suggestion follows the principle of *abstraction.* [16] Abstraction is the process by which some larger concept is derived from specific incidences. In this sense, all theological reflection is based upon abstraction. The theological writings of Paul, for example, are reflections abstracted from more specific observations of the ways of God among the people of Israel and in the early church. These condensed statements contain a world, a world of past, present, and future experience; they offer a new horizon of promises and claims.

Sermon "themes" or "points" are abstractions, too, from reflection on biblical or contemporary events. The problem with the older, more argumentative sermon forms was not that they contained "points" but that the whole sermon was virtually an abstraction that, by its endless dividing and subdividing of ideas, moved farther and farther away from the determining events of Story.

For our purposes, *we will look for the promises or claims of the narrative of our text, which will serve as the directing insight or theme* of the sermon. Or, if our text is already a theological insight by Paul or the writer of Hebrews, we will look for *the context of the situation that produced it.* That will provide us with the setting, characters, and plot incidents necessary for structuring our sermon according to "narrative logic."

We then *begin with the end:* this insight into the larger world of the gospel becomes the end of the sermon, its goal or intent, its theme. This end of exegesis, both biblical and contemporary, becomes the beginning place of the sermon. All else, all movement within the sermon, all means employed—whether descriptive narrative or "points" of theological insight—are for the purpose of making this Real-World with its Word available to the congregation.

When we interpret the text in this way, it is important that listeners be invited to go along with us on the journey. Eduard Schweizer, speaking of parables, writes that "the preacher comes totally to the encounter with the hearer; he penetrates his world; he invites him to go with him, step by step, up to that point at which the parable invites the hearer to encount the reality of God. . . . The hearer [must] walk with the one who speaks and follow him in order to have access to the meaning, while objective listening would not lead to real understanding."[17]

If the congregation journeys along with us through this world, it may well be that they arrive at a different word or insight than ours. In fact, to some degree it must be a different word from ours, since their lives intersect with the gospel in their own unique ways. Nevertheless, this does not mean that their insights must be the opposite of our own, but certainly they will be modified by their own experience of the journey. Nor does this mean that the preacher should proceed without offering any insight. Every story is an interpretation, a selection of events by contraction and an explication of events by abstraction. To proclaim is to run the risk of interpretation: we must remember that we may guide on this journey, but in the long run only the Spirit of God can direct.

Locate reflection within the flow of narration. An important clue for some correspondence between older, more propositional, ideational sermons and more recent insights may be found in the observations of Don Wardlaw regarding contextual sermons. In contrast to the *traditional* discursive sermon organized predominantly in the reflective mode with "points," these sermons "major in narrative material, featuring scenes or clusters of scenes of things that happen to human beings. . . . Contextual sermon shapes do not so much banish reflection as they *relocate pondering within the flow of narration*" [emphasis mine]. Furthermore, this approach sets up "pauses for reflection amid the flow of narration" and thereby avoids the problems of noninterpreted narrative."[18]

This is, I believe, a significant insight. If pictured, traditional and contextual sermon forms might appear as in the accompanying diagram.

Traditional   Contextual

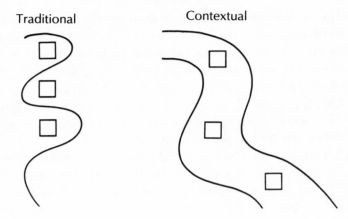

The difference in the two approaches should be clear. The traditional sermon form represents blocks of ideas, arguments, or propositions separated only by a thin trickle of illustrative material. *The contextual sermon is the flow or process of life, as understood from the biblical text and contemporary experience, with whatever theological reflection or sermon "ideas" are called for embedded in the flow itself.*

Though, as we have said, there will be exceptions, it is generally better to proceed descriptively rather than analytically. Rather than carving out granite blocks of "eternal principles" from the Bible as stepping-stones to truth, with a tiny trickle of experience flowing around and between them as illustrations, we do better to discover such stepping-stones within the larger river of experience. Speak of human life, life as those of us in the Tradition have experienced it both then and now. Let this story of life flow back and forth from the text to the contemporary, always within the banks of one river (the directing promise, claim, or "theme"). Floodplain sermons are usually as shallow as they are broad. Perhaps the flow of the river will only bring you to its destination at the end, at its conclusion; perhaps you will find stepping-stones, smaller insights that lead to a larger insight along the way.

I have analyzed a great many sermons of practitioners both classical and contemporary of this form of preaching. Though infinite in their variety of arrangements, some things remain constant. These sermons are built out of *historical* narrative/reflection and *contemporary* narrative/reflection. Historical narrative yields to historical reflection; contemporary narrative yields to contemporary reflection. Either may precede, either may follow. The one may alternate with the other throughout the sermon. But there is always unity and movement: unity of story or theme, movement through unfolding of meaning.

In my own experience, I have found three narrativelike structures to be most useful: narrative-only, initial narrative, and alternating narrative forms. *Narrative-only* forms were the least used in my four-year experience with narrative. Few texts seemed to contain sufficient narrative context to sustain a sermon without periods of theological reflection. And, to be honest, even those few that did required a certain expansion of the story for interpretive purposes. I do not feel comfortable inventing dialogue for biblical figures or describing scenes that are purely imaginative. If the added material is historically accurate (as to places, customs, characters), certainly a minimal expansion is acceptable. Within these limits, however, I found few texts that yielded narrative-only forms.

Initial narrative and *alternating narrative* are different cases. The first follows narrative with insight, the second alternates the two throughout the sermon. Either fits most texts in some fashion, but alternating narrative definitely requires more agility and smooth transitioning between narrative and insight. This becomes even more complex, as in the hands of the most skilled practitioners, where a *contemporary narrative* is alternated with a *biblical narrative*. (The fine sermons in *Preaching Biblically,* edited by Don Wardlaw, show several such examples.)

I would suggest, for those just beginning such forms, following a simple textual narrative with theological insights/contemporary understanding. And this form does not have to violate the best insights of inductive preaching theories, either. The reflective portion of the sermon should be as open and participatory as the narrative portion, utilizing rhetorical questions, dialogical reflections, "overheard" pondering. Nevertheless, our purpose is not to fit one preaching theory or another, but to declare the Good News so that it is heard. These methods may help in that.

Narrate honestly. At this point I feel I must say something regarding honesty in narrative. Life is not always neat, happy, or satisfying; some of it is disturbing, messy, and miserable. The stories from the Bible do not invariably present fresh-faced heroes and heroines like those in the world of TV, where we are secure in knowing that right always triumphs, the boy gets the girl, and our violence overcomes their violence just before the last commercial. The Bible is too honest for that. Nor does all true Christian preaching in the contemporary always lead to cheerful adjustment and positive thinking.

That, in Paul's language, is the thinking of the world. We do not need all of that to be true for God to be true. God is not so weak and impotent, and neither are we. We can hear the truth about our mortality and still believe that God is for us, come what will.

Part of our desire for such beautiful, happy coherance in the story stems from our misunderstanding of human life itself. Heinrich von Kleist, author of some of the finest German novellas, says through one of his characters, "We are all like packages on a moving van. We bump up against one another, we may even occasionally read one another's labels, but we rarely get to see the contents." Albert Camus says that we suffer from "nostalgia for the life of others. This is because seen from the outside, another's life forms a unit, whereas ours, seen from the inside, seems broken up. We are still chasing after an illusion of unity."[19] Preaching is not allowed such an illusion.

It was not in the wilderness wanderings that God was most remote from the Hebrews—the prophets remember that period as a time of intimacy with God and great growth for the child Israel. It was in the successful cities and the spacious Temple courts that Israel lost its vision of God. Telling the truth as it is does not present nearly so much a danger to the church as telling the truth as we would like it to be. If we falsify the Story, either in the past or in the present, we preach, as Paul said, "another gospel," which is no gospel (Gal. 1:6–7).

One of the hallmarks of biblical narrative is its honesty, especially in comparison with other classical literature. Eric Auerbach speaks on the strikingly realistic and antiheroic nature of the biblical narrative (he cites especially the accounts of Peter's denial).[20] And Robert McAfee Brown, commenting on the descriptive beauty of South Africa in Alan Paton's *Ah, But Your Land Is Beautiful,*[21] asks, "A beautiful book about ugliness, how can that be?" and answers, "I think Paton is saved in large part by his characters— characters who are not only creations of his heart and soul . . . but are also people he has really known. . . ."[22] The honesty of the gospel demands the honesty of preaching, where the nobility and ugliness of life alike are portrayed. Without that honesty, there is no true preaching. God *as God is* must come to humanity *as humanity is* in this day *as this day is.* Or else we preach a false god to a deceived person in an unreal day.

Preach from within the Tradition. There may be no more important word than this for our contemporary preaching. Preaching today must not stand *outside* of the ancient word, looking at it with cool, objective detachment, or stirring around in its dead ashes to see if underneath there yet might be a spark of life. We must hear the *preaching* of the text before we ourselves preach it. We must claim it, own it, allow it to own us.

Preachers who sound like semibored professors of religious studies cannot be proclaimers of the gospel. Of course this does not mean that we lose our objective facilities, that we only approach the text in "initial naiveté," that we do not know the complications and dilemmas of the text even better than "objective" outsiders. But we must position ourselves as one with the community: as one with the community of the past, in their struggles to see the truth and proclaim it, as one with the community of the present, in their struggles to live the gospel in this time and place, and even as one with the community of the future, in their struggles to fulfill the future opened in Jesus Christ.

I believe this to be much of the strength of black preaching, this preaching from within the Tradition, and the secret of much of the impressive power of that preaching even when specifically heard by the white community alone.[23] But is this not the secret of all true preaching? Can any preaching succeed that does not use every means to lead the congregation to participate imaginatively in the past events of faith? Can any preaching lead to transformation that does not preach as one within the community to whom it preaches? Can any preaching open a future for the gospel that does not itself believe the promise of that future and claim it as a present reality through Jesus Christ? If we do not preach from within the Tradition, no "plotting," no "narrative logic," no "telling a story" will save us.

Of course it is "I" who approaches the sermon; it is "I" who interprets the text; it is "I" who reflects on the text. I do approach the preaching task as an "I," but as a self-aware one. I must be aware of my own cultural bias and also aware of that bias in all interpreters of the Story, both past and present. But that encourages me all the more to be a part of the larger community of faith, which includes not only "me and mine," but others whose experience is quite different from my own. I do not reject community, therefore, on that basis; I acknowledge my place within it and seek to be taught from it.

This is the ultimate value of "worldly preaching": by embracing a wider context in its understanding, such preaching holds the miraculous hope of embracing a wider community in its promise.

IV. SAYING THE SERMON

14. Jesus as Communicator

If there was anything the friends and enemies of Jesus agreed on, it was his ability to communicate. Rich and poor, old and young, insiders and outsiders, the noblest of society and the worst of the streets, all were spellbound by Jesus. The common people "heard him gladly" (Mark 12:37), while the scribes and lawyers listened enraged. But they listened.

"No one ever spoke like this man," they said, shaking their heads (John 7:46). From the teachers in the Temple when he was twelve years old to the thief on the cross when he was dying, the words of Jesus reached across all barriers of age and class. Even children were frequently in his circle, sometimes to the consternation of his disciples (Matt. 18:5, Mark 10:13).

He was equally at home speaking to one person or a thousand. At times, the crush of the crowd was so great that he had to get into a boat to speak to the throng beside Lake Galilee (Mark 4:1). Sometimes he talked quietly with one person, sitting on the curb of a well or visiting in the house of a friend. Other times he spoke with impassioned zeal and vigorous action, as he did in the Court of the Gentiles in the Temple, or when he confounded the scribes and Pharisees who surrounded him like a pack of snarling animals.

These words of Jesus have become the subject of a thousand times a thousand books. *What* he said that so captivated his world has been often studied; *how* he said it has been scarcely noticed. But the manner of his speech can hardly be a matter of indifference. Read the words of Jesus in one way, and they are full of love and grace; read them in another way, change the tone and stance, and even his most loyal disciples would not stay around—much less children. What then, can we learn of Jesus as communicator? And what can that say to us who now seek to communicate with audiences almost as diverse as his, almost as difficult?

Although the New Testament witness varies somewhat, particularly in the Gospel of John, overall the Gospels yield a remarkably uniform picture of the oral communication of Jesus. A study of the preaching and teaching of Jesus, as well as his more informal interviews with individuals, suggests several prominent characteristics that should typify our communication of his gospel.

IDENTIFICATION AND PARTICIPATION

The communication of Jesus was marked by identification and participation. He was involved with life; he was involved with *people's* lives. He did not speak abstractly. He never sounded like an outsider with a bad case of moral superiority. The moral wonder of his life has been called the greatest miracle of Jesus. But the greatest miracle of his life, it seems to me, was that so many ordinary people would listen to one whose life and thoughts moved on such a different, higher path.

But they listened, because he was one of them. "Is he not the carpenter's son?" (Matt. 13:55). Yes, and to some that meant they could not believe. After all, who paid any attention to carpenters' sons? His credentials were not in order—at least, not for the Jerusalem crowd.

Nevertheless, for others less pretentious, that was exactly *why* they listened. He was one of them and his speech, like that of Peter in the courtyard, betrayed him. It betrayed his humanity, his kinship with their flesh, their loneliness, their longing. He was like them in all respects—even in suffering—and his sympathetic suffering bound him to them, and to us (Heb. 2:17–18).

Yet his speech also betrayed his oneness with the purposes of Israel, the prophets of Israel, and even the God of Israel. The effect of his luminous life among them was only possible because he was one of them and because the dreams he projected had become real in him, their brother.

Jesus turned the limitation of location into the validation of his witness. He lived a little while, in a little land. In comparison to other world figures, it is startling how few people ever saw him or heard him. But he so vested himself in the people he did meet, as one with them in their quest, that his people, the people we now call the church, could not and cannot stop talking about it.

Jesus showed an unmatched empathy across a wide spectrum of humanity. He was involved with thinkers and doers, with philosophers and fishermen. He was followed by children and sages, by widows and prostitutes. His disciples were a crazy quilt of ordinary folk, people like Martha and Mary, Peter, James and John; they also included the culturally correct, such as Joseph of Arimathea, Nicodemus, and Nathanael; and the strange lot, such as Simon Zealotes, Mary Magdalene, and even Judas.

How did he communicate with such a range of human personality? How could anyone reach so diverse a group of individuals? He touched them and touches us by his identification and participation with life, real, human life. And so must everyone who communicates his gospel.

APPROPRIATE AUTHORITY

Jesus spoke with appropriate authority. The Bible says that he "spoke as one having authority, not as their scribes" (Matt. 7:29). He spoke as one who knew what he was talking about. And because he clearly knew what he was talking about when he spoke of fields and fishing, of prodigals and waiting fathers, of desperate widows and lost lambs, they began to believe he knew what he was talking about when he spoke of kingdoms to come, and of God.

He spoke as one having authority, not as the scribes; that is, he did not speak in footnotes. The rabbis were famous for citing other, more famous rabbis: "Rabbi-So-and-So said, Rabbi-So-and-So said . . ." Their immediate authority was the rabbi they cited or the decisions of the Great Sanhedrin; their more distant authority was the Law, and behind the Law was Moses. Even the Messiah, when he came, would say nothing of himself but would only interpret the Law of Moses. This early fundamentalism not only robbed the rabbis of authority, but ultimately it robbed God of authority since all that God had to say had been said.

Imagine their outrage, if you can, when Jesus came saying, "You have heard it said . . . but I say unto you . . ." (Matt. 5:31–39). Who was this one to tell them anything? Worse yet, who was he to modify Moses?

Yet the people clung to him, hung on his words, fed on them, like the other wilderness wanderers before them. He claimed to stand in the true succession of Israel's prophets and Israel's God. His speech was a balance of Scripture and experience, of "objective" text and "subjective" experience. But since Jesus believed that God was still active in the world, no text—no matter how time honored and fixed its meaning—was safe from fresh interpretation.

Although Jesus did not rest his authority upon the traditions of his spiritual ancestry, neither did he rest it apart from that tradition. "I have not come to destroy the law," said Jesus, "but to fulfill it" (Matt. 5:17–18). By establishing continuity with the tradition of Israel, Jesus was heard as a part of that tradition. Yet he also projected powerful, contemporary images of the meaning of that tradition. By so doing, he moved them from the dead past into the living present.

Our authority, of course, is not the same as the authority of our Lord. Yet we too deal with "objective" text and "subjective" experience. We too must show the balance that acknowledges the wisdom of the past of our faith, while at the same time it insists on the freedom of the Spirit to interpret those texts afresh for us and for our world. Appropriate authority for today's preacher of the gospel is neither the fixed certainties of past interpreters nor the whimsical vagaries of modern experience. Appropriate authority, whether in this century or any other, rests upon a careful understanding of the ways of God in the history of our faith, translated and even fulfilled through an interpretation of that faith for these times. We must determine "valid modes of seeking the meaning of the biblical text in its own setting, and then determining a valid mode of expression of that meaning in contemporary settings."[1] For those who preach today, appropriate authority

must move beyond past-tense footnoting to present-tense proclaiming.

APPROPRIATE AFFECT

Jesus communicated with appropriate affect. To begin with, he
showed a normal range of emotions. Unlike some preachers in
subsequent centuries, Jesus had no problem showing anger, celebration, or grief, depending on his experience. He did not confront
life with a perpetual scowl, but he didn't face it with a pasty grin
either. He did not bound through life with boundless (and ground-
less) optimism, nor did he drag through life with perpetual gloom.
His preaching was not a fierce triumphalism, nor was it a mousy
defeatism. Jesus was not so insecure as to have to adopt any one
emotion as a defense against criticism or a strategy for persuasion.
When people hurt, he hurt; when a wedding party was in progress,
he rejoiced. He showed anger at injustice, grief at sorrow, celebration at joy, ironic humor at pretense.

His emotions were never stagy or calculated; he never showed
contrived enthusiasm or piety. In short, his emotions were real.
They came from honest reactions to real situations. He could be
a gentle shepherd with his lambs, the children, or the roaring Lion
of Judah with the money changers in the Temple. In every case,
his words fit the occasion, and his emotions fit his words.

Frankly, it would be impossible to imagine Jesus preaching with
the tone and manner of some preachers. The preacher whose view
of pastoral piety compels him or her to smile serenely through
every pronouncement, no matter how sad or serious its content;
the preacher whose vein-bulging platform performances cause
children to hide their faces in mother's lap; the egocentric pulpit
orator with patent leather phrases and plastic emotions—these
preachers are not showing the emotions of those who are children
of the Christ of the Gospels.

No matter what our sentences say, we will never communicate
the gospel of Jesus Christ unless our emotions are appropriate for
the content of our messages. We may be persuasive, successful,

"effective" at accomplishing our objectives, but we can never be effective at accomplishing *his* objectives.

EARTHY

The communication of Jesus was also earthy. That may sound strange, but it is true. He was never crude, but he was human, graphic, tactile. He was never prim or prissy, effete or elegant, ethereal or otherworldly. There was a *reality* about his speech. It was workmanlike, direct. Jesus was never brusque or abrupt, but he was frank. There was nothing churchy about his speech, nothing cathedral-like about his tone.

That crowd couldn't stand him—the ones who made long prayers for effect, who embroidered elegant scriptures on their garments while inside they were "full of dead men's bones" (Matt. 23:27)—they despised him. His down-to-earthness showed up their higher-than-heavenness. Spurgeon warned his students against a "stilted, fussy or pretentious" style in their speech and an air of ministerial superiority, or what he called "ministerial starch," in their manner.[2]

It does make one stop to think, doesn't it, how much difficulty we have reaching *his* audience—the outsiders, the working class, the poor, the young, the neglected, the outcasts, the rebellious—and how little difficulty we have reaching *their* audience—the insiders, those with vested interests, the officially righteous, the politically advantaged? Could it be that we have moved from our origins, from our station as lowly representatives of an out-of-favor religion, to the position of superior advocates of a favored majority? Have we become like the archly aristocratic woman whose Sunday School class of street urchins once startled a visitor by chirping the prayer she had taught them, that God should "confirm the wealthy in their riches and restrain the vicious poor"?

The earthiness of Jesus called a spade a dirty shovel and didn't care whose private garden he was disturbing. Real people liked that. The common people "heard him gladly." (Mark 12:37).

Maybe if we want more of that kind in our congregations, we'd better tell the truth we know in a way it can be understood.

IMAGE–ORIENTED

The preaching of Jesus was vivid, pictorial, colorful, narrative. He used ideational language, too, but in his method of communication, these expressions were subordinated to more image-oriented language.

By so doing, Jesus stood in the tradition of the prophets. Just as they took the *mashal,* or the proverb of Widsom literature, and developed it into the "parable" of their proclamations and prophesy, so Jesus took the parable of the Palestinian rabbis and advanced it through his "wealth of imagination, the power of short and realistic depiction, in the spiritual force that he presented."[3]

He was most picture-oriented when presenting the most difficult or abstract ideas. For example, in the presentation of his complex concept of the kingdom of God, Jesus used a dozen pictures to convey its meaning. The kingdom of God, he said, is like a pearl of great price, a grain of mustard seed, a seed growing of itself, leaven in meal, a field with tares and wheat, a treasure hidden in a field, a net filled with fish, a merciful king and his unjust servant, a wedding feast, and a land manager who equally rewards workers hired at the eleventh hour as those hired earlier.

Recent approaches to preaching have returned, in a greater or lesser degree, to this image-oriented communication concept of Jesus. Both in the use of parabolic story and in the use of graphic language, preaching today has moved increasingly toward that colorful, graphic speech Jesus used.

We do not do that simply out of slavish devotion to the methodology of Jesus. It is a matter of linguistic fact that when we speak of God or the things of God, we stand at the boundaries of language itself. We must then describe what we cannot define; we must sketch what we cannot calculate. This preaching sticks in the mind. It opens new horizons; it awakens dreams.

Image-oriented preaching more nearly corresponds to reality than our efforts to reduce reality to abstract absolutes. Definition is not superior to description in preaching, nor is the tightly argued, analytically ordered message superior to a more descriptive one. Austin Farrer says in *A Rebirth of Images,* "There is a current and exceedingly stupid doctrine that symbol evokes emotion and exact prose states reality. Nothing could be further from the truth: exact prose abstracts from reality, symbol presents it."[4] Rather than being inferior to its ideational precursors, pictorial preaching is a superior communicator in the spiritual search.

EXPLICIT AND IMPLICIT

The preaching and teaching of Jesus were both explicit and implicit. That is, sometimes he gave the meanings of his messages explicitly to his disciples, with a stated conclusion or a specific call to action or decision: "Follow me . . ." (Matt. 4:18); "therefore do not be anxious about tomorrow . . ." (Matt. 6:34); "for everyone who exalts himself will be humbled, and he who humbles himself will be exalted" (Luke 14:11). At other times the meanings or conclusions to Jesus' teachings were frequently only implicit in the message. He drew no conclusions for his listeners; he gave them no explicit orders. They were left to their own perceptions for the meaning: "He who has ears to hear, let him hear" (Luke 14:35). Sometimes the disciples were confused about the audience intended for the message: "Peter said, 'Lord, are you telling this parable for us or for all?' " (Luke 12:41). Frequently the messages remained mysterious to them: "But they did not understand this saying . . . they were afraid to ask him about this saying" (Luke 9:45); "This is a hard saying; who can hear it?" (John 6:60); "They questioned within themselves what the rising from the dead should mean" (Mark 9:10).

We understand more readily the reason for the explicit teachings of Jesus. That seems to be the role of the teacher or preacher, we think; we think we are suppose to tell people what things mean, or to tell people what to do. That is certainly the conventional meaning of "to preach" in our society today. But how do we understand his implicit conclusions? Why did he teach in such a manner that the disciples themselves were sometimes unsure of the intent or meaning of his message? And did not the Yale Studies in Communication come to the rather surprising conclusion that people prefer explicit conclusions in speeches to implicit ones, and that this result held true regardless of the educational level of the listener?[5]

First of all, Jesus realized that some things could be learned only through experience and that no amount of reasoning could make it otherwise. So he said to them, "Go and learn what this means, 'I desire mercy and not sacrifice' " (Matt. 9:13). Although he explicitly told them to "go and learn," he only implicitly pointed them to the meaning of "those who are well have no need of a physician, but those who are sick" (Matt. 9:12). Without common presuppositions and a common experiential base from which to learn, he knew they could not hear his meaning.

Furthermore, implicit conclusions are thought provoking; they facilitate the growth process. Preachers or teachers who only give their listeners cut-and-dried conclusions bear all of the responsibility for the message; the listeners are only passive recipients of their active speaking. Because implicit conclusions demand participation, they involve the listeners in the understanding process.

Every audience represents virtually infinite fields of experience; therefore many levels of understanding are possible. But a preacher who provides neat answers to all questions robs the congregation of the variety of applications they can give to the gospel's message in daily life. Even if the listeners accept my conclusions and follow my orders, what they do is limited to only my understanding of my experience. My interpretation can draw only from my observations, but their understanding can draw from many fields of experience unknown to me, and their actions can move into fields of effort unimagined by me.

Granted, the listener does need some clue into my understanding of the matter or of the purpose of the message in the first place. That is why the listeners in the Yale Studies preferred the conclusiveness of the explicit ending to the vagueness of a lengthy recital of facts with no conclusion. But that does not mean that only dogmatic speeches are effective or that more open-ended approaches are always ineffectual.

As Fred Craddock points out, "overhearing" the gospel through story or narrative allows persons to reach conclusions through inductive means.[6] The listeners do seek resolutions to the story, however, because in any true preaching of the gospel, something vital is at stake. Without resolution a sense of incompletion results, and the listeners are frustrated.[7] (It is important to note that "resolution" does not always or even primarily mean a neat solution or happy ending; the paradox and tension in the gospel must not be removed.) Nonetheless, the explicit actions to be taken on the basis of the story are largely implicit in its resolution.

Frequently, more analytical or ideational sermons require more explicit conclusions simply because they are so loaded with facts that the listeners have no idea what to make of them. Therefore they become confused or even irritated if the speech ends without an explicit conclusion. What are they to *do* with all that information?

But if our sermons, like the sermons of Jesus, are more pictorial and suggestive, explicit conclusions may not be needed. The story itself may linger in the mind, pointing to horizons previously unseen. Then, through the activity of the Holy Spirit, the combination of images, events, and ideas in the sermon may link together with their experience, sometimes much later, with results that surpass the limited intent of the speaker.

Of course, that can be a dangerous process because it places part of the responsibility for proper action on the part of the listeners. That requires maturity on the part of listeners, and some preachers are so authoritarian or paternalistic that they never trust others to think for themselves. At a certain point in the human life cycle that kind of paternal direction is appropriate, but who would want a thirty-five-year-old child who has to call home every hour to ask mother or father what to do? (Unfortunately, some of those kinds of children have been produced!) There is risk in giving autonomy to the child, but without that kind of responsibility, maturity can never be reached.

The same is true for the Christian congregation. Preachers, whether fundamentalist or liberal, with high control needs are careful to spell out all conclusions to the letter. They fear that their congregations will reach conclusions contrary to theirs if left to their own interpretations. Yet adolescence is a necessary stage in growth, even Christian growth; and that means that our listeners, like those of Jesus, must be allowed to grow through the struggle to understand the meaning of the Christian message for themselves. The *message* of the gospel should be clear; the specific and detailed meanings of that message for listeners must be discovered in their own lives.

At this point a very valid question may be raised. What do you do about a congregation that has many different levels of maturity in it? What do you do when some people have great understanding of the Christian faith and others could draw the wrong conclusions to almost anything if it were not spelled out for them? First of all, the preacher must analyze the degree to which members of the congregation may be typified as either mature in their understanding or beginners in the faith. The messages may then be tipped somewhat toward more or less explicit conclusions. Overall, however, pictorial, descriptive preaching once again commends itself to us, since it permits multileveled communication in the same message.

That is, a child and a professor may hear the same story and perceive quite different levels of meaning; an amateur and an art critic may look at the same painting and each fully appreciate it yet find different levels of significance. Ideational language, on the other hand, demands definition; if you don't know the definitions of the words, you can't know their meanings (like "ideational"). But a descriptive sermon can communicate to many different levels of experience without exceeding the information of some or offending the intelligence of others. Then the true profundity of the message is left where it should be, in the historical promise of God and the contemporary depth of insight that brought the sermon into being, rather than in the vocabulary of the speaker.

In every respect, then, the communication of Jesus was both plain and provocative. It was plain in its use of the familiar— familiar human images and familiar human problems. Likewise, the identification of Jesus with the problems of his listeners and his empathy with them, matched by the appropriate affect of human emotion, spoke plainly to his listeners. His appropriate use of authority showed them plainly that he was one with them in their history and one with them in their contemporary experience. Yet his image-oriented and earthy preaching provided provocative stimulus for their thinking. His preaching was both explicit enough to show plainly the principles of the gospel and implicit enough to provoke people to thinking and growth.

That kind of preaching, whether in that century or in this one, always has the same result: the "common people" listen gladly.

15. "Some Said It Thundered": Upper Garble and Lower Garble

Perhaps it is some primitive appendage, a kind of religious appendix, that causes us to continue to confuse thunder with the divine voice. When the voice from heaven spoke to Jesus shortly before his last Passover, a voice which Jesus explicitly said "came not because of me, but for your sakes," the people who stood by and heard it "said that it thundered: others said, an angel spoke to him" (John 12:23–30).

Unfortunately that misunderstanding is not an isolated phenomenon. It happens every Sunday, somewhere, for both clergy and laity. The occasional church visitor and perpetual pew-sitter alike have great difficulty in identifying the Word among so many words. What does the true voice from God sound like?

That question also haunts us preachers, afflicted on the one hand with the uneasy suspicion that we are human and on the other hand with the uncomfortable assignment of believing that somehow God can speak the Word through our mouths. Unless our approach to preaching is fully incarnational, our speech will betray us worse than that of Simon Peter in the courtyard.

Our futile attempts to sound less like ourselves and more like God may take one of two directions. We may alter our speech into a more authoritarian, hence more thunderous, tone in an effort to sound more self-assured and therefore less vulnerable. After all, who would be impressed if we used our own normal, often fallible voices in the pulpit? ("Do we not know this man? Is he not the carpenter's son?") There must be a kind of *ex-cathedra* ring to it if anyone is to imagine that God is somehow speaking through it. Or else we may seek the more elegant, high-flown speech of the celestial regions, complete with the faintest suggestion of a rustling of angel's wings in the background. Invariably these attempts impress people as either meaningless noise or less than human verbalism. In neither case, however, is the word of God recognized.

That is not to say that these efforts are without results. They obviously impress somebody favorably or they would not go on. The fact is, they are largely although not exclusively the result of the demands of the laity. The person in the pew must share the blame for the artificiality of pulpit speech. It is true that the young preacher often cultivates these accents as a kind of ministerial union card. But it is equally true that many an otherwise human young minister has been driven into unnatural speech because of the insistence that "our preacher should sound like a preacher," which means, of course, that he or she is to sound holy, to sound different in order to be respected.

This is another chicken-and-egg syndrome: generations of preachers have gotten by, if not succeeded, by using the tone the congregation recognizes as "religious," which in turn conditions another generation of lay people to what pulpit speech ought to sound like. Who started what is not important. *The continuing lack of faith on the part of both preachers and lay people alike that God can and will speak through normal human beings is to blame.*

Actually there are two reasons for the remote dialects of the pulpit, although both are only opposite sides of the same fault. The first is this desire for quasi-divine speech, this preoccupation of both laity and clergy with the search for the divine note that will unmistakably be perceived as heavenly. But the second is like unto it—in fact, it is difficult to imagine that the first could have occurred without it—the isolation of the pulpit.

Isolation breeds dialect. The more isolated the region, the more obscure the dialect. And if the isolation is acute enough, another language emerges. This is true of remote island peoples and primitive jungle tribes with their unique languages, but it is equally true of isolated sections of advanced nations such as the United States or Germany. (Even today in Germany, for example, there are villages no more than two miles apart where the inhabitants can instantly recognize one another due to a peculiar tone on one sound or another.)

There is a certain romance to dialect, a certain nostalgia at its passing. There is presently a kind of speech ecology movement dedicated to protecting the uniqueness of dialect and to preventing its falling victim to speech generalization, an effort closely akin to preserving the ivory-billed woodpecker or the whooping crane. Accents add variety and color to life; they may be quaint, or even amusing. But there is a less than funny side to dialect also, as when it hinders or absolutely blocks communication, or when it causes bitter sectionalism and thereby isolates and separates human beings from true community.

The pulpit, like all isolated regions, has its own peculiar dialects. Likewise, it has suffered from all of the problems associated with dialect separation. This separation of the pulpit is not primarily a geographical or spatial isolation, though that plays some role. There are two sources of pulpit separation, and each has produced its own distinctive dialect.

The first of these is *attitudinal separation,* an isolation consciously or unconsciously chosen by provincial preachers, those preachers who are provincial because of their remoteness either to the world or to the Word. It is equally as provincial to ignore the significance of the Word as to ignore the significance of the world. The truest mark of provincialism is still that of loving "every age but this and every culture but your own," in the words of Gilbert and Sullivan. This means that the most sophisticated and spatially involved preacher may be as provincial, and therefore as dialect-separated, as the most geographically or sectarially isolated preacher.

Both "liberal" and "fundamentalist" wings of the church use jargon equally. Too intense preoccupation with the historical given produces cultic speech; too intense preoccupation with the existential given produces ultimately meaningless speech. Only midpoint, incarnational preaching, produces speech that is truly intelligible.

But dialect separation may also exist where there is no serious attitudinal problem on the part of the preacher, but where a *methodological breakdown* has occurred. This is the second source of pulpit separation. It is where preachers struggle helplessly to escape the nonspeech of pulpit dialect but cannot because they simply do not know what it is in their language or method that is isolating them. Here the problem is not primarily due to disjointed theology of proclamation, but to faulty technique in preaching.

Thus the pulpit has produced two distinct dialects: Upper Garble and Lower Garble. *Upper Garble* is that dialect produced by attitudinal separation; *Lower Garble* results from faulty technique. Of course neither of these dialects is entirely independent of either attitude or technique, but at least the two are sufficiently distinct as to be described. Perhaps it would be interesting to note the principles for these two varieties of pulpit dialect, Upper Garble and Lower Garble.

UPPER GARBLE

1. *Never uses a short word when a long one would be more impressive.* This is the key to Upper Garble: impressiveness. Language can conceal as well as reveal. When we do not feel sufficiently impressive as preachers, Upper Garble can compensate for our insecurity. Short words can be used on every street corner; lengthy words are more complex and therefore more suggestive of the mysterious, the more-than-human, the profound. Upper Garble users seem never to notice that Jesus spoke simply.

Jacques Barzun illustrates this desire for impressiveness, which government leaders, who must never appear mortal or fallible, seem to share in common with preachers: "A single word gives us away, as when President Eisenhower said: 'Marshall Zhukov and I *operated* together very closely' (*New York Times,* July 18, 1957). Not *worked*—'operated.' Why 'operated'? Because it is loftier, more abstract, more suggestive of complex doings, more praiseworthy because more pretentious—one senses the careful effort that goes into operating closely together. And when a plain, straightforward army man falls unknowingly into pretentiousness, one can gauge how powerful the cultural pressure is to be a pedant."[1]

Even the simplest expressions can be rendered unintelligible: "A mass of concentrated earthly material perennially rotating on its axis will not accumulate an accretion of bryophytic vegetation. (A rolling stone gathers no moss.) That prudent *Aves* which matutinally deserts the cosiness of its abode will ensnare a vermiform creature. (The early bird catches the worm.) Aberration is the hallmark of *homo sapiens* while longanimous placability and condonation are the indicia of supramundane omniscience. (To err is human, to forgive, divine.)"[2]

The basic fault of Upper Garble is not that it can only be understood by intellectuals and therefore has a limited audience. Its real error is that it does not say sharply what it means, which opens it to the question of whether it *understands* sharply what it means. "What this theology explicates . . ." "Explicates" is like bringing an aardvark into the room and asking who knows what it is; or better, it is like shoving an empty trunk into the room and asking who knows what's in it.

Through long years of careful practice, the user of Upper Garble can systematically replace every short word in his or her vocabulary with a longer one that will be more difficult to understand. With a little luck, we may get so obscure that no one will confuse us with human beings.

2. *Always uses theo-philosophic language.* Every vocation has its professional jargon and its professional manner. The doctor does, as he or she sweeps through hospital corridors trailed by an entourage of nurses and interns, pausing briefly to "explain" a medical situation in terms that often leave the patient or family more confused than before; so does the counseling psychologist whose manner of speech has become so nondirective and clinical that it has the sound of someone tiptoeing on eggshells.

Both vocabulary and manner are the carefully cultivated practices of the ages, and they are especially employed by those who are often expected to do the impossible and are unwilling to face the reality of their own humanity and fallibility.

Theology has a long head start in this respect over all other professions. Our professional jargon is multicenturies old and is not merely hidden in the mysteries of the complex workings of the body or the mind, but the "soul." Therefore we have more at stake. The expertness of the theological specialist cannot be as easily established as that of a surgeon through a successful operation, or that of a psychologist through a successful counseling experience. We have no licensing boards to prevent other Christians from practicing theology as doctors do to prevent lay people from practicing medicine. Religion is like politics: everybody is an expert.

As a result, we preachers have a particularly hard time maintaining our authority. We may be tempted to use obscure jargon to prove our expertness.

The professional training of any specialist is a process of encoding, that is, an input into his or her mind of technical terms useful to that specialty. There is nothing basically wrong with that. It is necessary to facilitate technical communication between specialists. But problems develop when an encoded specialist tries to communicate without decoding his or her information. Then the person who has not had the benefit of encoding is bewildered, if somewhat impressed. This kind of encoded communication is perfectly understandable among fellow specialists, even if it is cryptic to outsiders. That is the reason two theologians in conversation resemble nothing so much as two computers talking to one another. But if the computer wants to talk to human beings, it must use a language people can understand.

The preacher, who is trained by theologians and similarly encoded, can never quite escape the mysterious glamour of the complex world of the theological laboratory. Even though we must talk to lay people, mere "commoners" in the art of theological speech, we are tempted to show the lofty regions of our training by our dialect. We want to prove to a world of secular godlings —doctors, scientific types, insurance underwriters—that we are specialists too. So we pull out all the stops. We speak of surd evil and patripassionism; we quote obscure theologians and cite the proceedings of ancient church councils; we drop what few Greek and Hebrew phrases we remember.

By doing so, we gets the best of both worlds. Our credibility is high as fully accredited scientific specialists whose long years of technical training are obviously in evidence, and our knowledge of the mysterious God we purport to represent is safely cloaked under a cloud of obscurity the layperson can admire, if not understand.

That attitude is typified by the old woman who came out of church shaking her head in wonderment and saying, "Our pastor must be a smart man—we can't understand a word he says!"

That preacher only made one mistake, and so did the old woman: they both confused obscurity with profundity. Jesus was profound, never obscure. He had profound thoughts and simple language. We are just the opposite: we have profound language and simple thoughts. In Spurgeon's lectures to his students, he once told them that preachers who were admired for being "deep" reminded him of a well: "You look down into a well; if it be empty it will appear to be very deep, but if there be water in it you will see its brightness. I believe that many 'deep' preachers are simply so because they are like dry wells with nothing whatever in them, except decaying leaves, a few stones, and perhaps a dead cat or two."[3]

3. *Strives for elevated or inflated language.* Polysyllabic language, theophilosophic language, and inflated language are three different means of sounding impressive. Polysyllabic language is impressive simply because it uses big words (like "polysyllabic"). Theophilosophic language is impressive because it is the exclusive property of the theological specialist. But inflated language has its own special function. Through a careful use of adjectives, the most ordinary event can be turned into a spectacle. That is, particularly useful to preachers who do not want their parishioners to mistake the noble realm of the religious world with everyday life.

For example, everything must become "marvelous," "wonderful," "glorious." By connecting the ministerial air hose, the preacher of Upper Garble can inflate the simplest and most solid words into swollen, great bloated things to be released and go floating out over the heads of a gaping congregation. If the choir sang well, it was "glorious." If the last meeting of the deacons or elders concluded without a fistfight, it was "wonderful" (that may not be overly inflated!).

This language is particularly useful among preachers. For example, if questioned about last Sunday's services, the upper-garbling preacher can reply, "Marvelous!"—when what he or she really means is, "Mediocre." (Actually, the only thing "marvelous" about the service is that there was anybody there at all!)

The effect of these words is even more enhanced when they themselves are inflated by prolonging the initial vowel, as in "maarvelous," "wuunderful," and "gloorious." A particularly pious sound can be rendered by giving the same treatment to the name of Jesus—"Jeesus." The longer, the holier. Similar tricks can be played with consonants, too, for some reason long lost in the archives of Upper Garble—as "Holy Spidit," for "Holy Spirit," as though one had extreme nasal blockage.

Many staunchly evangelical preachers who would never turn their collar around backward have compensated for their lack of clerical identification by turning their voices around backward. At first, of course, this kind of speech is only laughable, if a little pathetic. Young people, for example, usually snicker at the spectacle of Brother Puffing-Adder or Reverend Blowfish. But there must be something addicting about it, because if fed on a steady diet of verbal soufflé the teeth of a congregation become unable to chew anything more substantial, and its taste seems to run to nothing else.

Unfortunately, however, such inflated language, like inflated currency, eventually becomes worthless. Nobody wants it; it is even hard to give away.

4. *Employs the grand manner.* Preachers who have become adept at the use of such elegant and complex language could scarcely be expected to act normally. They must find a manner to match their speech. Their gestures, their expressions, their platform manner, their bearing, all must match their language.

Depending on their theological persuasion, this usually takes one of two courses: either they become Elizabethan or Cool ("Cool" being defined as whatever is acceptable in those sophisticated in-circles that have rejected the out-circles; usually a carefully studied underplaying of the role). There are avid collectors of either manner, quite parallel to taste in furniture, either antique or modern.

For example, preachers who are the usual old-style Upper Garblers, those who prefer pious tones with matching theology, those whose rumbling basso or penetrating tenor energetically inflate words into grandiose proportions are likely to be Elizabethan in style. These preachers need an immense stage to be displayed upon to be viewed in proper proportion. As one layman described his pastor, he seemed "too big for any one room." The effect is overwhelming: large of gesture, expansive in warmth (sometimes also in girth), these preachers resemble a ministerial Falstaff—arms akimbo, arms crossed; fingers stabbing the heavens; head cocked; face in a scowl, now beaming like the sun; lips drawn back in a passable imitation of a smile; posturing and posing, gesticulating and declaiming. Their vocabulary is even more archaic, dating back to Beowulf or the Venerable Bede.

This Elizabethan manner is quite adaptive, too, suiting many locales and confessional situations. The traditionalist of almost any denomination can employ it anywhere. It is equally at home in the pulpit of an elegant cathedral where it is polished for upper-class tastes, or in a rural backwoods setting where it is energetically pursued by the typical backslapping, chicken-chomping, icebox-raiding, old-style parson. The benign paternalism it conveys is equally appreciated by the insecure, authority-needing church member at either end of the social spectrum.

On the other hand, preachers who are avant-garde Upper Garblers—and there are at least as many of those as traditionalists—will be Cool rather than Elizabethan. But they are no less impressive, no less elegant. Every movement speaks of sophistication, of poise, of casual correctness. Their awesome awareness of contemporary "in-ness" is no less intimidating than the ancient authoritarianism of the traditionalist. Their expressions are serene, detached, rather than bluff and hearty. Only traces of emotion show—most noticeably, perhaps, when denouncing emotion. They project an indefinable air of sexiness along with their nonchalance and urbanity. Their total manner is carefully calculated to keep them at the front of nondirective churchly fashion, the leaders of those who cannot be led.

Perhaps the two are not really centuries apart in approach. After all, the world has never known an era of more elegant dandies and culture-conscious sophisticates than the Elizabethan age.

5. *Always uses involved reasoning.* There are times, even for the accomplished practicioners of Upper Garble, when the most naive parishioners begin to see through their language and manner. Then it is necessary for the Upper Garbler to lose them in the dark woods of complex reasoning. If they cannot follow the tracks of inference and deduction no matter how carefully they trace the intricate patterns, then the mystery is safe and the authority of the Upper Garbler is secure.

Plainness is one virtue that Upper Garble shuns like the plague. Nothing is more humiliating than being understood (particularly if what is said is meaningless).

But by going around in endless circles of logic, even the most attentive hearers can be thrown off the track. At last they will give up the chase and go mentally home, baffled and fatigued, perhaps even irritated, but still impressed that something profound has been said which they somehow missed. How long, of course, they will continue to follow the hounds at the Sunday hunt is open to question. From the persistently declining attendance at worship, it is apparent that many people have already enjoyed all of the sport they can stand.

Nevertheless, the use of involved reasoning is a tested and true method of remaining impressive, particularly if administered in small doses, and should be mastered by every user of Upper Garble. As long ago as 1883, Austin Phelps described the practice in his classic work *English Style in Public Discourse,* as he told of a German philosopher who rewrote part of a manuscript because he found it understandable.[4] With its long and impressive history, the device should not be overlooked.

6. *Overstates when confused.* Closely akin to the use of involved reasoning is the practice of overstating when confused. No one could be expected to be right *all* of the time, but superiority is difficult to maintain in the presence of error. It smacks too much of humanity. And infallibility is impossible.

The Bible has the unfortunate habit of putting us preachers into waters over our heads. What are we to do then? Admit that we face a truth we cannot understand? Confess that there are spiritual realities we have not yet experienced? And thereby admit that we are only very human Christians among others?

Not likely! Better to overstate, to explain everything, to eliminate paradox, to claim divine insight, to allude to personal spiritual triumphs. The more emphatically said, the better. A bit of verse expresses it well: "When in danger or in doubt, run in circles, scream and shout."

Helmut Thielicke warns against this kind of arrogance on the part of the minister. We must confess our helplessness at certain points in interpreting the word of God. We must confess that there are truths that are still beyond us and yet be able to point both ourselves and others to them. We can speak of these truths—indeed, we must—we are bound to the whole truth of Scripture, even those parts which we have not yet experienced as a certainty in our own lives.

But we must not exaggerate; we must acknowledge without shame those truths we are still waiting to apprehend and confess them as expected truths. Then we testify that the truth of the Scripture is greater than our own experience or understanding. "But woe to him who acts as if he already 'saw' all things, as if everything were equally clear to him, as if he were looking without blinking into the thousand-watt lamp of the whole truth."[5]

But such an approach requires humility, and humility is the essence of the incarnational experience. Unless we are willing to make that kind of sacrifice, we would do better to practice Upper Garble.

7. *Loses its humanity in its divinity.* Upper Garble is guilty of homiletical Docetism. Those who practice it imagine that their humanity is an illusion, that their spiritual nature alone is real. That is heresy. The effects of this modern Docetic error are far more widespread and deadly than its ancient counterpart. It is no minor problem, no insignificant misuse of elocution, no matter how comical certain aspects of it. Upper Garble is a serious symptom of a deeply underlying problem, an indicator of an acute spiritual sickness. It is the outward expression of an inner disorder that can only lead to an abnormal existence for both preacher and congregation.

This final principle of Upper Garble is actually not a separate characteristic. It is rather a summary of the total error involved in the dialect. This fault results from a false concept of authority, an insecurity on the part of the preacher which feeds on the insecurities of the congregation. It is marked by an almost total absence of genuine humanity in language and style.

These preachers have failed to grasp the essential humility required of the servant of God. They have failed to notice that Jesus himself took on the form of a human being in his incarnation and humbled himself to communicate and become one with us. We still need to be reminded that "the servant is not greater than his lord" (John 13:16). Jesus constantly struggled to conceal sufficiently his messianic nature so that he would not force a warped obedience on others. This struggle is reversed with insecure preachers; instead of a "messianic secret," they are involved in a "human secret" in an effort to gain authority by concealing their weaknesses.

There is a distinct risk involved in humanity. Perhaps those preachers who attempt to conceal their humanity in Upper Garble once had their authority severely challenged and were so frightened and intimidated that they decided, perhaps unconsciously, that it was far safer to rise a step above the human.

But with no common ground under their feet, with no dust upon their shoes, preachers cannot walk and talk with people. They are as safe, and as isolated, as the Greek gods. And as unreal.

LOWER GARBLE

Lower Garble is not free of attitudinal problems, of sins of the spirit, but basically this dialect is caused by faulty technique. The most humble and authentic preachers can still have great difficulty in projecting their genuine humanity as they proclaim the gospel. If they do, they may unconsciously suffer from one or more of the technical errors of Lower Garble that separate the pulpit from the Word or the world.

1. *Locates the sermon in ancient history.* This fault particularly plagues those preachers who attempt to be "biblical" in their preaching. Their very concern to be faithful to the text may cause them to do little more than deliver a first-century history lecture. They become lost in Canaan and never find their way into the twentieth century. They are almost totally preoccupied with ancient grammar, historical footnoting, and background studies.

It was most certainly a Lower Garbler about whom Fosdick wrote, "Only the preacher proceeds still upon the idea that folk come to church desperately anxious to discover what happened to the Jebusites."[6] It is good to visit Canaan, but too many preachers enter the pulpit carrying waterpots on their heads.

Nevertheless, background studies and historical information are essential to a correct interpretation of the biblical text. Otherwise the significance of the text may be totally lost when isolated from its historical context. Without a historical and critical understanding of the Scripture, the sermon invariably degenerates into a mere subjective discourse on whatever the preacher particularly wants to say. But this historical data itself cannot become the exclusive *focus* of the sermon.

Original language studies are also basic to an understanding of the Scripture. Bonhoeffer says, "No sermon should be produced without use of the original text."[7] But any preacher who uses Greek and Hebrew words in the pulpit, whether to demonstrate expertness or simply as a misguided attempt to "clarify" a difficult text, has missed the point. Charles R. Brown writes, "The expository sermon is a product of exegesis, but not an exhibition of it. It is altogether wise to dig beforehand with your Greek spade and your Hebrew shovel but not to be digging while you are preaching."[8]

The results of original language exegesis and word studies should be brought into the pulpit, but the tools should be left in the study. Instead of saying, "The words *agape* and *phileo* are two different Greek words for love," it is better to say, "The New Testament describes love in two ways," and then describe it. The point is to communicate the biblical concept, not to display knowledge. Even when innocently done, the practice is distracting and confusing and often opens the motivations of the preacher to suspicion.

But if the sermon is not to wander around longer in the historical wilderness than the Israelites trying to find the Promised Land, the cure of this malady is also not to reduce the sermon to the six o'clock news report. The total absence of the historical is as great a fault as preoccupation with it. Our congregations simply need more than the time, the weather, and a vaguely religious commentary upon the headlines.

Fosdick himself balanced his criticism of historical preoccupation with this remark: "If people do not come to church anxious about what happened to the Jebusites, neither do they come yearning to hear a lecturer express his personal opinion on themes which editors, columnists, and radio commentators have been dealing with throughout the week."[9]

2. *Speaks to no one in particular about nothing in particular.* The motto of this kind of preaching is, "I shot a sermon in the air, it fell to earth, I know not where." The title of some sermons could be, "Some Good Things to Do," or "And Another Thing . . ."!

Lower Garble suffers from an incurable vagueness. It speaks about people, not to people. It cannot clearly focus its eyes upon any one object. Every sermon is a hopeless collection of religious generalizations. No matter what text is chosen or what topic is announced, the course of the sermon eventually meanders around the same geography.

This kind of preaching is usually caused by a limited and preconceived notion of what the gospel really is. The preachers of Lower Garble really have only one sermon, or at most two, which their prior insights have strongly impressed upon them. This previous experience has so programmed them that when their preaching buttons are pressed, the congregation hears the same prerecorded message. The preachers may be dimly aware of this limitation and may even struggle feebly against it for a while, but eventually they give up and resort to a mere shuffling of illustrations, titles, and texts to provide a spurious variety in preaching.

Almost every Christian has one or two sermons his or her own experiences in the faith have yielded, but this subjective base is far too narrow for balanced Christian proclamation. Preachers must keep both the biblical and the contemporary in sharp focus, or else they will aimlessly cross the same dull terrain, having neither a specific message nor a specific party to deliver it to. They must pay more attention to what the Bible and the people are trying to tell them. In short, they need to listen more and talk less.

Some preachers excuse their endless generalizations by insisting that more specific preaching misses too many people. The general theory seems to be that by shooting at nothing you can hit everything. They are afraid that no one in the immediate audience may identify with a specific situation from either the Bible or contemporary life.

But a person does not need to have suffered the loss of a brother to identify with the grief of Mary and Martha or the pain of a runaway son to identify with the waiting father. In both cases, however, these specifics are more tangible than vague assurances murmured in the general direction of grief. Everyone has suffered loss and known grief; and almost all churchgoers can and will immediately translate a specific grief situation into applicable terms for their own experience. Then the Scripture's assurance becomes their assurance, the biblical hope becomes their hope. Otherwise the gospel remains a historical abstraction not spoken to them, the sermon, a pointless arrow fired into midair.

3. *Lacks vividness because it never becomes involved.* Closely related to

generalized preaching, and yet distinct from it, is uninvolved preaching. Much preaching is vague and generalized because the preacher is personally uninvolved. This does not mean that he or she does not tell enough personal illustrations, or that the gospel should be established on the basis of personal experiences. It means two things: first, that his or her preaching lacks perspective; and second, that it focuses on subjects rather than on people, that it is third-person preaching.

As Helmut Thielicke has pointed out, vividness is a matter of perspective. For example, a trip through the mountains is exciting, crossing a plain is dull and uninteresting. The difference is that the mountains provide a changing perspective; the plain is constantly flat. Unless preachers often position themselves and their audiences relative to issues and to life, listening to their sermons will be like driving for hours through Kansas wheat fields or across Texas plains, hoping every moment to see some hill or tree stick up on the horizon to break the monotony of the landscape.

Thielicke says: "Perspective means that what I see and what I communicate to others is related to the observer's standpoint and that it always communicates my relationship to things too. . . . You have no 'perspective' in your theology; it is all flat. And that means, first, that there is no distinction between what is nearer and what is more remote, between what is primary and what is secondary, and so there is no focal point; and second, you do not reveal your own relationship or attitude to these things, that is, you do not emerge as perspective center. And the result is that there is no vividness."[10]

There is also no reality, and often no honesty. Preachers must be willing to take a true stance, their own stance with reference to the issues of life. Every stance will gain a following anyhow. Preachers might as well pick one that is truly theirs—they may have to live with it for a long time.

Without perspective, everything is distorted. Unless preachers honestly position themselves and the doctrines they preach relative to the Bible and to life, mountains become molehills and an ordinary person becomes a spiritual giant. We must not appear to stand equidistant to all spiritual reality.

This does not mean that we are to be forever parading our spiritual shortcomings or our theological confusion, or that we are to join an honesty cult. It does mean that we are not to make every biblical admonition sound equally easy, and that we do not have to pretend to understand everything in the Bible or to have accomplished every spiritual challenge.

Nor is it necessary to say, "I never pray for others, but you should." Honesty only demands that a true perspective be given: "Praying for others is not easy. At least not for me, and perhaps not for you either." Rather than lowering our credibility, this kind of perspective preaching gives the preacher believability and the sermon a great increase in vividness.

Lower Garble also lacks vividness because it is always talking about "it," never about "you" and "me." Again, this is not a question of application, but of focus. In Lower Garble, the subject of the sermon is its subject, not its hearers. That may seem logical enough, but it is a great fault. Of course the sermon must have a unifying concern, and the preacher ought to stick to it and not preach all over the known world. But if we focus on our subject instead of on the people for whom the message of the gospel is intended, we begin a monologue with ourselves. We become infatuated with ideas and may be guilty of theme worship.

It is as though we turned ninety degrees away from our audience to address the subject. If the audience likes, they may look at the subject with us. But only we and the subject are in dialogue; the hearers are passive spectators. We are like a juggler of colored balls; our ideas are the balls, and our total concentration is required to keep them all up in the air at the same time. A few years of this kind of preoccupied preaching, and the whole congregation could get up and silently tiptoe out without ever being missed.

A congregation, however, long accustomed to the role of mere passive observers, usually resents more active involvement and contents itself with merely applauding good performances:

"Doesn't our preacher preach as well as anybody you've ever seen?" What the preacher is doing, of course, is another question. And this kind of performing, more than anything else, is responsible for the generations of pew-critics who regard their sole business in church as that of being entertained and of passing sour-faced judgments on poor performances.

This third-person, "it"-centered preaching removes vividness from the sermon because the congregation is not involved. It fosters an impersonal attitude on the part of both preacher and congregation and promotes oratory rather than conversation. It deceives the congregation into believing that the worship hour, or at least the preached part of it, is a time for the passive observation of an oratorical performance that takes place external to them and largely external to the preacher. (The effect is heightened if the preacher reads a manuscript.)

At best it is briefly entertaining, at worst, deadly dull. But whatever it is, the sermon is never a vital, living encounter between God and people.

4. *Lacks imagination totally.* This is the chief creative error of Lower Garble. It is marked by obvious words, ordinary ideas, and predictable order. Lower Garble is "ho-hum" preaching. It may avoid the rococo speech of Upper Garble with its endless flourishes and fretwork, but its own blockhouse style is scarcely an improvement.

To begin with, its words are obvious. A word does not need to be long, or technical, or inflated to avoid the obvious. It can simply be fresh, vivid, angular, tactile. With thought, the simplest words can spark.

In fact, as overblown and pseudotheological as American pulpit speech has become, *any* simple word is usually exciting. The obscure has now become the expected in the pulpit. Concrete speech is a solid contrast and a welcome relief from the vague fog that usually envelops the pulpit and pew.

Furthermore, the ideas of Lower Garble are ordinary. Not ordinary, as in "understandable," but ordinary as in "trite." In fact, they are usually nothing but a string of religious clichés. The lower-garbling preacher may protest, "But I am no creative genius! What do they *expect,* anyhow?" It isn't genius that's lacking, however. It's usually work—plain old ordinary, common work. Plus an attention to the Scripture, with its abundance of still-unheard ideas and yet-unthought thoughts.

The more we depend upon our own creative topical efforts, the more ordinary our ideas become. The usual young preacher, fresh from the seminary, loaded (we think) with creative ideas, is usually in for a shock. We discover that we only have three ideas anyway; and of these, everybody has heard two already, and the third isn't true. We have only two alternatives: trust in the Bible to provide ever-fresh, ever-meaningful ideas or go on repeating our collection of inherited clichés.

Finally, the order of Lower Garble sermons is always predictable. First comes the text, then the introduction, then three points and a poem. Or first a problem, then a solution. The traditional preacher is predictably rigid, the avant-garde preacher predictably amorphous. The evangelistic preacher is predictably authoritarian and hortatory, the counseling preacher predictably nondirective. It becomes obvious that the form of the sermon is not the least bit influenced by the Scripture it generally claims to proclaim, but entirely by the life-style and theological bias of the preacher.

Again, the only cure for the predictable sameness of Lower Garble is for the preacher to take seriously both the real Word and the real world, and that will inevitably lead us to freshness and discovery.

5. *Vaporizes each statement into a forceless mass.* Stylistically, Lower Garble is hopeless. A dialect that is historically antique, uninvolved, talking with no imagination whatsoever to no one in particular about nothing in particular could scarcely be expected to speak with impact. What causes its language to be so punchless?

(a) It avoids proper nouns and personal pronouns. This is the inevitable result of third-person preaching. Lower Garble identifies no "us," no "we," no "you," or "I," only "it." This pseudo-objectivity loses not only personality, it loses the uniqueness of the present. Language struggles to express the unique. It cannot do so apart from the use of the *proper name,* which indicates without attempting definition or description. Casserly explains:

There is a sense in which all our words are shoddy and second-hand, used too often before, and by too many people, to be worthy of the exquisite individuality of the present event. . . . Let some modern Socrates ask John, an angelically patient John, why he loves Matilda. "Because of her brown eyes and auburn hair." "Because she is honest and kind and good." "But Ethel is all these things outstandingly." "Because she loves me." "But so does poor Joan." The conversation may continue till John's patience is exhausted, but it is certain that he will never succeed in telling his interrogator why he loves Matilda. If he is subtle enough John may say that he loves Matilda because of her "Matildaness"—in Christian theological and philosophical terms, the *hypostasis* or "hecceity" of Matilda—and this reply may terminate the conversation, but it will hardly answer the question. John has experienced "Matildaness" vividly enough, no doubt, but can he either describe or define it?[11]

Only preaching that names names, identifies places, and uses pronouns appropriately can hope to communicate personally and uniquely.

(b) It shuns action verbs. Lower Garble depends upon the various forms of "to be," the weakest verb in the English language. For example, rather than saying, "He believes," Lower Garble prefers "It is his belief that." If it can avoid the verb altogether, so much the better: "Prior to the congregation's consideration of the suggestion," rather than, "Before the church considered the suggestion."

Whenever possible, Lower Garble adds to its general vagueness by using the more remote Latinate forms of verbs—"employ" instead of "use," "stated" instead of "said," "ensue" instead of "follow"—or else it changes them from verbs altogether: as "reflection" for "reflect," "consideration" for "considered," "investigation" for "investigate," and so on. Noun constructions and noun-adjectives replace vulgar verbs.

When they cannot be avoided, verbs can always be smothered by putting them in the passive voice. Inverting the sentence helps, too.

(c) It never uses simple adjectives or modifying phrases. For example, "psychological research" is too simple; "research of a psychological character" is much better. Putting adjectives after the nouns in prepositional phrases adds to the confusion: not, "it was a religious war," but "it was a war of a religious nature."

Categories should be added to all adjective complements: gigantic in size; triangular in shape; pure white in color. Otherwise, the listeners might never figure this out for themselves.

(d) It is wordy. Lower Garble never says one word when three would do just as well. It prefers "due to the reason that," not "because"; "in a manner similar to," not "like" or "as"; "in the event that," not "if." These phrases are not only longer, they are less precise. Lubricating phrases are dropped into the words to make the sentences slip along more smoothly: facilitate, effectuate, expedite, utilize; feasible, plausible, acceptable. The useless phrase, "the fact that," is constantly in use: "The fact that it rained hurt attendance," not, "The rain hurt attendance."

The pulpit must overcome the dialect barriers of Upper Garble and Lower Garble to be heard. No doubt it can go on being a vaguely amusing and somehow comforting anachronism, a quaint remembrance of the good old days of virtue and innocence, of Sunday bandstands in the park and Fourth of July rhetoric, an occasionally pleasant pastoral interlude far from the "real world," the outside world. But if it does so, it can only expect amused tourists, not committed disciples.

Already thousands of the churches of the world have either become city monuments, brief stopovers for tour buses and curious visitors, or else obscure covens of the Society of the Same where only the dwindling number of initiates understand the strange dialect still doggedly spoken.

Not that the church should lose entirely the distinctiveness of its speech in a mere self-conscious effort to deny its heritage, in a silly attempt to "come home" to a world that is not its own; indeed, that is not even truly a *world,* but a *religion,* and a religion that is utterly foreign to its own faith. But it must break down the dialect walls that block its speech from reaching the world, the

274 / SAYING THE SERMON

communication barriers that wall itself in and others out.

Dialect can only be eliminated by conversation. Only true conversation, conversation not with itself but with others, can overcome the regionalism of the pulpit. When conversation occurs, dialect disappears and understanding grows.

For the pulpit and pew, or for the preacher and layperson, this interchange requires a peculiar grace, a unique humility. It requires a proper understanding of the diversity of gifts within the body of Christ, an acceptance of the function of the ministry and the importance of the laity. Both preacher and layperson must stand beneath the Word; both must listen, and both must speak.

But how can the preacher so speak that she or he also hears, and is heard? And how can the layperson so listen that he or she also speaks? There is a grace of hearing, and there is a gift of speaking. Unless preacher and congregation alike pray for both, no true dialogue can take place, and all of the external adjustment of its services or its speech cannot save it.

16. "They Listened the More Willingly"

Delivery is not an art form; it is a communication channel. Being a good speaker is not particularly important; being a good communicator is. Of course, good communicators are good speakers—but the opposite is not always true. What usually happens when we set out to be a "good speaker" is that we focus on all the wrong things: eloquent diction, precise enunciation, dramatic gestures, impressive facial expression, resonant tone, even correct breathing. By the time we are ready to speak, we are either paralyzed or galvanized. On the platform we resemble either a chalk dummy or a hyperactive robot.

An incarnational approach to sermon delivery is at least as important as an incarnational approach to sermon theory. When delivery is not fully integrated theologically into preaching, one of two things happens: either it preoccupies itself with the audience, which is the result of a false subjectivity, or it preoccupies itself with its material, which is the result of a false objectivity.

SUBJECTIVITY AND OBJECTIVITY IN DELIVERY

When delivery is treated as an art form to be mastered, a false subjectivity arises. These preachers believe that their skill is responsible for making the Word effective. Then we are treated to the spectacle of orating, gesticulating, posturing preachers. Their delivery may be country-crude or city-slick, but they are still guilty of the same theological error: their attention is focused on themselves and their effect rather than on the gospel and the congregation.

They may talk a great deal about the power of the Word or the authority of the Bible, but their every movement makes it apparent that their only trust is in themselves, in their own ability to persuade or captivate. They have no confidence in the presence of God in the Word, or else they would trust themselves to it more and less to their stage effects. If they really believed that the Bible possesses the power they are eternally asserting it has, they would not find it necessary to keep on blowing their trumpets so loudly or marching around the pulpit seven times to make the walls of Jericho fall down.

On the other hand, when delivery is treated homiletically as the illegitimate stepchild of the sermon or as a mere afterthought, an interesting elective if one is so inclined, then another bad thing happens to preaching. Philosophically, it becomes Greek rather than Hebrew. The manuscript is the pure soul; delivery is the embarrassing body. Eventually only the soul is important, and the more disembodied it can remain, the better. Therefore the manuscript is usually read word for word—preferably in an unemotional monotone—to keep personality out of preaching as much as possible. (But then why not mimeograph the sermon and mail it to the congregation, thereby sparing them the boredom of hearing it badly read?)

There is a false objectivity at work here, as if manuscripts written by very subjective human beings are any less tainted with subjectivity than their speaking of them. But somehow the objectification of ideas on paper seems pure, whereas the delivery of these ideas orally introduces a corrupt and fallible subjectivity. The pure ideal, so cooly remote and mysteriously authoritative, has to undergo the humiliation of taking on shape and form with the attendant risk that someone will identify the preacher of it as a human being.

It is as if "Oz, the great and terrible" had to step out from behind his screen where he is furiously cranking wheels and pulling levers and show Dorothy that he is nothing more than a genial old man; or as when Alice screamed at the mad court, "You're nothing but a pack of cards!" and the whole thing tumbled together.

But poor delivery is no pure virtue, and saying a sermon badly is no evidence that God is in it. Monotone cannot prevent manipulation, and at least as many people have been deceived by false ideas as by false rhetoric.

CONTACT POINT

Delivery must partake of the incarnational approach to preaching. Just as the interpretation of the Scripture must stand at midpoint between the historical and the existential, so delivery must stand at midpoint between the objective and the subjective, between a self-conscious withdrawal and an aggressive authoritarianism.

The *contact point* of the preached message is of utmost importance. The sermon must not take place behind the pulpit, nor on top of the pew, but at midpoint. True preaching only occurs when the preacher and congregation meet halfway in dialogue.

This means that proper delivery neither attacks the congregation nor hides behind the pulpit. If the preacher is too aggressively outgoing, the audience may be impressed with the first few blasts of pure personality, but eventually, they get tired of leaning backward to get his or her face out of theirs and withdraw altogether. This kind of pulpit-pounding, Bible-twisting, Lord's Supper table-leaping preacher can stun the most faithful into a blank-faced, mindless withdrawal. But if the preacher is too withdrawn, too passive, the people may move forward at first to encourage him or her to come out of hiding, but finally they will get tired of the chase around the pulpit and decide it is not worth the effort. Let the preacher burrow up in his or her notes; they have better things to do.

To establish the contact point of the sermon correctly, preachers must maintain the proper linear distance relative to their material and their audience. This can only happen if they have the proper degree of confidence in both. If they are uncertain or insecure about their material or their audience, they will either get lost in their ideas or try to cover up their insecurity with a showy display of meaningless fireworks. But if they have too much self-assurance in their own brilliant ideas or their own magnetic personality, the same thing happens. They become so fascinated with their own profound thoughts that they conduct a narcissistic love affair with them in plain sight of the audience, or else they trust their own persuasive personalities to the degree that they ignore the biblical message and depend upon dazzling the audience with a grand presence.

We must believe in both the Word and our hearers. Then our delivery can be confident without being overconfident, natural without being forced, persuasive without being seductive. When we trust God rather than ourselves, our confidence in our message is properly placed and our natural assurance grows. Likewise, when we respect the integrity of our congregations we do not attempt to overwhelm them or deceive them, but neither are we intimidated by them or afraid to share ourselves with them.

Sometimes the actual physical distance between the pulpit and the pew makes the proper contact point difficult to establish. But the mental stance of the preacher is far more important than his or her spatial location. *We should imagine ourselves standing at least one-third of the way down the rows of pews,* as much in the midst of the people as possible. This psychological stance is highly important. It prevents aloof, remote, abstract speech. It also makes it impossible to take on a false platform manner or to shout or use grotesque gestures. (Only the most seriously imbalanced preacher could stand in the midst of friends and orate or shout in the face of someone only two feet away.)

This stance also permits the sermon to find its correct contact point. Since it neither hides from the audience nor overwhelms them, this kind of preaching encourages the people to meet the preacher halfway. They do not feel that the preacher is doing it all for them, and so they do not merely sit there as passive spectators. Likewise, they do not feel that we have nothing to say, or that we are unsure of ourselves and unable to say anything with certainty, and so they do not feel that listening to us is a waste of time. Instead, the preacher preaches so that the sermon event takes place at midpoint, exactly halfway between the eagerness of the preacher to declare the message and the willingness of the congregation to hear it.

It is amazing what a transformation this simple mental positioning can cause in sermon delivery, in the naturalness and humanity it can bring to pulpit speech. And it is likewise amazing what it can do for the attentiveness of the congregation.

There is nothing like the sound of a familiar voice to catch attention. As Paul was being dragged toward the tower of Antonius (Acts 21), having just been rescued by the Roman guards from a Jewish mob who believed he had desecrated the Temple, he asked the soldiers if he might speak to the crowd. They agreed; and when the people realized that he spoke their own language, they stopped their shouting, and "they listened the more willingly" (Acts 22:2).

If people ignore speech that is unnatural and peculiar, they are powerfully arrested by someone who speaks their own language. But "speaking their own language" involves more than voice or vocabulary, though of course these are involved. It is the complete impression conveyed from the pulpit. As such, it means that preachers must talk about things that really matter to the people, that they must do so naturally and understandably, and that they must do this as one of them, not as an outsider. In short, they must practice conversational delivery. But what is that?

CONVERSATIONAL DELIVERY

Conversational delivery is no new concept. It is one of the most familiar phrases in homiletics. Some preachers enthusiastically believe in it and recommend it, while others just as soundly oppose it. But few terms are used more glibly and with less understanding of their meaning than "conversational preaching." What does it really mean? Or perhaps better, what *should* it mean?

The concept has a long history. It could be traced back to the ancient preachers who encouraged speech that the audience could understand, or even further, to the Greek orators who urged their pupils to use intimate, familiar speech. But apparently the primary origin of the modern concept dates back to Richard Baxter. In *The Reformed Pastor,* he wrote: "A great matter also with the most of our hearers doth lie in the very pronunciation and tone of speech. . . . Especially see that there be no affectation, but that we speak as familiarly to our people as we would if we were talking to any of them personally. The want of a familiar tone and expression is as great a defect in most of our deliveries as anything whatsoever, and that which we should be very careful to amend. When a man hath a reading or declaiming tone, like a schoolboy saying his lesson or an oration, few are moved with anything that he saith."[1]

Later preachers also took up this approach. It probably explains the appeal of Phillips Brooks better than anything else. A contemporary of his said, "He spoke to his audience as *a man might speak to his friend. . . .* The listeners never thought of style or manner, but only of the substance of his thoughts."[2] Charles R. Brown, dean of Yale Divinity School, said, *"The tone of dignified conversation* furnishes the staple method for effective delivery. It wears better than any other style of speech."[3] Harry Emerson Fosdick believed strongly in the conversational approach, but he never believed that he mastered it.[4] Helmut Thielicke stressed the importance of mastering one's sermon material to achieve conversational delivery: "Only he who is very familiar with and close to what he is saying can talk about it *quite naturally and in a conversational tone."*[5]

Other preachers either strongly endorsing or known for practicing conversational delivery include John A. Broadus, who was a master of it, Charles Finney, John Henry Jowett, Dwight Moody, S. Parkes Cadman, Ralph Sockman, Clovis Chappell, and Leslie Weatherhead.

But what does conversational preaching involve? Before identifying some characteristics of the conversational style, let us first be plain about what it is *not.* It is not uninvolved, matter-of-fact, indifferent speech. It is not poorly articulated, overly quiet, mumbling speech. It is not inanimate, gestureless, expressionless speech. It is not a self-conscious monologue.

Conversational preaching, very simply, is exactly like a good conversation. Watch any two friends in conversation. Are they passive, expressionless? Or are they flamboyant and oratorical? Not if they are really having a conversation instead of holding alternating monologues. The amazing thing about conversation is that it can be so animated and lively without once appearing forced or unnatural. The whole business proceeds naturally.

This is the key to conversational preaching, and leads us to our first principle:

1. *Conversational preaching is natural because it is internally motivated.* We must not plan expressions, gestures, inflections. Rather, we must allow these things to proceed naturally from the subject we are discussing. If we are fully involved with our subject, and at the same time completely engaged with our audience, the inevitable result will be a natural, animated style.

2. *Conversational preaching speaks in its natural tone of voice.* Conversation is the speech norm. Everyone has a natural pitch of voice he or she uses in daily conversation. That same tone should be carried to the platform. This does not mean that the voice may not need to be louder. Actually, the very physical difference between speaking to one person three feet away and five hundred people many feet away may demand more volume. But the secret is to use the same *tone,* even at a higher volume. This will require some practice at first, but it can be mastered if the preacher is really absorbed in genuine conversation. Do not elevate the pitch or fall into an oratorical cadence, the famous "ministerial tune." (This tune can actually be played on the piano: two notes the same, two notes one step higher, and then the first two notes repeated—try it sometime. On the piano—not the congregation!)

A voice pattern invariably results from a preset inflection un-related to the content of the material being delivered. *This tone must be avoided at all costs.* Nothing so terminates a conversation as the opening note of an oratorical solo, and nothing so prevents a conversation from ever getting started as the pious singsong of Reverend Holier-Than-Thou.

3. *Conversational preaching talks with its audience, not to them, or at them.* It does so by including them in the thought process. The preacher is not talking *to* the congregation about *his or her* subject; he or she

is talking *with* them about a mutual interest. Talking to the audience suggests too strongly a one-sided performance. We are certainly not talking *at* them either, as if they were bad children who needed scolding, or even children at all, who needed someone to tell them what to do.

Preaching is not telling someone what to do; it is a mutual hearing of the word of God, as both speaker and listener stand beneath its truth.

One useful means of achieving conversation with the audience is the rhetorical question. Flat assertions have a way of shutting off discussion. (You can observe that in any daily conversation.) As much as possible, the preacher should raise questions to engage her or his congregation in mental dialogue: "How can we love our neighbor? Isn't that really unrealistic and impossible? And who is our neighbor, anyhow?" Or, "What do you understand Christ to be saying in this Scripture? It seems to me that he is asking . . ." The sermon should be a mental conversation: "I suppose it was something like that that caused David to say . . ." These sentences invite the congregation to join in the decision-making process.

4. *Conversational preaching is constantly aware of the audience.* Since we are in conversation with our congregations, we are not oblivious to their response. We should never be out of touch with their feelings, not even for a moment. With practice, we should be able to detect instantly the feelings our audiences are constantly transmitting to us: if our interpretation of the Scripture has struck a particularly deep chord of response, we should know it; if boredom and restlessness is spreading through the congregation, we should know it. (One particularly accurate indication of not listening is that blank look of solemn attention when the congregation is sitting stone-still and motionless, as in a hypnotic trance—but if you waved a hand in front of their eyes, nobody would blink.)

We must be so in control of our material that we can devote our full attention to conversation with our audiences and reacting to their responses. Chrysostom was so in touch with his congregation that he lengthened or shortened each section of his exposition depending upon the response of the audience.[6] Any preacher who has such a healthy respect for the reaction of his or her hearers will soon learn how to speak so that people listen willingly.

Understood in this way, conversational preaching is very closely akin to the dialogue sermon. It is not necessary to replace one with the other. The dialogue sermon is a special sermon *form,* and an excellent one, and depending upon the interest of the preacher and his congregation, may be used almost exclusively or very seldom.

But conversational preaching is a fundamental *approach* to the minister's role in the proclamation of the gospel. It can be used in every sermon, regardless of its form. It permits a distinct quality of dialogue even in traditional preaching where the minister alone speaks.

If the sermon does not engage the audience in mental dialogue, it is highly unlikely that actual physical dialogue can be structured after the sermon—or during it, for that matter, if we are so flatly monological in our responses or questioning that we squelch a scheduled dialogue session. After all, merely physically arranging a dialogue sermon is no guarantee that dialogue will actually take place. Who hasn't sat through a miserable session that advertised itself as a dialogue experience, but in fact was nothing but a series of alternating monologues?

Bonhoeffer insists that dialogue could, and in fact, must occur in every true sermon:

What is the sociological relation of the congregation to the preacher? Is he drawn into their fellowship as one questioner among others? Or is he the bearer of unconditioned truth, and is he their teacher, answering their questions? Should the sermon be a dialogue or a monologue? . . . In answering this question . . . there has been a great deal of one-sided argument. It is characteristic of the preacher that he simultaneously questions and proclaims. He must ask along with the congregation, and form a "Socratic" community—otherwise he could not give any reply. But he can reply, and he must, because he knows God's answer in Christ. . . . It is a pre-supposition of a Christian congregation that it comes together as a questioner, and at the same time it is the strength of the congregation that each individual learns of the knowledge and the truth that belongs to the congregation.[7]

But this kind of dialogue through conversational preaching can be easily blocked. The preacher must avoid or remove those barriers that can block the communication channel.

BARRIERS IN THE COMMUNICATION CHANNEL

All of the barriers to true conversation have one thing in common: they are various forms of a *separation* between the speaker and the hearer. In order to participate in true dialogue with the congregation, the preacher must avoid each of these causes of separation:

1. *Material separation.* When we are preoccupied with our material or else have not sufficiently mastered it, material separation occurs. We get lost in our content and lose sight of the audience. This may be called "talking within the cylinder"; the preacher looks like a person in a phone booth reading the directory aloud to himself or herself.

This fault has one of two causes. It will always occur if the preacher regards the sermon as a performance, as the delivery of a body of material, and so talks *about it* rather than *with the people.* But we can also be separated from our audiences by our material if we must spend most of our time rummaging around in our mental attics trying to remember what in the world it was we wanted to say. Only adequate preparation and a proper focus can prevent this error. (Needless to say, preachers who obviously read their sermons with their noses buried in a notebook haven't got a chance to begin with. Their material separation is absolute.)

2. *Idea separation.* Idea separation is closely akin to material separation. But in this case is it not the material in general that causes the problem, but the presentation of abstract ideas. In other words, as long as we are talking about personal events or are involved in narration, we are in close contact with the audience. Our tone is natural, our manner friendly and relaxed. But if we begin to present a theory, a doctrine, or an abstract idea, then we usually lapse into impersonal oratory. These presentations sound exactly like two different sermons delivered by two entirely different people.

This schizoid presentation can be avoided if the preacher realizes that all doctrines were given for people and that each idea must be grasped by people. No part of the sermon should be thought of as theoretical; the most profound concepts have the most practical significance for people. Jesus always spoke most concretely and humanly when presenting his most eternal truths.

3. *Mood separation.* Frequently the preacher begins on a higher level of emotional intensity than the audience. We have been thinking about the text and the sermon long enough—let's hope —that we have become genuinely excited about it and eager to communicate it. We may be tempted into a dramatic opening that strikes the audience as forced or unnatural simply because they do not as yet have any reason to be as fired about the subject as the preacher. Then when we realize that we have overshot the audience, we may panic at their lack of response and turn up the emotional level even higher in an attempt to whip the audience into enthusiasm. We may be guilty of *homiletical overkill:* emotion in excess of content, volume level in excess of space. But rather than stirring emotion, just the opposite results. The congregation sits coldly watching a desperate performance, and the one who has begun on a shout ends in a whisper.

Dynamism at the beginning of a sermon can be easily overdone. The preacher will do better to give the audience time and cause to be excited. We must realize that our own enthusiasm originated from the word of God and our study of it, and if properly presented it will do the same for the congregation. No hard and fast rule can be given in this area, but generally speaking an easy opening is an asset for gaining attention and a dynamic one a liability, whereas later in the sermon, dynamism may be appropriate and a casual stance less so.

It is also a mistake to begin to urge too soon in the sermon. In conversation, we never begin with exhorting. If we are ever led to urge or exhort a friend in conversation, such exhortation comes slowly and it is always marked by understanding, even humility. To be heard and heeded when we urge something upon a congregation of fellow Christians, we must first have demonstrated that we speak out of genuine interest in their well-being, that we profoundly care about them and understand them. Then our most serious words will be taken as the genuine concern of a real friend.

4. *Pace separation.* Famous speakers have demonstrated a great variety in rate of delivery: Webster spoke at 80–100 words a minute; Lincoln, 100; Franklin Roosevelt, 117; Henry Clay, 160; and Phillips Brooks, 215 words a minute. Some people can obviously speak clearly and effectively at a much higher rate than others. But Brigance concludes, "In general a rate of more than 150 words a minute is too fast; and, if you slow down to 100 words a minute, there is danger of the audience losing interest—unless you speak with exceptional force and with effective pauses."[8]

Obviously it is possible to speak so rapidly that no one can follow or so slowly that no one wants to follow. Static rate figures, however, are not nearly so important for the speaker as a varied pace. Does her or his rate suit the subject matter? Is it internally motivated and natural, or artificial and forced? Does it ever vary, or is it uniformly hammering or uniformly dragging?

Floating is a pleasant sensation in water, but an extremely unpleasant one in preaching. The audience will invariably get restless and irritated if we drift aimlessly between thoughts, floating around and paddling along until we can think of something else to say. On the other hand, *racing* is equally irritating and nerve-racking. The preacher who leaps to the platform with tongue racing is trying to pump into the sermon artificially the appearance of that conviction it lacks naturally. Rate normally rises with enthusiasm or interest, but it should do so on its own, not as a device employed by the preacher to simulate fervor.

If we are aware that our rate of delivery is naturally slow and deliberate, we can eliminate overly drawn-out pauses and add variety. Checking our energy levels will be more productive than artificially increasing rate; sometimes a too-slow rate is the result of an inadequate involvement with the sermon itself.

If we speak too rapidly, we can employ more pauses—the "white space" in oral delivery. Setting off sentences in print with "white space" separates them and emphasizes them. Pauses will do the same for the rapid speaker. We might also check our output of nervous energy. It could be that we lack the certainty and assurance God has promised those who proclaim the Word.

PREACHING AND CONVENTIONAL SPEECH CONCERNS

But what of the conventional concerns of "public speaking" classes—articulation, resonation, phonation, breathing, gestures, posture, and so on? Generally speaking, *these things are only important if they get in the way.* If communication is hindered by some fault in one of them, then the obstacle that is interfering must be removed from the communication channel. Enormous amounts of energy and time have been wasted by preachers and preaching classes in really pointless efforts to "master the arts" of gestures, articulation, breathing, and voice projection.

If the communication of the sermon is not being hampered by one of these elements, *no attention should be given to them whatsoever.* In fact positive harm can be done to preachers and their proclamation by making them self-conscious about their speech. Then they focus on the *externals* of the sermon rather than the *internal* matters from which good delivery proceeds. Even when a real problem is discovered, a point of diminishing returns is reached very quickly in efforts devoted to such "speech arts."

Artificiality can be easily created in the total delivery of a speaker who may suffer from poor articulation, for example, but who is otherwise completely natural and engaging. Instead of a very natural and earnest preacher of the gospel whose communication was really excellent except for rare occasions when faulty articulation blocked understanding, we are left with an overly precise and very self-conscious, artificial pulpit orator who is anything but human and whose communication with the congregation is almost always bad. If that is improvement, the church doesn't need it.

The difficult problem is knowing whether we have a speech problem that is interfering with the communication of our messages and if so, how to remove it. Our college speech courses or seminary delivery courses should have at least indicated the problem. If not, then we must ask someone who knows us well enough to answer.

As for removing the problem, this first step is the hardest—suspecting that it is there and asking. After that, the second step is conscious attention to eliminating the fault. This effort will have the undesirable but inescapable effect of making us self-conscious for a while. We will simply have to put up with that until the fault is gone. In the meantime, the best thing we can do is try to keep the rest of our delivery as natural as possible. The self-attention required to overcome a problem is a drastic cure, but if the fault is serious enough it may be warranted.

Finally, a few positive suggestions in each of these speech areas may be of some additional help.

1. *Body language.* Almost nobody worries about gestures anymore, but body language has become a topic of real interest. There are still many preachers who are either grotesque or frozen in the pulpit. The total absence of bodily involvement is as much a distraction to an audience as constant arm-waving or repetitious finger-stabbing. The use of the body, like all of delivery, must be internally motivated. Everyone uses gestures naturally in conversation because they are only done spontaneously; but put the same natural gesturer on the platform, and we may freeze or flap. We won't if we are really set free through genuine conversation with our audiences.

Body language, then, can never be planned. It happens. How can a natural use of the body be encouraged?

(a) *By not studying gestures.* Nothing is more fatal than practicing in front of a mirror or studying "upper, middle, and lower plane" gestures. That kind of planning is a sure-fire way to artificiality. Whoever thought of planning a gesture for conversation? "Let's see—this afternoon when I tell Tom about my flight from New York, I think I'll point heavenward!"

(b) *By not preventing body involvement.* Body involvement is only totally absent if prevented. If we mask our faces to hide our feelings or stand woodenly to avoid making a mistake, we make a mistake. Sometimes the problem lies in the feeling level of the preacher, too. If we are indifferent, we rarely gesture. The only body movements that should be prevented are meaningless, grotesque, or repetitious gestures that may be habitual but are never natural.

(c) *By avoiding overkill.* Homiletical overkill—emotion in excess of content, volume level in excess of space—always results in exaggerated, artificial expressions and movements. Forcing emotion forces gestures, often wildly inappropriate and poorly timed, but funny.

(d) *By becoming involved with the issue.* Involvement with the subject matter of the sermon leads to spontaneous, appropriate body movement—just as it does in conversation.

(e) *By becoming involved with the audience.* Body language is often produced in conversation because of our relationship with our listeners: we smile or frown because of the feelings we share; we point toward her or left or right of her; we stretch our hands to measure for him; we shrug to indicate a feeling we can't verbalize to her.

(f) *By becoming involved with the pictures.* When we are really visualizing our subject or when we are absorbed in narration, we use our bodies unselfconsciously. These are usually totally spontaneous expressions of the most appropriate sort. The more we visualize our ideas, the more visible they become to the audience.

(g) *By stretching yourself.* A few preachers are too big for any platform, but many are too small. They simply feel awkward holding a lively conversation with more than one person. Often they feel that they are overly gesturing and that their facial expressions are already almost too much. Usually the opposite is true. Just as a larger room requires more volume, a larger conversation can stand broader movement without becoming unnatural.

One good exercise for the really inhibited preacher is telling made-up stories to children. Expressiveness and natural body use always result from this kind of fun. And if you don't have any children of your own to tell stories to, rent some!

2. *Articulation, resonation, phonation.* Each of these terms has to do with speech sounds. *Phonation* is simply producing sound. *Articulation* is shaping it. *Resonation* is amplifying it.

The sound produced by the vibration of the vocal folds has a definite pitch, largely determined by the length and thickness of those folds. Most people produce adequate sound for speech. Endless amounts of needless effort have been devoted by preachers to developing a "deeper" voice. Many women, especially, do so to sound less "feminine" and to increase their authority. For their trouble, both men and women are usually rewarded only with a monotone. The sole requirement for a good voice is that it be interesting. Variety in tone accomplishes that. And variety results from internally motivated speech. Virtually the only time that a voice needs to be lowered is when it is artificially elevated by tension.

Nothing is worse for Christian proclamation than for preachers to become enamored with their own sounds. But they should be alert for persistent hoarseness, which may indicate constant voice abuse through harsh, strident misuse, but which can also be a symptom of serious throat problems. A doctor should always be consulted immediately if hoarseness persists longer than two weeks.

Resonation, or the amplification of the voice, is largely accomplished in the upper resonating chambers behind the nose, although the mouth plays some part. If the preacher's voice lacks adequate resonation, or the famous "voice projection," all he or she usually needs to do is open the mouth. Proper tone placement is impossible with teeth clenched. Nasality is also prevented in the same way. If either of these is a problem, a good exercise is to speak with the front teeth at least one-half inch apart: practice speaking with a notched eraser, cut to the proper length, held between the front teeth. (This is about as odd as speech exercises get, but it will correct severe nasality or inadequate voice projection.)

Articulation has to do with the cleanness and distinctness with which words are shaped. As long as all of the sounds in a word are easily understandable, articulation is adequate. Overly precise articulation, or the strange pronunciation of the speech purist who insists on saying all of the letters in a word—even those that shouldn't be pronounced, such as the "i" in "glacier" or "marriage"—sounds prissy and pendantic.

But if some words are not coming across clearly to the audience because of slurred vowels or dropped consonants, then articulation needs attention. The problem is usually either regional speech faults (dropping final g's, as in "runnin' " or dark vowels, such as "dork" for "dark"), or that the preacher is lip-lazy. More active, precise use of the lips and tongue in clipping off sounds will correct the problem.

3. *Breathing.* Unless the preacher is gasping like a guppy or running out of air in the middle of sentences, no attention needs to be given to breathing. Only the miracles of Lourdes are a more fascinating mystery than the fabled diaphramatic breathing. It would be interesting to know how many hours have been spent by preachers standing around with their hands on their middles, panting like puppy dogs; or how many sermons have been delivered in an absent-minded way by preachers lost in the mysterious contemplation of "packing their tones around their belt"—whatever that means.

If preachers will simply not preach at such a ridiculous rate that they sounds like someone simultaneously running to a fire and delivering the Gettysburg Address; or if they will not studiously cultivate that curious gasping sound before every sentence that is supposed to simulate religious passion; or if they will not speak out of half-exhausted lungs, sipping teaspoonsful of air between words; then they need not worry about mastering the mysteries of diaphramatic breathing or avoiding the curse of "upperclavicular breathing" (which, to everyone's pleasure, will remain undefined).

4. *Posture and platform manner.* The last of the classical speech concerns to be discussed here are posture and platform manner, which require the least comment of all. Unless a preacher is either rigid with fright or is possessed with a length of rubber hose for

a backbone, posture is insignificant. Common sense should take care of platform manner. A few "don'ts" should suffice:

(a) Don't bound to the platform like an escaped kangaroo, nor drag to the platform like someone going to the block.

(b) Don't slump across the pulpit as if unable to remain awake (others may join you).

(c) Don't stand ramrod stiff and rigid, as though afraid of setting off a bomb.

(d) Don't fix your gaze on the ceiling, the floor, or one side of your audience alone. (Eye contact in conversation is natural; it doesn't need promoting, just not preventing.)

(e) Don't rock back and forth or sway hypnotically from side to side like a cobra about to strike. (This is a hard habit to break, if habitual. Try anchoring one leg against the back of the pulpit. That is a frightfully unnatural stance, but it is much less distracting than the preacher who has got into a "weaving way." In time, it can be easily abandoned.)

In summary, delivery should be natural. It will be, if internally motivated. Conversation is its model because it is the basic speech norm. It is a style of speech exactly suited to the Christian message. Conversational preaching avoids both false subjectivity and false objectivity and permits the most intimate communication of the word of God.

Approached in this way, the delivery of the sermon stands miles apart from the Emerson School of Elocution tradition, the self-conscious mastery of an impressive art form. Sermon delivery must be anchored on its subjective side to communication theory, and on its objective side to incarnational preaching. Otherwise it will falsify its theological basis at the same time it is failing to communicate.

But when the living Word becomes incarnate in the living situation—even as it takes on flesh and blood in the most practical saying of the sermon—then the preaching event occurs, and Christ once again comes to the people.

Notes

PREFACE

1. Julius Schniewind, *Die geistliche Erneuerung des Pfarrerstandes,* 2d ed. (Berlin: Verlag Haus und Schule, 1949), 7.
2. Gustaf Wingren, *The Living Word* (Philadelphia: Fortress, 1960), 24.
3. Ibid., 23–24.
4. Joseph Sittler, *The Anguish of Preaching* (Philadelphia: Fortress, 1966), 7.
5. Ibid., 10.
6. Ibid., 12.
7. Rudolf Bohren, *Preaching and Community,* trans. David E. Green (Richmond, VA: Knox, 1965), 42.
8. David James Randolph, *The Renewal of Preaching* (Philadelphia: Fortress, 1969), 21. We cannot agree with David Randolph at this point when he places the ax in the hands of venerable John A. Broadus, who may have compounded the crime but certainly was not responsible for it. That atrocity was committed long before Broadus asserted that homiletics was a branch of rhetoric.

1. WHAT CAN PREACHING DO?

1. Elie Wiesel, *Legends of Our Time* (New York: Avon, 1968), 31.
2. See Paul Ricoeur, *The Conflict of Interpretations* (Evanston, IL: Northwestern University Press, 1974), 11–24.
3. Paul Ricoeur, "Structure, Word, Event," trans. Robert Sweeney, *Philosophy Today* 12 (1968):119.
4. Karl-Heinrich Bieritz, "Patterns of Proclamation," trans. Geoffrey Wainwright, *Studia Liturgica* 15, no. 1 (1982–83):19.
5. Walker Percy, *The Message in the Bottle* (New York: Farrar, Straus and Giroux, 1979), 114–49.
6. Ibid., 120–25.
7. Edward Schmidt, "Another Look at Christ in Preaching," *Worship* 55 (1981):-433.
8. For a description of the meaning of this passage from a Third World perspective, see Robert McAfee Brown, *Unexpected News: Reading the Bible with Third World Eyes* (Philadelphia: Westminster, 1984), 89–104.
9. Fred B. Craddock, *Overhearing the Gospel* (Nashville, TN: Abingdon, 1978), 47.
10. Bieritz, "Patterns of Proclamation," 19.
11. Jürgen Moltmann, *The Power of the Powerless* (San Francisco: Harper & Row, 1983), ix.

2. THE STUBBORN PULPIT

1. William D. Thompson, ed., *Abingdon Preacher's Library* (Nashville, TN: Abingdon, 1980), 9.
2. Fred B. Craddock, *As One Without Authority* (Enid, OK: Phillips University Press, 1971), 1.
3. T. Harwood Pattison, *The History of Christian Preaching* (Philadelphia: American Baptist Publication Society, 1903), 88.
4. Yngve Brilioth, *A Brief History of Preaching,* trans. Karl E. Mattson (Philadelphia: Fortress, 1965), 21ff.
5. Pattison, *History of Christian Preaching,* 57.
6. Brilioth, *Brief History of Preaching,* 95.
7. Ibid., 79–81.
8. Clyde E. Fant, Jr., and William M. Pinson, Jr., *20 Centuries of Great Preaching,* 13 vols. (Waco, TX.: Word, 1971), 1:232.
9. Ibid.
10. Brilioth, *Brief History of Preaching,* 129ff.
11. Pattison, *History of Christian Preaching,* 211.
12. Richard Baxter, *The Reformed Pastor,* ed. Hugh Martin (Richmond, VA: Knox, 1956), 89.
13. Pattison, *History of Christian Preaching,* 248.
14. Stopford Brooke, ed., *Life and Letters of Frederick W. Robertson,* 2 vols. (Boston: Ticknor and Fields, 1865), 2:59–60.
15. Ibid.
16. Joseph Fort Newton, *Some Living Masters of the Pulpit* (New York: Doran, 1923), vii–viii.
17. *Spectator,* 91:85–86.
18. *Current Literature,* 42:312–14.
19. Ibid., 44:94–95.
20. *Harper's Weekly,* 55:6.
21. *Hampton's Magazine,* 27:223–32.
22. *Current Opinion,* 69:511–12.
23. *Literary Digest,* 83:34.
24. *Literary Digest,* 87:31–32.
25. *Century Magazine,* 111:1–19.
26. *Harper's Magazine,* 157:133–41.
27. *Christian Century,* 49:114–16.
28. *Catholic World,* 144:6–8.
29. Joseph Sittler, *The Anguish of Preaching* (Philadelphia: Fortress, 1966), 26.
30. Clyde Reid, *The Empty Pulpit* (New York: Harper & Row, 1967), 25–33.
31. Reuel Howe, *Partners in Preaching* (New York: Seabury, 1967), 26–33.
32. Gene E. Bartlett, "The Preaching and Pastoral Roles," *Pastoral Psychology* 3 (March 1952): 21–28.
33. Pierre Berton, *The Comfortable Pew* (New York: Lippencott, 1965), 96ff.
34. Peter Berger, *The Noise of Solemn Assemblies* (Garden City, NY: Doubleday, 1961).
35. Rodney Stark et al., "Sounds of Silence," *Psychology Today* 3, no. 11 (April 1970):38ff.
36. James E. Dittes, *Minister on the Spot* (Philadelphia: Pilgrim, 1970), 77–78.
37. Reuel Howe, *The Miracle of Dialogue* (New York: Seabury, 1963), 32.

38. Berton, *The Comfortable Pew*, 101–102.
39. Horst Symanowski, *The Christian Witness in an Industrial Society* (Philadelphia: Westminster, 1964), 20.
40. August Wenzel, "Criticisms of Preaching in Current Writings," *Lutheran Quarterly* 20 (November 1968):393.
41. Theodore Wedel, "Is Preaching Outmoded?" *Religion in Life* 35 (Autumn 1965): 535.
42. Harvey Cox, *The Secular City* (New York: Macmillan, 1965), 122.
43. Helmut Thielicke, *The Trouble with the Church,* trans. and ed. John W. Doberstein (New York: Harper & Row, 1965), xi.
44. Robert Jensen, *A Religion Against Itself* (Richmond, VA: Knox, 1967).
45. Gerhard Ebeling, *Theology and Proclamation,* trans. John Riches (Philadelphia: Fortress, 1966).
46. Thielicke, *Trouble with the Church,* cf. 9ff.
47. Allan Boesak, *The Finger of God,* trans. Peter Randall (Maryknoll, NY: Orbis, 1982), 10.
48. Sittler, *Anguish of Preaching,* 27.

3. THE STUBBORN HOPE

1. Amos N. Wilder, *The Language of the Gospel* (New York: Harper & Row, 1964), 18–19.
2. Ibid., 14.
3. Ibid., 15.
4. Robert H. Mounce, *The Essential Nature of New Testament Preaching* (Grand Rapids, MI: Eerdmans, 1960), 16–18.
5. Yngve Brilioth, *A Brief History of Preaching* (Philadelphia: Fortress, 1965), 3.
6. W. B. Sedgwick, "The Origins of the Sermon," *Hibbert Journal* 45 (January 1947):162.
7. Yngve Brilioth, *Landmarks in the History of Preaching* (London: S.P.C.K., 1950), 2–3.
8. Floyd V. Filson, *The New Testament Against Its Environment* (Chicago: Regnery, 1950), 11.
9. P. T. Forsyth, *Positive Preaching and the Modern Mind* (Grand Rapids, MI: Eerdmans, 1964), 1.
10. Filson, *New Testament Environment,* 26.
11. Thorleif Boman, *Hebrew Thought Compared with Greek* (Philadelphia: Westminster, 1960), 206.
12. P.H. Menoud, "Preaching," *The Interpreter's Dictionary of the Bible,* 4 vols. (Nashville, TN: Abingdon, 1962), 3:868.
13. Jerome Murphy-O'Connor, *Paul on Preaching* (New York: Sheed & Ward, 1964), 51.
14. Wilder, *Language of the Gospel,* 28.
15. Ibid., 21.
16. Mounce, *New Testament Preaching,* 28.
17. Wilder, *Language of the Gospel,* 21.
18. Ibid., 22–23.

19. Hugh Kerr, *Preaching in the Early Church* (New York: Revell, 1948), 14.
20. Wilder, *Language of the Gospel*, 20.
21. Clemens E. Benda, "Language, Consciousness and Problems of Existential Analysis (Daseinsanalyse)," *American Journal of Psychotherapy* 14, no. 2 (April 1960):262.
22. Robert W. Funk, *Language, Hermeneutic, and Word of God* (New York: Harper & Row, 1966), 7.
23. Karl Barth, *The Preaching of the Gospel*, trans. B. E. Hooke (Philadelphia: Westminster, 1963), 9.
24. Ibid., 12, 14.
25. Ibid., 54–55.
26. Ibid., 37.
27. Carl E. Braaten, "The Interdependence of Theology and Preaching," *Dialog* (Winter 1964):15.
28. Fred B. Craddock, *As One Without Authority* (Enid, OK: Phillips University Press, 1971), 39.
29. Rudolf Bultmann, *Theologie des Neuen Testaments*, 3 vols. (Tübingen: Mohr, 1948), 1:297.
30. Rudolf Bultmann, "Reply," *The Theology of Rudolf Bultmann*, ed. Charles W. Kegley (New York: Harper & Row, 1966), 260–61.
31. Ibid., 273.
32. Rudolf Bultmann, "Preaching: Genuine and Secularized," *Religion and Culture, Essays in Honor of Paul Tillich*, ed. Walter Leibrecht (New York: Harper, 1959), 240.
33. Rudolf Bultmann, *Offenbarung und Heilsgeschehen*, vol. 7 of *Beiträge zur evangelischen Theologie*, ed. E. Wolfe (Munich: Evangelischer Verlag, Albert Lempp, 1941), 7:66.
34. For further documentation of this assertion, see my work *Bonhoeffer: Worldly Preaching* (Nashville, TN: Nelson, 1975).
35. Dietrich Bonhoeffer, *Gesammelte Schriften*, ed. Eberhard Bethge, 5 vols. (Munich: Chr. Kaiser Verlag, 1961), 4:7.
36. Ibid., 4:8.
37. Ibid., 4:12.
38. Ibid., 4:240.
39. Gerhard Ebeling, *The Problem of Historicity in the Church and Its Proclamation*, trans. Grover Foley (Philadelphia: Fortress, 1967), 22.
40. Gerhard Ebeling, *Word and Faith*, trans. James Leitch (Philadelphia: Fortress, 1963), 425.
41. Heinrich Ott, *Theology and Preaching*, trans. Harold Knight (Philadelphia: Westminster, 1965), 19.
42. Heinz Zahrnt, *The Question of God: Protestant Theology in the Twentieth Century*, trans. R. A. Wilson (New York: Harcourt, Brace & World, 1969), 299.
43. Gustaf Wingren, *The Living Word* (Philadelphia: Fortress, 1960), 13.
44. P. T. Forsyth, *Positive Preaching and the Modern Mind* (Grand Rapids, MI: Eerdmans, 1964), 1.
45. Emil Brunner, *Revelation and Reason* (Philadelphia: Westminster, 1946), 142.
46. H. H. Farmer, *The Servant of the Word* (New York: Scribner, 1942), 24.
47. Martin E. Marty, *Second Chance for American Protestants* (New York: Harper & Row, 1963), 158–59.
48. Harvey Cox, *The Secular City* (New York: Macmillan, 1965), 241.

49. John Bright, *The Authority of the Old Testament* (Nashville, TN: Abingdon, 1967), 162, 164.
50. Nels F. S. Ferré, "The Place of Preaching in the Modern World," *The Pulpit* (December 1962): 10.
51. Clyde Reid, *The Empty Pulpit* (New York: Harper & Row, 1967), 37–38.
52. Joseph Sittler, *The Anguish of Preaching* (Philadelphia: Fortress, 1966), 7–8.
53. Peter L. Berger, "A Call for Authority in the Christian Community," unpublished manuscript (mimeo COCU: 71, Denver No. 9), pp. 9ff.
54. Peter L. Berger, *The Precarious Vision* (Garden City, NY: Doubleday, 1961), 184.
55. Reid, *Empty Pulpit,* 86.
56. Gerhard Ebeling, *The Nature of Faith,* trans. Ronald Gregor Smith (Philadelphia: Muhlenberg, 1961), 189.
57. Ibid., 190.

4. PROCLAMATION, MANIFESTATION, AND ACTION

1. Paul Ricoeur, "Manifestation and Proclamation," *Journal of the Blaisdell Institute* (Winter, 1978): 13–35.
2. H. Richard Niebuhr, *The Kingdom of God in America* (New York: Harper, 1959), 193.
3. Ricoeur, "Manifestation and Proclamation," 19–21.
4. David Tracy, *The Analogical Imagination* (New York: Crossroad, 1981), 193ff.
5. See James Buchanan, "Creation and Cosmos: The Symbolics of Proclamation and Participation," in *Cosmology and Theology,* ed. David Tracy and Nicholas Lash (New York: Seabury, 1983), 37–43.
6. Tracy, *The Analogical Imagination,* 203.
7. Ibid., 222.
8. Ibid., 379.
9. Ibid., 210.
10. Ibid., 215.
11. Gustavo Gutierrez, *The Power of the Poor in History,* trans. Robert R. Barr (Maryknoll, NY: Orbis, 1984), 37.
12. Ibid., 17.
13. Gustavo Gutierrez, "Liberation, Theology and Proclamation," trans. J. P. Donnelly, in *The Mystical and Political Dimension of the Christian Faith,* ed. Claude Geffre and Gustavo Gutierrez (New York: Herder and Herder, 1974), 75.
14. Tracy, *The Analogical Imagination,* 390.
15. For a further discussion of this subject, see Tracy, *The Analogical Imagination,* 390–91.
16. Jürgen Moltmann, *The Power of the Powerless* (San Francisco: Harper & Row, 1981), ix.
17. Gutierrez, "Liberation, Theology and Proclamation," 69.
18. Allan Boesak, *The Finger of God,* trans. Peter Randall (Maryknoll, NY: Orbis, 1982), 4.
19. Gutierrez, *The Power of the Poor in History,* 37.
20. Justo and Catherine Gonzalez, *Liberation Preaching: The Pulpit and the Oppressed* (Nashville, TN: Abingdon, 1980) 96.
21. Ibid.

22. For a study of the mutual concerns of women and blacks regarding sexism and racism, see "Racism, Pluralism, Bonding," in Janet Calven and Mary I. Buckley, eds., *Women's Spirit Bonding* (New York: Pilgrim Press, 1984), 67–136.
23. Letty M. Russell, "Introduction: The Liberating Word," in *The Liberating Word: A Guide to Non-Sexist Interpretation of the Bible,* ed. Letty M. Russell (Philadelphia: Westminster, 1976), 14–15.
24. Rosemary Radford Ruether, *Sexism and God-Talk: Toward a Feminist Theology* (Boston: Beacon, 1983), 201.
25. Letty M. Russell, *The Liberating Word,* 110.
26. Ruether, *Sexism and God-Talk,* 194.
27. Ibid., 195.
28. Ibid. For a thorough presentation of these possibilities, see Elizabeth Fiorenza, *In Memory of Her: A Feminist Theological Reconstruction of Christian Origins* (New York: Crossroad, 1983).
29. Ruether, *Sexism and God-Talk,* 281.
30. This raises particularly acute questions for Baptist tradition as established by their long-held dictum, "Apostolicity is proved not by succession but by possession."
31. Nancy A. Hardesty, "Minister as Prophet? Or as Mother?" in *Women in New Worlds,* 2 vols., ed. Rosemary Skinner Keller, Louise L. Queen, and Hilah F. Thomas (Nashville: Abingdon, 1981), 1:91.
32. Ibid., 88ff.
33. Lareta Halteman Finger, "Women in Pulpits," *The Other Side* (July 1979):14.
34. Janet S. Everhart, "Maggie Newton Van Cott," in *Women in New Worlds,* ed. Skinner, et al., 2:315.
35. Ibid, 311.
36. From Kathryn Kish Sklar, "The Last Fifteen years," in *Women in New Worlds* ed. Skinner, et al., 1:48ff.
37. Ibid.
38. Barbara Welter, "The Cult of True Womanhood," *American Quarterly* 18/2 (Summer 1966).
39. For amplification of these issue, see the strong essays in "Racism, Pluralism, Bonding" in Calven and Buckley, *Women's Spirit Bonding,* 67–136.
40. See Joan Jacobs Brumberg, "The Case of Ann Hasseltine Judson," in *Women in New Worlds* ed. Skinner, et al., 2:248.
41. See Clarence G. Newsome, "Mary McLeod Bethune as Religionist" in *Women in New Worlds,* ed. Skinner, et al., 1:102–116.
42. For a critical yet appreciative appraisal of Georgia Harkness, see Joan Chamberlain Engelsman "The Legacy of Georgia Harkness," in *Women in New Worlds,* ed. Skinner, et al., 2:338–58.
43. Henry H. Mitchell, *The Recovery of Preaching* (San Francisco: Harper & Row, 1977), 23.
44. Ibid.
45. Ibid.
46. Sonja H. Stone, "Oral Tradition and Spiritual Drama: The Cultural Mosaic for Black Preaching," *Journal of the Interdenominational Theology Center* 8 (Fall 1980): 19.
47. For a further discussion, see Warren H. Stewart, *Interpreting God's Word in Black Preaching* (Valley Forge, PA: Judson, 1984).
48. Paul Carter Harrison, *The Drama of Nommo: Black Theatre in the African Continuum* (New York: Grove Press, 1972), 197.

49. Stone, *Oral Tradition and Spiritual Drama,* 26.
50. James H. Cone, "Sanctification, Liberation, and Black Worship," *Theology Today* 35 (July 1978): 142.
51. James Sanders, *God Has a Story Too* (Philadelphia: Fortress, 1979), 17–19.
52. Henry Mitchell, "Black Preaching," *Review and Expositor* 70 (1973): 338.
53. Cone, "Sanctification, *Liberation, and Black Worship,"* 143.
54. Howard Thurman, *Jesus and the Disinherited* (Nashville, TN: Abingdon, 1949), 30–31.

5. TOWARD INCARNATIONAL PREACHING

1. Peter L. Berger, "A Call for Authority in the Christian Community," unpublished manuscript (mimeo COCU: 71, Denver No. 9), pp. 6, 11.
2. Jürgen Moltmann, *Theology of Hope* (New York: Harper & Row, 1965), 172–73.
3. Jules Moreau, *Language and Religious Language* (Philadelphia: Westminster, 1961), 194.
4. H. Richard Niebuhr, *Christ and Culture* (New York: Harper & Row, 1951), 11.
5. For his discussion of this subject, see Gustaf Wingren, *The Living Word* (Philadelphia: Fortress, 1960), 25ff.
6. Wingren, *The Living Word,* 26.
7. Paul Tillich, *Theology of Culture,* ed. Robert C. Kimbell (New York: Oxford University Press, 1959), 204.
8. Ibid., 207.
9. Ibid., 207–208.
10. Wingren, *Living Word,* 211.
11. Tillich, *Theology of Culture,* 42.
12. Harvey Cox, *The Secular City* (New York: Macmillan, 1965), 241.
13. Emil Brunner, *The Divine-Human Encounter* (Philadelphia: Westminster, 1943), 85.
14. H. H. Farmer, *The Servant of the Word* (New York: Scribner, 1942), 45.
15. Kyle Haselden, *The Urgency of Preaching* (New York: Harper & Row, 1963), 24.
16. Eberhard Bethge, *Bonhoeffer in a World Come of Age,* ed. Peter Vorkink II (Philadelphia: Fortress, 1968), 50. But it is interesting to see his remark on the next page, "repetition has emptied the words" of preaching, which is certainly a criticism of its method of communication of the message.
17. Ronald E. Sleeth, "Theology vs. Communication Theories," *Religion in Life* 32 (Autumn 1963): 547–52.
18. Tillich, *Theology of Culture,* 201.
19. Ibid., 213.

6. "WE ARE HUMAN BEINGS LIKE YOURSELVES"

1. Helmut Thielicke, *The Trouble with the Church,* trans. and ed. John W. Doberstein (New York: Harper & Row, 1965), 9–10.
2. George Buttrick, *Jesus Came Preaching* (New York: Scribner, 1932), 170.

3. Charles H. Spurgeon, *Spurgeon's Lectures to His Students,* ed. David Otis Fuller (Grand Rapids, MI: Zondervan, 1945), 147.

4. P. T. Forsyth, *Positive Preaching and the Modern Mind* (Grand Rapids, MI: Eerdmans, 1964), 41.

5. Dietrich Bonhoeffer, *Life Together,* trans. and intro. John W. Doberstein (New York: Harper, 1954), 108.

6. Dietrich Bonhoeffer, *Gesammelte Schriften,* ed. Eberhard Bethge, 5 vols. (Munich: Chr. Kaiser Verlag, 1961), 4:282.

7. Jaroslav Pelikan, *The Preaching of Chrysostom* (Philadelphia: Fortress, 1967), 24.

8. John Octavius Johnston, *The Life and Letters of Henry Parry Liddon* (New York: Longmans, Green, 1904), 55.

9. D. T. Niles, *Preaching the Gospel of the Resurrection* (Philadelphia: Westminster, 1953), 45.

10. Karl Barth, *The Word of God and the Word of Man,* trans. Douglas Horton (New York: Harper, 1957), 129.

11. Paul Scherer, *For We Have This Treasure* (New York: Harper, 1944), 23.

12. Brand Blanshard, *On Philosophical Style* (Bloomington, IN: Indiana University Press, 1954), 18.

13. John Kelman, *The War and Preaching* (New Haven, CT: Yale University Press, 1919), 9-10.

14. Clyde E. Fant, Jr., and William M. Pinson, Jr., *20 Centuries of Great Preaching,* 13 vols. (Waco, TX.: Word, 1971), 5:51.

15. Blanshard, *Philosophical Style,* 52-53.

7. CREDIBILITY AND CHARISMA

1. This material follows the approach of C. I. Hovland, I. L. Janis, and H. H. Kelley in *Communication and Persuasion* (New Haven, CT: Yale University Press, 1966), 19-53. Other approaches of interest, with only slight variations, are given by C. H. Marple in the *Journal of Social Psychology* 4 (1933): 176-86 and Erwin Bettinghaus, *Persuasive Communication* (New York: Holt, Rinehart, & Winston, 1968), 105ff.

2. J. Edgar Park, *The Miracle of Preaching* (New York: Macmillan, 1936), 148.

3. See Clyde E. Fant, Jr., and William M. Pinson, Jr., *20 Centuries of Great Preaching,* 13 vols. (Waco, TX.: Word, 1971), 4:112 and 6:10.

4. Phillips Brooks, *Lectures on Preaching* (New York: Dutton, 1898), 5.

5. Nathaniel J. Burton, *In Pulpit and Parish* (New York: Macmillan, 1925), 96.

6. Helmut Thielicke, *The Trouble with the Church,* trans. and ed. John W. Doberstein (New York: Harper & Row, 1965), 23-24.

7. Ann Ruth Willner, *Charismatic Political Leadership: A Theory* (Princeton, NJ: Center of International Studies, 1968), 16.

8. Erwin Bettinghaus, *Persuasive Communication* (New York: Holt, Rinehart & Winston, 1968), 117.

9. Willner, *Charismatic Political Leadership,* 4.

10. Ibid., 9.

11. Ibid., 61ff.

12. Ibid., 9.

9. THE WORD BECOMES FLESH

1. Karl Barth, *The Preaching of the Gospel,* trans. B. E. Hooke (Philadelphia: Westminster, 1963), 77.
2. Ibid., 18.
3. Harry Emerson Fosdick, *The Living of These Days* (New York: Harper, 1956), 95, 98.
4. Charles H. Spurgeon, *Spurgeon's Lectures to His Students,* ed. David Otis Fuller (Grand Rapids, MI: Zondervan, 1945), 66.
5. Heinrich Ott, *Theology and Preaching,* trans. Harold Knight (Philadelphia: Westminster, 1965), 68.
6. Edmund Holt Linn, *Preaching as Counseling: The Unique Method of Harry Emerson Fosdick* (Valley Forge, PA.: Judson, 1966), 55.
7. Paul Tillich, *Theology of Culture,* ed. Robert C. Kimbell (New York: Oxford University Press, 1959), 74.
8. John Killinger, ed., *Experimental Preaching* (New York: Abingdon Press, 1973), 15.
9. Rudolf Bultmann, *Jesus Christ and Mythology* (New York: Scribner, 1958), 41, 42.
10. Killinger, *Experimental Preaching,* 14.
11. Ibid., 13.
12. Ibid.
13. Ibid., 9, 10.

10. OUT OF THE GUTENBERG GALAXY

1. Howard H. Martin, "Puritan Preachers on Preaching: Notes on American Colonial Rhetoric," *Quarterly Journal of Speech* 50, no. 3 (October 1964): 285.
2. For a discussion of the differences between oral and written style, see William Norwood Brigance, *Speech Composition* (New York: Appleton-Century Crofts, 1953), 200ff.; Raymond F. Howes, "The Talked and the Written," *Quarterly Journal of Speech* 26 (April 1940): 231ff.; C. H. Woolberton, "Speaking and Writing—A Study of Differences," *Quarterly Journal of Speech Education,* June 1922, 272ff.; and Glenn A. Capp, *How to Communicate Orally* (Englewood Cliffs, NJ: Prentice-Hall, 1961), 212ff.
3. Marshall McLuhan and Edmund Carpenter, eds., *Explorations in Communication* (Boston: Beacon, 1960), 125–26.
4. Marshall McLuhan, *The Gutenberg Galaxy, the Making of a Typographic Man* (Toronto: University of Toronto Press, 1962), 20.
5. Marshall McLuhan, *Understanding Media, the Extensions of Man* (New York: McGraw-Hill, 1964), 79.
6. McLuhan, *Gutenberg Galaxy,* 23.
7. Ibid., 98.
8. For a complete discussion of this question, see "A Study of the Effects of Certain Elements of Oral Style on the Intelligibility of Informative Speeches," unpublished dissertation by Gordon L. Thomas, Northwestern University, June 1952.

9. Karl Barth, *The Preaching of the Gospel,* trans. B. E. Hooke (Philadelphia: Westminster, 1963), 77.
10. Fred Craddock, *Preaching* (Nashville, TN: Abingdon, 1985), 191–92.
11. Eugene L. Lowry, *Doing Time in the Pulpit* (Nashville, TN: Abingdon, 1985), 102.

12. ONCE UPON A TIME . . .

1. Richard Lischer, "The Limits of Story," *Interpretation,* 38, no. 1 (January 1984): 26.
2. For example, Richard A. Jensen, *Telling the Story* (Minneapolis, MN: Augsburg, 1980); and Edmund Steimle, Morris Niedenthal, and Charles Rice, *Preaching the Story* (Philadelphia: Fortress, 1980).
3. Eugene L. Lowry, *Doing Time in the Pulpit* (Nashville, TN: Abingdon, 1985) and *The Homiletical Plot* (Atlanta, GA: Knox, 1980); Don M. Wardlaw, ed., *Preaching Biblically* (Philadelphia: Westminster, 1983); Fred B. Craddock, *As One Without Authority* (Nashville, TN: Abingdon, 1979) and *Overhearing the Gospel* (Nashville, TN: Abingdon, 1978).
4. See Dan O. Via, *The Parables* (Philadelphia: Fortress, 1967); John Dominic Crossan, *In Parables* (New York: Harper & Row, 1973) and *Cliffs of Fall: Paradox in Polyvalence in the Parables of Jesus* (New York: Seabury, 1980); Sallie McFague TeSelle, *Speaking in Parables* (Philadelphia: Fortress, 1975); Robert W. Funk, *Language, Hermeneutic, and Word of God* (New York: Harper & Row, 1966) and *Jesus as Precursor* (Philadelphia: Fortress, 1975).
5. Daniel and Aline Patte, *Structural Exegesis: From Theory to Practice* (Philadelphia: Fortress, 1978); Roland Barthes, *Critical Essays* (Evanston, IL: Northwestern University Press, 1972); Northrop Frye, *Anatomy of Criticism* (New York: Atheneum, 1969); E. D. Hirsch, *Validity in Interpretation* (New Haven, CT: Yale University Press, 1967).
6. Roland Barthes, "Science Versus Literature," *Introduction to Structuralism,* ed. Michael Lane (New York: Basic Books, 1970), 411.
7. Stephen Crites, "The Narrative Quality of Experience," *Journal of the American Academy of Religion* 39 (September 1971): 297–302.
8. Frank Kermode, *The Sense of an Ending* (London: Oxford University Press, 1966).
9. Paul Ricoeur, "The Narrative Function," *Semeia* 13 (1978): 195.
10. Philip Wheelwright, *Metaphor and Reality* (Bloomington, IN: Indiana University Press, 1962), 101–109.
11. Gabriel Fackre, *The Christian Story* (Grand Rapids, MI: Eerdmans, 1978); Wesley Kort, *Narrative Elements and Religious Meaning* (Philadelphia: Fortress, 1975); James B. Wiggins, ed., *Religion as Story* (New York: Harper & Row, 1975); Brian Wicker, *The Story-Shaped World* (Notre Dame, IN: University of Notre Dame Press, 1975).
12. Henry Mitchell, *The Recovery of Preaching* (San Francisco: Harper & Row, 1977), 155–56.
13. See Brevard S. Childs, *Biblical Theology in Crisis* (Philadelphia: Westminster, 1970), *The Book of Exodus: A Critical, Theological Commentary* (Philadelphia: West-

minster, 1974), and *Introduction to the Old Testament as Scripture* (Philadelphia: Fortress, 1979); also, James A. Sanders, *God Has a Story Too: Biblical Sermons in Context* (Philadelphia: Fortress, 1979).

14. Richard Lischer, "Preaching and the Rhetoric of Promise," *Word and World* 8, no. 1 (Winter, 1988), forthcoming.
15. Crites, "Narrative Quality of Experience," 297.
16. In Wicker, *Story-Shaped World*, 47.
17. Claus Westermann, "From the Old Testament Text to the Sermon," *Review and Expositor* 72 (1975):170.
18. Lowry, *Doing Time*, 58.
19. Thomas G. Long, "Shaping Sermons by Plotting the Text's Claim Upon Us," in Wardlaw, *Preaching Biblically*, 90–91.
20. Ronald J. Allen, "Shaping Sermons by the Language of the Text," in Wardlaw, *Preaching Biblically*, 31.
21. For a similar list, see Lowry, *Doing Time*, 27.
22. See Philip Wheelwright, *Metaphor and Reality*, 45–46.
23. For assertions along this line, see Wardlaw, *Preaching Biblically*, 21; Craddock, *As One Without Authority* 153; and Leander E. Keck, *The Bible and the Pulpit: The Renewal of Biblical Preaching* (Nashville, TN: Abingdon, 1978), 106.
24. Lischer, "The Limits of Story," 26–27.
25. Ibid., 27.
26. Mary Ann Tolbert, *Perspectives on the Parables: An Approach to Multiple Interpretations* (Philadelphia: Fortress, 1979), 91.
27. Lischer, "The Limits of Story," 29.
28. Ibid., 30.
29. Kermode, *The Sense of an Ending*, 4.
30. Lischer, "Preaching and the Rhetoric of Promise."
31. Lischer, "The Limits of Story," 30.
32. Sallie McFague TeSelle, "Parable, Metaphor, and Narrative," *Homiletic* 2 (1977):vi.
33. Don Wardlaw, "Shaping Sermons by the Context of the Text," in Wardlaw, *Preaching Biblically*, 70–71.
34. Lischer, "The Limits of Story," 30.
35. Ibid., 34.
36. Ibid.
37. Lischer, "Preaching and the Rhetoric of Promise."
38. Ibid.
39. See Lischer, "The Limits of Story," 37; Fred B. Craddock, *Preaching* (Nashville, TN: Abingdon, 1985), 155, 188–189; and Lowry, *Doing Time*, 22.
40. Lowry, *Doing Time*, 99.
41. Ibid., 101.
42. Craddock, *Preaching*, 155.
43. Lowry, *Doing Time*, 79–80: "I believe the term *nonpropositional* does not mean *anti-propositional*. To claim the biblical record to be largely nonpropositional is not to claim there are no biblical propositions. It is to say, first of all, that the Christian revelation as experienced historically in the corporate body of Christ, the church, simply cannot be contained in propositional form."

44. Craddock, *Overhearing the Gospel,* 135.
45. Ibid., 136–37.
46. Ibid., 137. We might question whether narrative should be conducted "as though the presence of the listeners were not essential to its process," especially in light of Werner H. Kelber's recent work on the original oral nature of the gospel, in which he shows that oral forms of speech are "negotiable in social contexts and by interaction of speaker with hearers" and that parabolic speech is "peculiarly dependent on oral, social contextuality. . . . Contrary to modern aesthetics of literature, parable is first and foremost a speech act delivered by speaker to hearers." Werner H. Kelber, *The Oral and the Written Gospel* (Philadelphia: Fortress, 1983), 62.
47. Via, *The Parables,* 100–101.
48. Don Wardlaw has proposed this suggestive idea. See Wardlaw, *Preaching Biblically,* 63–71.
49. David Tracy, *The Analogical Imagination* (New York: Crossroad, 1981), 200.
50. Markus Barth, "Biblical Preaching Today," *Review and Expositor* 72 (1975): 165.
51. See Charles E. Reagan and David Stewart, eds., *The Philosophy of Paul Ricoeur* (Boston: Beacon, 1978).
52. Ibid., 213.
53. Ibid., 223.
54. Ibid., 231ff.
55. Ibid., 101.
56. Ibid., 224.
57. Ibid., 125.
58. Jürgen Moltmann, *Perspectiven der Theologie: Gesammelte Aufsätze* (Munich: Christoph Kaiser Verlag and Mainz: Matthias Grunwald Verlag, 1968), 125.
59. Ibid.
60. Reagan and Stewart, *Philosophy of Paul Ricoeur,* 144.
61. Ibid., 145.
62. Paul Ricoeur, *Interpretation Theory: Discourse and the Surplus of Meaning* (Fort Worth, TX: Texas Christian University Press, 1976), 30.
63. George A. Lindbeck, *The Nature of Doctrine* (Philadelphia: Westminster, 1984), 118–19.
64. Moltmann, *Perspectiven,* 115.
65. Fred B. Craddock, "The Sermon and the Uses of Scripture," *Theology Today* 42 (April 1985): 8.
66. Craddock, *Overhearing the Gospel,* 74.
67. Westermann, "From the Old Testament Text to the Sermon," 170.
68. Gerhard von Rad, "Typologische Auslegung des Alten Testaments," *Evangelische Theologie* (1952): 29.
69. Moltmann, *Perspectiven,* 123.
70. Craddock, "The Sermon and the Uses of Scripture," 11.
71. Barth, "Biblical Preaching Today," 166.
72. Ernesto Cardenal, *The Gospel in Solenteiname* (Maryknoll, NY: Orbis, 1976–82), 3:98.
73. See Markus Barth, *Conversation with the Bible* (New York: Holt, Rinehart, & Winston, 1964).
74. Kelber, *The Oral and the Written Gospel,* xvi.
75. Ibid., 62.

76. Ibid., 62–63.
77. Craddock, *Overhearing the Gospel,* 76.
78. See Hans Frei, *The Eclipse of Biblical Narrative,* (New Haven, CT: Yale University Press, 1974).
79. Hermann Diem, "Kierkegaard's Bequest to Theology," in *A Kierkegaard Critique,* Howard Johnson and Niels Thulstrup, eds., trans. Thora Moullon (New York: Harper & Row, 1962), 260.
80. Justo L. Gonzalez and Catherine Gunsalus Gonzalez, *Liberation Preaching* (Nashville, TN: Abingdon, 1981), 100–101.
81. Juan Luis Segundo, *The Liberation of Theology* (Maryknoll, NY: Orbis, 1976), 9.
82. Reagan and Stewart, *The Philosophy of Paul Ricoeur,* 237.
83. Søren Kierkegaard, *The Last Years: The Kierkegaard Journals 1883–1855,* trans. Ronald Gregor Smith (New York: Harper & Row, 1965), 303.
84. Moltmann, *Perspectiven,* 126.
85. Ibid., 127.

13. WORLDLY PREACHING: FROM THIS-WORLD TO REAL-WORLD

1. See *The Philosophy of Paul Ricoeur,* Charles E. Reagan and David Stewart, eds., (Boston: Beacon, 1978), 213–45.
2. Paul Ricoeur, "Biblical Hermeneutics," *Semeia* 4 (1975): 86.
3. Reagan and Stewart, *The Philosophy of Paul Ricoeur,* 225.
4. Ibid., 226.
5. For a fuller discussion, see Reagan and Stewart, *The Philosophy of Paul Ricoeur,* 227–31.
6. Ibid., 228.
7. Ibid.
8. Ibid., 230.
9. Ibid., 231.
10. Paul Ricoeur, *Time and Narrative,* vol. 1, trans. Kathleen McLaughlin and David Pellaeur (Chicago: University of Chicago Press, 1984), 65–67.
11. Robert Coles, *The Political Life of Children* (New York: Atlantic Monthly Press, 1986), 17.
12. See Frederick Buechner, *The Hungering Dark* (San Francisco: Harper & Row, 1985), and *The Magnificent Defeat* (New York: Seabury, 1979).
13. Robert Coles, *The Moral Life of Children,* (New York: Atlantic Monthly Press, 1986), 250.
14. The Monks of New Skete, *How to Be Your Dog's Best Friend* (Boston: Little, Brown, 1978), xiii.
15. Ibid., 88.
16. Stephen Crites, "The Narrative Quality of Experience," *Journal of the American Academy of Religion* 39 (September 1971): 308.
17. Eduard Schweizer, "From the New Testament Text to the Sermon," trans. James W. Cox, *Review and Expositor* 72 (1975): 181.
18. Don Wardlaw, "Shaping Sermons by the Context of the Text," in Don Wardlaw, ed., *Preaching Biblically* (Philadelphia: Westminster, 1983), 70.

19. Albert Camus, *Notebooks 1942–1951,* trans. Justin O'Brien (New York: Harcourt Brace Jovanovich, 1965), 27.
20. Eric Auerbach, *Mimesis* (New York: Doubleday, 1953), 35–43.
21. Alan Paton, *Ah, But Your Land Is Beautiful* (New York: Scribner, 1981).
22. Robert McAfee Brown, *Saying Yes and Saying No* (Philadelphia: Westminster, 1986), 99–100.
23. See Henry Mitchell, *The Recovery of Preaching,* (San Francisco: Harper & Row, 1977), 92, for further discussion of this interesting question.

14. JESUS AS COMMUNICATOR

1. James A. Sanders, *God Has A Story Too: Biblical Sermons in Context* (Philadelphia: Fortress, 1979) 14–15
2. Charles H. Spurgeon, *Spurgeon's Lectures to His Students,* ed. David Otis Fuller (Grand Rapids, MI: Zondervan, 1945), 149.
3. Friedrich Hauck, "Parabole," trans. Geoffrey W. Bromiley, *Theological Dictionary of the New Testament,* ed. Gerhard Kittel and Gerhard Friedrich, 10 vols. (Grand Rapids, MI: Eerdmans, 1967), 5:754.
4. As quoted in R. E. C. Browne, *The Ministry of the Word* (Philadelphia: Fortress, 1976), 86.
5. See C. I. Hovland, I. L. Janis, and H. H. Kelley, *Communication and Persuasion* (New Haven, CT: Yale University Press, 1966).
6. See particularly Fred B. Craddock, *Overhearing the Gospel* (Nashville, TN: Abingdon, 1978), 101ff.
7. Eugene L. Lowry, *Doing Time in the Pulpit* (Nashville, TN: Abingdon, 1985), 64–69.

15. "SOME SAID IT THUNDERED": UPPER GARBLE AND LOWER GARBLE

1. Jacques Barzun, *House of Intellect* (New York: Harper, 1959), 222.
2. Jerome Herbert Perlmutter, *A Practical Guide to Effective Writing* (New York: Random House, 1965), 9.
3. Charles H. Spurgeon, *Spurgeon's Lectures to His Students,* ed. David Otis Fuller (Grand Rapids, MI: Zondervan, 1945), 200.
4. Austin Phelps, *English Style in Public Discourse* (New York: Scribner, 1883), 341.
5. Helmut Thielicke, *The Trouble with the Church,* trans. and ed. John W. Doberstein (New York: Harper & Row, 1965), 54.
6. Harry Emerson Fosdick, *The Living of These Days* (New York: Harper, 1956), 92.
7. Dietrich Bonhoeffer, *Gesammelte Schriften,* ed. Eberhard Bethge, 5 vols. (Munich: Chr. Kaiser Verlag, 1961), 4:260.
8. Charles R. Brown, *The Art of Preaching* (New York: Macmillan, 1922), 42.
9. Fosdick, *Living of These Days,* 93.

10. Thielicke, *The Trouble with the Church,* 58.
11. Julian Victor Langmead Casserley, *The Christian in Philosophy* (New York: Scribner, 1951), 178–79.

16. "THEY LISTENED THE MORE WILLINGLY"

1. Richard Baxter, *The Reformed Pastor,* ed. Hugh Martin (Richmond, VA: Knox, 1956), 97ff.
2. Alexander V. G. Allen, *The Life and Letters of Phillips Brooks,* 3 vols. (New York: Dutton, 1901), 3:393.
3. Charles R. Brown, *The Art of Preaching* (New York: Macmillan, 1922), 168.
4. See Clyde E. Fant, Jr., and William M. Pinson, Jr., *20 Centuries of Great Preaching,* 13 vols. (Waco, TX.: Word, 1971), 9:24–25.
5. Helmut Thielicke, *Encounter with Spurgeon* (Philadelphia: Fortress, 1963), 32.
6. See Fant and Pinson, *20 Centuries,* 1:58ff.
7. Dietrich Bonhoeffer, *The Communion of Saints,* trans. R. Gregor Smith (New York: Harper & Row, 1963), 165.
8. William Norwood Brigance, *Speech Communication* (New York: Appleton-Century Crofts, 1947), 58.

Index

Transitional setences, 184
Truth, Sojourner, 61

VanCott, Maggie Newton, 61
Via, Dan, 203
Von Rad, Gerhardt, 208

Wardlaw, Don, 193, 200, 235
Weber, Max, 121
Welter, Barbara, 61–62
Wesley, John, 60
Wheelwright, Philip, 194
Whitefield, George, 63–64
Wiesel, Elie, 10
Wilder, Amos, 34

Willard, Francis, 60
Wingren, Gustav, xii, 44, 85
Women: female Baptist preachers, 59; Holiness tradition and preaching, 59–60; preaching and, 57–63; Wesley's permission to preach, 60
Word: first century understanding of, 222–23; flesh and, 5; priority over image, 34–37, 39; standing beneath the, 83–84
Words, essential in life of Jesus, 86–87; power of, 10
Worship, 17–18

Zion, language of, 37, 39, 75, 132